CompTIA®
Linux+ and LPIC
Practice Tests

CompTIA®
Linux+ and LPIC
Practice Tests
Exams LX0-103/LPIC-1 101-400, LX0-104/LPIC-1 102-400, LPIC-2 201, and LPIC-2 202

Steven Suehring

SYBEX®
A Wiley Brand

Senior Acquisitions Editor: Kenyon Brown
Development Editor: Gary Schwartz
Technical Editor: Kevin Ryan
Production Editor: Rebecca Anderson
Copy Editor: Linda Recktenwald
Editorial Manager: Mary Beth Wakefield
Production Manager: Kathleen Wisor
Executive Editor: Jim Minatel
Book Designer: Judy Fung and Bill Gibson
Proofreader: Nancy Carrasco
Indexer: Ted Laux
Project Coordinator, Cover: Brent Savage
Cover Designer: Wiley
Cover Image: ©Getty Images Inc./Jeremy Woodhouse

To Jakob and Owen.

Acknowledgments

After a certain point, writing acknowledgements becomes more difficult than writing the book itself. I've reached that point. I've stared at this page longer than any other one in this book. It's impossible to thank adequately everyone who contributes, directly or indirectly, to something like a book. So I won't. Well, okay, I will a bit.

Thanks to everyone at Delta Dental. I had a great experience, and it was an honor coming back. To the faculty at UWSP, thank you for welcoming and helping a new faculty member. Thank you Ken Brown and Gary Schwartz; it's been a pleasure working with you both on another book.

Thanks to everyone at Ski's, for providing the best of the best in both food and service. Of course, no acknowledgements section would be complete without a thank-you to Patti, Jess, Rob, Jim, and Tim at Partners, without whom these pages would have taken longer to write. And always, thank you Kent Laabs for keeping my gear habit going. Looking forward to the year.

About the Author

Steve Suehring is an Assistant Professor of Computing and New Media Technologies at the University of Wisconsin—Stevens Point. Prior to joining the faculty in 2015, Steve gained 20 years of field experience in a variety of technical engineering, system and network administration, and system architectural roles. Steve has written several books and has served as an editor for *LinuxWorld* magazine.

Contents

CompTIA.

Becoming a CompTIA Certified IT Professional is Easy

It's also the best way to reach greater professional opportunities and rewards.

Why Get CompTIA Certified?

Growing Demand

Labor estimates predict some technology fields will experience growth of over 20% by the year 2020.* CompTIA certification qualifies the skills required to join this workforce.

Higher Salaries

IT professionals with certifications on their resume command better jobs, earn higher salaries and have more doors open to new multi-industry opportunities.

Verified Strengths

91% of hiring managers indicate CompTIA certifications are valuable in validating IT expertise, making certification the best way to demonstrate your competency and knowledge to employers.**

Universal Skills

CompTIA certifications are vendor neutral—which means that certified professionals can proficiently work with an extensive variety of hardware and software found in most organizations.

 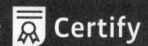 

Learn more about what the exam covers by reviewing the following:

- Exam objectives for key study points.

- Sample questions for a general overview of what to expect on the exam and examples of question format.

- Visit online forums, like LinkedIn, to see what other IT professionals say about CompTIA exams.

Purchase a voucher at a Pearson VUE testing center or at CompTIAstore.com.

- Register for your exam at a Pearson VUE testing center:

- Visit pearsonvue.com/CompTIA to find the closest testing center to you.

- Schedule the exam online. You will be required to enter your voucher number or provide payment information at registration.

- Take your certification exam.

Congratulations on your CompTIA certification!

- Make sure to add your certification to your resume.

- Check out the CompTIA Certification Roadmap to plan your next career move.

Learn more: **Certification.CompTIA.org/linuxplus**

* Source: CompTIA 9th Annual Information Security Trends study: 500 U.S. IT and Business Executives Responsible for Security
** Source: CompTIA Employer Perceptions of IT Training and Certification

Introduction

CompTIA Linux+ and LPIC Practice Tests is a companion volume to the *CompTIA Linux+ Study Guide*. This book helps you to prepare for the certification exams by testing your knowledge of the concepts and terminology being used on the exam. Within the book are 1,201 questions, answers, and explanations covering the range of topics necessary for the exams.

Each of the chapters within the book contains questions specific to a section of the exam. There are also four longer practice exams that encompass questions from a given domain. This book is intended to be used in conjunction with the corresponding certification-related books, and it can be used to find areas that you may need to emphasize for further study.

Linux+ Certification

CompTIA certifications are notable for the added benefits that can be found by certificate holders. Linux+ certification is a way to prove that you possess the knowledge necessary to perform job-related duties for Linux administration.

The Linux+ certification covers several important topics for Linux administration, and it helps to prepare you for the things you'll need to do with a Linux server. Included among the areas tested are installation, compiling and installing server software, and security. These topics are vital to the everyday job of a Linux administrator.

Importantly, the certification exams are not tied to a particular distribution but rather to the broad Linux ecosystem. This better prepares you for the variety of Linux flavors that you'll encounter at a given employer or job.

How This Book Is Organized

This book consists of two sections, each based on one of the two exams involved in the Linux+ and LPIC certification series. The book has a chapter dedicated to each of the relevant domains. At the end of the book, there are also four longer practice exams corresponding to a given set of domains.

Each chapter begins with a list of the objective domains covered in that chapter. While the questions themselves draw from those objectives, you can expect to draw on other knowledge relevant to being a Linux administrator.

The review questions and final review tests included in this book are *not* derived from the actual Linux+ exam questions. They serve to provide exposure to the underlying content and to deliver a comparable testing vehicle for you to prepare for the exam. It will not be a useful exercise to memorize the answers to these questions and assume that doing so will enable you to pass the exam. The underlying subject matter is the important focus of your studies so that you will be able to pass the exam.

Congratulations on the decision to demonstrate your Linux administration skills with this certification.

How to Use This Book and the Interactive Online Learning Environment and Test Bank

This book includes 1200 practice test questions, which will help you get ready to pass the Linux+ and LPIC exams. The interactive online learning environment that accompanies the CompTIA Linux+ and LPIC Practice Tests provides a rubust test bank to help you prepare for the certification exams and increase your chances of passing them the first time! By using this test bank, you can identify weak areas up front and then develop a solid studying strategy using each of these robust testing features.

The test bank also offers four practice exams. Take these practice exams just as if you were taking the actual exam (without any reference material). When you've finished the first exam, move on to the next one to solidify your test-taking skills. If you get more than 90 percent of the answers correct, you're ready to take the certification exams.

 The Sybex Interactive Online Test Bank can be accessed at
http://www.wiley.com/go/Sybextestprep.

CompTIA Linux+ Practice Tests: Objective Map

Objective	Chapter Number
101 System Architecture	1
101.1 Determine and configure hardware settings.	1
Enable and disable integrated peripherals	1
Configure systems with or without external peripherals such as keyboards	1
Differentiate between the various types of mass storage devices	1
Know the differences between coldplug and hotplug devices	1
Determine hardware resources for devices	1
Tools and utilities to list various hardware information (e.g., lsusb, lspci)	1
Tools and utilities to manipulate USB devices	1
Conceptual understanding of sysfs, udev, dbus	1
101.2 Boot the system.	1
Provide common commands to the boot loader and options to the kernel at boot time	1
Demonstrate knowledge of the boot sequence from BIOS to boot completion	1
Understanding of SysVinit and systemd	1
Awareness of Upstart	1
Check boot events in the log file	1

Objective	Chapter Number
Remove files and directories recursively	3
Use simple and advanced wildcard specifications in commands	3
Use find to locate and act on files based on type, size or time	3
Usage of tar, cpio and dd	3
103.4 Use streams, pipes and redirects.	**3**
Redirecting standard input, standard output and standard error	3
Pipe the output of one command to the input of another command	3
Use the output of one command as arguments to another command	3
Send output to both stdout and a file	3
103.5 Create, monitor and kill processes.	**3**
Run jobs in the foreground and background	3
Signal a program to continue running after logout	3
Monitor active processes	3
Select and sort processes for display	3
Send signals to processes	3
103.6 Modify process execution priorities.	**3**
Know the default priority of a job that is created	3
Run a program with higher or lower priority than the default	3
Change the priority of a running process	3
103.7 Search text files using regular expressions.	**3**
Create simple regular expressions containing several notational elements	3
Use regular expression tools to perform searches through a filesystem or file content	3

Objective	Chapter Number
105.2 Customize or write simple scripts.	5
Use standard sh syntax (loops, tests)	5
Use command substitution	5
Test return values for success or failure or other information provided by a command	5
Perform conditional mailing to the superuser	5
Correctly select the script interpreter through the shebang (#!) line	5
Manage the location, ownership, execution and SUID rights of scripts	5
105.3 SQL data management	5
Use of basic SQL commands	5
Perform basic data manipulation	5
106 User Interfaces and Desktops	**6**
106.1 Install and configure X11.	**6**
Verify that the video card and monitor are supported by an X server	6
Awareness of the X font server	6
Basic understanding and knowledge of the X Window configuration file	6
106.2 Set up a display manager.	**6**
Basic configuration of LightDM	6
Turn the display manager on or off	6
Change the display manager greeting	6
Awareness of XDM, KDM and GDM	6

Objective	Chapter Number
109.2 Basic network configuration.	**9**
Manually and automatically configure network interfaces	9
Basic TCP/IP host configuration	9
Setting a default route	9
109.3 Basic network troubleshooting.	**9**
Manually and automatically configure network interfaces and routing tables to include adding, starting, stopping, restarting, deleting or reconfiguring network interfaces	9
Change, view or configure the routing table and correct an improperly set default route manually	9
Debug problems associated with the network configuration	9
109.4 Configure client side DNS.	**9**
Query remote DNS servers	9
Configure local name resolution and use remote DNS servers	9
Modify the order in which name resolution is done	9
110 Security	**10**
110.1 Perform security administration tasks.	**10**
Audit a system to find files with the suid/sgid bit set	10
Set or change user passwords and password aging information	10
Being able to use nmap and netstat to discover open ports on a system	10
Set up limits on user logins, processes and memory usage	10
Determine which users have logged in to the system or are currently logged in	10
Basic sudo configuration and usage	10

Objective	Chapter Number
110.2 Set up host security.	**10**
Awareness of shadow passwords and how they work	10
Turn off network services not in use	10
Understand the role of TCP wrappers	10
110.3 Securing data with encryption.	**10**
Perform basic OpenSSH 2 client configuration and usage	10
Understand the role of OpenSSH 2 server host keys	10
Perform basic GnuPG configuration, usage and revocation	10
Understand SSH port tunnels (including X11 tunnels)	10
200 Capacity Planning	**11**
200.1 Measure and Troubleshoot Resource Usage	**11**
Measure CPU usage.	11
Measure memory usage.	11
Measure disk I/O.	11
Measure network I/O.	11
Measure firewalling and routing throughput.	11
Map client bandwidth usage.	11
Match / correlate system symptoms with likely problems.	11
Estimate throughput and identify bottlenecks in a system including networking.	11
200.2 Predict Future Resource Needs	**11**
Use monitoring and measurement tools to monitor IT infrastructure usage.	11
Predict capacity break point of a configuration.	11

Objective	Chapter Number
212.2 Managing FTP servers	**23**
Configuration files, tools and utilities for Pure-FTPd and vsftpd	23
Awareness of ProFTPd	23
Understanding of passive vs. active FTP connections	23
212.3 Secure shell (SSH)	**23**
OpenSSH configuration files, tools and utilities	23
Login restrictions for the superuser and the normal users	23
Managing and using server and client keys to login with and without password	23
Usage of multiple connections from multiple hosts to guard against loss of connection to remote host following configuration changes	23
212.4 Security tasks	**23**
Tools and utilities to scan and test ports on a server	23
Locations and organisations that report security alerts as Bugtraq, CERT or other sources	23
Tools and utilities to implement an intrusion detection system (IDS)	23
Awareness of OpenVAS and Snort	23
212.5 OpenVPN	**23**
OpenVPN	23

CompTIA
Linux+/LPIC-1

PART

I

Chapter

1

System Architecture (Domain 101)

THE FOLLOWING COMPTIA LINUX+/LPIC-1 EXAM OBJECTIVES ARE COVERED IN THIS CHAPTER:

✓ **101.1   Determine and Configure hardware settings**

- Enable and disable integrated peripherals
- Configure systems with or without external peripherals such as keyboards
- Differentiate between the various types of mass storage devices
- Know the differences between coldplug and hotplug devices
- Determine hardware resources for devices
- Tools and utilities to list various hardware information (e.g. lsusb, lspci, etc.)
- Tools and utilities to manipulate USB devices
- Conceptual understanding of sysfs, udev, hald, dbus
- The following is a partial list of the used files, terms, and utilities:
  - /sys
  - /proc
  - /dev
  - modprobe
  - lsmod
  - lspci
  - lsusb

✓ **101.2   Boot the System**

- Provide common commands to the boot loader and options to the kernel at boot time
- Demonstrate knowledge of the boot sequence from BIOS to boot completion

- Understanding of SysVinit and systemd
- Awareness of Upstart
- Check boot events in the log file
- The following is a partial list of the used files, terms and utilities:
  - dmesg
  - BIOS
  - bootloader
  - kernel
    - initramfs
    - init
    - SysVinit
    - system

✓ **101.3   Change runlevels/boot targets and shutdown or reboot system**

- Set the default runlevel or boot target
- Change between runlevels/boot targets including single user mode
- Shutdown and reboot from the command line
- Alert users before switching runlevels/ boot targets or other major system events
- Properly terminate processes
- The following is a partial list of the used files, terms and utilities:
  - /etc/inittab
  - shutdown
  - init
  - /etc/init.d
  - telinit
  - system
  - systemctl
  - /etc/systemd/
  - /usr/lib/system/
  - wall

1. A Serial ATA (SATA) disk will use which of the following identifiers?

    A. `/dev/hdX`

    B. `/dev/sataX`

    C. `/dev/sdX`

    D. `/disk/sataX`

2. Which command enables you to view the current IRQ assignments?-

    A. `view /proc/irq`

    B. `cat /proc/interrupts`

    C. `cat /dev/irq`

    D. `less /dev/irq`

3. Which device is typically connected as the first floppy disk?

    A. `/dev/hd0`

    B. `/dev/flop0`

    C. `/dev/fd0`

    D. `/dev/sda`

4. Configuration of udev devices is done by working with files in which directory?

    A. `/udev/devices`

    B. `/devices/`

    C. `/udev/config`

    D. `/etc/udev`

5. Which command is used to load a module and its dependencies automatically?

    A. `modprobe`

    B. `lsmod`

    C. `insmod`

    D. `rmmod`

6. Which command is used to obtain a list of USB devices?

    A. `usb-list`

    B. `lsusb`

    C. `ls-usb`

    D. `ls --usb`

7. When working with hotplug devices, what is the location of scripts that are executed when a given device is inserted into the computer?

    A. `/etc/usb`

    B. `/etc/usb-dev`

    C. `/dev/usb`

    D. `/etc/hotplug/usb`

8. Which option given at boot time within the GRUB configuration will boot the system into single-user mode?

    A. `single-user`

    B. `su`

    C. `single`

    D. `root`

9. During boot of a system with GRUB, which key can be pressed to display the GRUB menu?

    A. Shift

    B. E

    C. V

    D. H

10. Which command can be used to view the kernel ring buffer in order to troubleshoot the boot process?

    A. `lsboot`

    B. `boot-log`

    C. `krblog`

    D. `dmesg`

11. During the initialization process for a Linux system using SysVinit, which runlevel corresponds to single-user mode?

    A. Runlevel 5

    B. Runlevel SU

    C. Runlevel 1

    D. Runlevel 6

12. On a system using SysVinit, in which directory are startup and shutdown scripts for services stored?

    A. `/etc/init-d`

    B. `/etc/init`

    C. `/etc/sysV`

    D. `/etc/init.d`

13. Which command can be used to reboot a system?

    A. `init 6`

    B. `shutdown -h -t now`

    C. `init 1`

    D. `refresh-system`

14. Which command would you use if you make changes to the /etc/inittab file and want those changes to be reloaded without a reboot?

    A. init-refresh

    B. init 6

    C. telinit

    D. reload-inittab

15. Which command displays the current runlevel for a system?

    A. show-level

    B. init --level

    C. sudo init

    D. runlevel

16. Within which folder are systemd unit configuration files stored?

    A. /etc/system.conf.d

    B. /lib/system.conf.d

    C. /lib/systemd/system

    D. /etc/sysconfd

17. Which explanation best describes the following, gathered with the ls -la command?
    lrwxrwxrwx. 1 root root 35 Jul 8 2014 .fetchmailrc ->
    .configs/fetchmail/.fetchmailrc

    A. It is a file called .fetchmailrc, which is linked using a symbolic link.

    B. It is a file called .configs/fetchmail/.fetchmailrc, which is owned by lrwxrwxrwx.

    C. It is a directory called .fetchmailrc, which is owned by user Jul.

    D. It is a local directory called .configs/fetchmail/.fetchmailrc.

18. Which command is used with systemd in order to list the available service units?

    A. systemd list-units

    B. systemctl list-units

    C. systemd unit-list

    D. systemctl show-units

19. Which option to lspci is used to display both numeric codes and device names?

    A. -numdev

    B. -n

    C. -nn

    D. -devnum

20. Which command can be used to obtain a list of currently loaded kernel modules?

   A. `insmod`

   B. `modlist`

   C. `ls --modules`

   D. `lsmod`

21. Which option to the `modprobe` command shows the dependencies for a given module?

   A. `--show-options`

   B. `--list-deps`

   C. `--show-depends`

   D. `--list-all`

22. Which command can you use to send a message to all users who are currently logged into a system?

   A. `cat`

   B. `wall`

   C. `tee`

   D. `ssh`

23. Which of the following is a good first troubleshooting step when a hard disk is not detected by the Linux kernel?

   A. Unplug the disk.

   B. Check the system BIOS.

   C. Restart the web server service.

   D. Run the `disk-detect` command.

24. Within which directory is information about USB devices stored?

   A. `/etc/usbdevices`

   B. `/var/usb`

   C. `/lib/sys/usb`

   D. `/proc/bus/usb`

25. Which option can be added to a GRUB configuration line to set or change the root partition at boot time to `/dev/sda2`?

   A. `rootpartition={hd0,2}`

   B. `root=/dev/sda2`

   C. `root={hd0,3}`

   D. `rootpartition=/dev/sda2`

26. Which key combination will enable you to edit the kernel options and then boot when using GRUB Legacy?

A. ESC for editing and Return to boot

B. V for editing and then Return to boot

C. E for editing and then B to boot

D. V for editing and then B to boot

27. The system on which you're working recently had a hard drive failure. A new hard drive has been installed, and it has had Linux restored from backup to the drive. However, the system will not boot and instead shows a grub > prompt. Within the grub > prompt, which command will show the current partitions as seen by GRUB?

A. ls

B. showPart

C. partitionlist

D. ps

28. If the kernel ring buffer has been overwritten, within which file can you look to find boot messages?

A. /var/log/bootmessages

B. /var/log/mail.info

C. /var/adm/log/boot.info

D. /var/log/dmesg

29. Which command and option can be used to determine whether a given service is currently loaded?

A. systemctl --ls

B. telinit

C. systemctl status

D. sysctl -a

30. Which command on a systemd-controlled system would place the system into single-user mode?

A. systemctl one

B. systemctl isolate resuce.target

C. systemctl single-user

D. systemctl runlevel one

31. Which command on a system controlled by Upstart will reload the configuration files?

A. initctl reload

B. systemd reload

C. upstart --reload

D. ups -reload

32. When working with a SysV system, which `chkconfig` option will display all services and their runlevels?

   A. `--reload`

   B. `--list`

   C. `--all`

   D. `--ls`

33. A drive connected to USB will be considered to be which type of device?

   A. Medium

   B. Coldplug

   C. Hotplug

   D. Sideplug

34. During the boot process, what is the next step after the kernel has taken over the initialization process and initializes devices?

   A. The system BIOS initializes devices.

   B. The system is placed in multi-user mode.

   C. The boot loader initializes the kernel.

   D. The root partition is mounted.

35. A legacy PATA disk is used to boot the system. You recently added an internal DVD drive to the computer, and now the system will no longer boot. What is the most likely cause?

   A. The BIOS has identified the DVD drive as the first disk, and therefore the system can no longer find the Linux partition(s).

   B. The hard drive became corrupt when the DVD drive was installed.

   C. The hot swap option has not been enabled in the BIOS.

   D. The DVD drive is not detected by the computer and needs to be enabled first in the BIOS and then in Linux prior to installation.

36. The system is using a temporary flash USB disk for data mounted at `/dev/sda1`. You need to remove the disk. Which of the following commands will enable the disk to be safely removed from the system?

   A. `usbstop /dev/sda`

   B. `umount /dev/sda1`

   C. `unmount /dev/sda1`

   D. `dev-eject /dev/sda1`

37. Within which partition will the EFI system partition typically be mounted?

   A. `/etc/efi`

   B. `/efi`

   C. `/sys/efi`

   D. `/boot/efi`

38. Assuming that a USB disk contains a single partition and is made available on /dev/sdb, which command mounts the disk in /media/usb?

A. mount /dev/sdb1 /media/usb

B. usbconnect /dev/sdb0 /media/usb

C. mount /dev/sdb0 /media/usb

D. usbmount /dev/sdb1 /media/usb

39. You have connected a USB disk to the system and need to find out its connection point within the system. Which of the following is the best method for accomplishing this task?

A. Rebooting the system

B. Viewing the contents of /var/log/usb.log

C. Connecting the drive to a USB port that you know the number of

D. Running dmesg and looking for the disk

40. Which of the following commands will initiate an immediate shutdown of the system?

A. shutdown -c

B. halt

C. systemd stop

D. stop-system

41. Which option within a systemd service file indicates the program to execute?

A. StartProgram

B. ShortCut

C. ExecStart

D. Startup

42. What is the command to display the default target on a computer running systemd?

A. systemctl defaults

B. update-rc.d defaults

C. systemctl runlevel

D. systemctl get-default

43. Which option of the systemctl command will change a service so that it runs on the next boot of the system?

A. enable

B. startonboot

C. loadonboot

D. start

44. Which of the following best describes the /proc filesystem?

    A. /proc contains information about files to be processed.

    B. /proc contains configuration files for processes.

    C. /proc contains information on currently running processes, including the kernel.

    D. /proc contains variable data such as mail and web files.

45. Which command will retrieve information about the USB connections on a computer in a tree-like format?

    A. lsusb -tree

    B. lsusb --tree

    C. lsusb -t

    D. usblist --tree

46. How many SCSI devices are supported per bus?

    A. 7 to 15

    B. 2 to 4

    C. 12

    D. 4

47. What is one reason why a device driver does not appear in the output of lsmod, even though the device is loaded and working properly?

    A. The use of systemd means that drivers are not required for most devices.

    B. The use of initramfs means that support is enabled by default.

    C. The system does not need a driver for the device.

    D. Support for the device has been compiled directly into the kernel.

48. Which option to rmmod will cause the module to wait until it's no longer in use to unload the module?

    A. -test

    B. -f

    C. -w

    D. -unload

Chapter 2

Linux Installation and Package Management(Domain 102)

THE FOLLOWING COMPTIA LINUX+/LPIC-1 EXAM OBJECTIVES ARE COVERED IN THIS CHAPTER:

✓ **102.1 Design hard disk layout**

- Allocate filesystems and swap space to separate partitions or disks
- Tailor the design to the intended use of the system
- Ensure the /boot partition conforms to the hardware architecture requirements for booting
- Knowledge of basic features of LVM
- The following is a partial list of the used files, terms and utilities:
  - /(root) filesystem
  - /var filesystem
  - /home filesystem
  - /boot filesystem
  - swap space
  - mount points
  - partitions

✓ **102.2 Install a boot manager**

- Providing alternative boot locations and backup boot options
- Install and configure a boot loader such as GRUB Legacy

- Perform basic configuration changes for GRUB 2

- Interact with the boot loader

- The following is a partial list of the used files, terms, and utilities

  - menu.lst, grub.cfg and grub.conf

  - grub-install

  - grub-mkconfig

  - MBR

✓ **102.3 Manage shared libraries**

- Identify shared libraries

- Identify the typical locations of system libraries

- Load shared libraries

- The following is a partial list of the used files, terms and utilities

  - ldd

  - ldconfig

  - /etc/ld.so.conf

  - LD_LIBRARY_PATH

✓ **102.4 Use Debian package management**

- Install, upgrade and uninstall Debian binary packages

- Find packages containing specific files or libraries which may or may not be installed

- Obtain package information like version, content, dependencies, package integrity and installation status (whether or not the package is installed)

- The following is a partial list of the used files, terms and utilities:

  - /etc/apt/sources.list

  - dpkg

  - dpkg-reconfigure

  - apt-get

  - apt-cache

  - aptitude

✓ 102.5 Use RPM and YUM package management

- Install, re-install, upgrade and remove packages using RPM and YUM

- Obtain information on RPM packages such as version, status, dependencies, integrity and signatures

- Determine what files a package provides, as well as find which package a specific file comes from

- The following is a partial list of the used files, terms and utilities:

  - rpm

  - rpm2cpio

  - /etc/yum.conf

  - /etc/yum.repos.d/

  - yum

  - yumdownloader

1. When partitioning a disk for a mail server running Postfix, which partition/mounted directory should be the largest in order to allow for mail storage?

   A. /etc

   B. /usr/bin

   C. /mail

   D. /var

2. Which option within GRUB Legacy is used to indicate that a root partition contains a non-Linux kernel?

   A. initrd

   B. non-linux

   C. rootnoverify

   D. root-win

3. Which option within a partition mounting command will cause the partition to be mounted in such a way as to prevent execution of programs?

   A. execless

   B. stoprun

   C. noexec

   D. norun

4. Which command will output a new GRUB 2 configuration file and send the output to the correct location for booting?

   A. update-grub > /boot/grub/grub.cfg

   B. update-grub boot > /boot/grub/grub.cfg

   C. grub-rc.d

   D. grub-boot

5. What is the maximum number of primary partitions available on an MBR partitioning system?

   A. Two

   B. Four

   C. One

   D. Five

6. Which command is used to update the links and cache for shared libraries on the system?

   A. ldcache

   B. cache-update

   C. link-update

   D. ldconfig

7. Which command and option are used to update a Debian system to the latest software?

   A. `apt-update`

   B. `apt-get upgrade`

   C. `dpkg -U`

   D. `apt-cache clean`

8. Which option given to a yum command will install a given package?

   A. `update`

   B. `configure`

   C. `install`

   D. `get`

9. What is the location of the home directory for the root user?

   A. `/home/root`

   B. `/home/su`

   C. `/root`

   D. `/`

10. When using rpm2cpio, by default, the output is sent to which location?

   A. STDOUT

   B. The file `cpio.out`

   C. The file `a.out`

   D. The file `/tmp/cpi.out`

11. When working with partitions on disk, you see the type 0x82. Which type of partition is this?

   A. Linux

   B. Linux swap

   C. NTFS

   D. FAT32

12. Which partition or directory structure typically holds most of the programs for a Linux system?

   A. `/etc`

   B. `/usr`

   C. `/home`

   D. `/var`

13. Your GRUB Legacy configuration includes a dual-boot option with Linux listed first and another operating system listed second. Which of the following options will boot to the Linux partition by default?

A. default=linux

B. default=0

C. default=1

D. default=other

14. Which file should you edit when using GRUB 2 in order to set things like the timeout?

A. /etc/default/grub

B. /etc/grub/boot

C. /etc/boot/grub.d

D. /grub.d/boot

15. Which yum option displays the dependencies for the package specified?

A. list

B. deplist

C. dependencies

D. listdeps

16. Which options for an rpm command will display verbose output for an installation along with progress of the installation?

A. -ivh

B. -wvh

C. --avh

D. --ins-verbose

17. Which of the following commands adds /usr/local/lib to the LD_LIBRARY_PATH when using Bash shell?

A. set PATH=/usr/local/lib

B. export LD_LIBRARY_PATH=$LD_LIBRARY_PATH:/usr/local/lib

C. LD_LIBRARY_PATH=/usr/local/lib

D. connectpath LD_LIBRARY_PATH=/usr/local/lib

18. Which command can be used to download an RPM package without installing it?

A. yumdl

B. yumdownloadonly

C. yumdown

D. yumdownloader

19. Which command will search for a package named zsh on a Debian system?

    A. `apt-cache search zsh`

    B. `apt-get search zsh`

    C. `apt-cache locate zsh`

    D. `apt search zsh`

20. Which option within `/etc/default/grub` is used to configure the default operating system for boot?

    A. `GRUB_OS`

    B. `GRUB_ON`

    C. `GRUB_DEFAULT`

    D. `DEFAULT_OS`

21. When found in a GRUB configuration file, what does the `ro` option indicate?

    A. Initially mount the root partition as read-only

    B. Mount the kernel as read-only

    C. Start the `init` program as read-once

    D. Mount the root partition in Raised Object mode

22. Within which directory will you find the repositories used by YUM?

    A. `/etc/yum.conf`

    B. `/etc/repos`

    C. `/etc/yum.conf.d`

    D. `/etc/yum.repos.d`

23. Which `rpm` option can be used to verify that no files have been altered since installation?

    A. `-V`

    B. `-v`

    C. `--verbose`

    D. `--filesum`

24. Which option for the `grub-mkconfig` command sends output to a file instead of STDOUT?

    A. `-STDOUT`

    B. `--fileout`

    C. `-o`

    D. `-f`

25. The presence of `menu.lst` within the filesystem typically indicates which condition?

    A. GRUB Legacy is in use on the system.

    B. GRUB 2 is in use on the system.

    C. An error has occurred creating the output to `menu.lst`.

    D. The options for rescue boot have been changed.

26. Which command is used to determine the libraries on which a given command depends?

   A. ldconfig

   B. librarylist

   C. listdeps

   D. ldd

27. Which of the following is true of Linux swap space?

   A. Swap is used to hold temporary database tables.

   B. Swap is used as additional memory when there is insufficient RAM.

   C. Swap is used by the mail server for security.

   D. Swap is used to scrub data from the network temporarily.

28. Which of the following is not typically used to store libraries?

   A. /lib

   B. /etc/lib

   C. /usr/lib

   D. /usr/local/lib

29. Which of the following commands updates the package cache for a Debian system?

   A. apt-get cache-update

   B. apt-cache update

   C. apt-get update

   D. apt-get upgrade

30. Within which file are details of the current package repositories stored on a Debian system?

   A. /etc/apt.list

   B. /etc/sources.list

   C. /etc/apt/sources.list

   D. /etc/apt.d/sources.list

31. Of the following choices, which size would be most appropriate for the /boot partition of a Linux system?

   A. Between 100 MB and 500 MB

   B. Between 1 GB and 10 GB

   C. /boot should not be partitioned separately.

   D. Less than 5 MB

32. Which of the following commands initializes a physical disk partition for use with LVM?

   A. lvmcreate

   B. pvcreate

    C. `fvcreate`

    D. `lvinit`

33. Which of the following commands installs GRUB into the MBR of the second SATA disk?

    A. `grub-install /dev/hdb2`

    B. `grub-install /dev/sda2`

    C. `grub-config /dev/sda`

    D. `grub-install /dev/sdb`

34. Which command should be used to make changes to the choices made when a Debian package was installed?

    A. `dpkg-reconfigure`

    B. `dpkg -r`

    C. `dpkg --reconf`

    D. `apt-get reinstall`

35. Which command is used to create a logical volume with LVM?

    A. `pvcreate`

    B. `lvmcreate`

    C. `lvcreate`

    D. `volcreate`

36. What is the logical order for creation of an LVM logical volume?

    A. Physical volume creation, volume group creation, logical volume creation

    B. Physical volume creation, logical volume creation, volume group creation

    C. Logical volume creation, physical volume creation, volume group creation

    D. LVM creation, format, partition

37. Which of the Debian package management tools provides a terminal-based interface for management?

    A. `apt-get`

    B. `dpkg`

    C. `apt-cache`

    D. `aptitude`

38. Which option for yum performs a search of the package cache?

    A. `seek`

    B. `query`

    C. `--search`

    D. `search`

39. Which command option for `rpm` can be used to show the version of the kernel?

   A. `rpm kernel`

   B. `rpm -q kernel`

   C. `rpm search kernel`

   D. `rpm --list kern`

40. Assuming a menu entry of "Debian" in your GRUB configuration, which option in `/etc/default/grub` would set that as the default operating system to boot?

   A. `GRUB_OS`

   B. `GRUB_OS_DEF`

   C. `GRUB_DEFAULT`

   D. `GRUB_CONF`

41. Which option in `/etc/yum.conf` is used to ensure that the kernel is not updated when the system is updated?

   A. `exclude=kernel*`

   B. `exclude-kernel`

   C. `updatekernel=false`

   D. `include-except=kernel`

42. Which partition type should be created for a Linux system non-swap partition?

   A. 82

   B. 83

   C. 84

   D. L

43. Which command should be run after making a change to the `/etc/default/grub` file?

   A. `grub`

   B. `grub-mkconfig`

   C. `grub-inst`

   D. `reboot`

44. Which command searches for and provides information on a given package on a Debian system, including whether or not the package is currently installed?

   A. `dpkg -i`

   B. `dpkg -s`

   C. `apt-cache`

   D. `apt-info`

45. Which command is used to search for physical volumes for use with LVM?

  A. `lvmcreate`

  B. `pvcreate`

  C. `lvmdiskscan`

  D. `lvmscan`

46. Which option added to `yumdownloader` will also download dependencies?

  A. `--deps`

  B. `--resolve`

  C. `--resdeps`

  D. `-d`

47. Which of the following installs a previously downloaded Debian package?

  A. `dpkg -i <package name>`

  B. `apt-install <package name>`

  C. `apt-slash <package name>`

  D. `dpkg -U <package name>`

48. A hard drive is reported as hd(0,0) by the GRUB Legacy configuration file. To which of the following disks and partitions does this correspond?

  A. `/dev/hdb2`

  B. `/dev/hda0`

  C. `/dev/disk1`

  D. `/dev/sda1`

Chapter

3

GNU and Unix Commands (Domain 103)

THE FOLLOWING COMPTIA LINUX+/LPIC-1 EXAM OBJECTIVES ARE COVERED IN THIS CHAPTER:

✓ **103.1 Work on the command line**

- Use single shell commands and one line command sequences to perform basic tasks on the command line
- Use and modify the shell environment including defining, referencing and exporting environment variables
- Use and edit command history
- Invoke commands inside and outside the defined path
- The following is a partial list of the used files, terms and utilities:
  - bash
  - echo
  - env
  - export
  - pwd
  - set
  - unset
  - man
  - uname
  - history
  - .bash_history

✓ 103.2 Process text streams using filters

- Send text files and output streams through text utility filters to modify the output using standard UNIX commands found in the GNU textutils package

- The following is a partial list of the used files, terms and utilities:

  - cat
  - cut
  - expand
  - fmt
  - head
  - od
  - join
  - nl
  - paste
  - pr
  - sed
  - sort
  - split
  - tail
  - tr
  - unexpand
  - uniq
  - wc

✓ 103.3 Perform basic file management.

- Copy, move and remove files and directories individually
- Copy multiple files and directories recursively
- Remove files and directories recursively
- Use simple and advanced wildcard specifications in commands
- Using find to locate and act on files based on type, size, or time

- Usage of tar, cpio, and dd
- The following is a partial list of the used files, terms and utilities:
  - cp
  - find
  - mkdir
  - mv
  - ls
  - rm
  - rmdir
  - touch
  - tar
  - cpio
  - dd
  - file
  - gzip
  - gunzip
  - bzip2
  - xz
  - file globbing

✓ **103.4   Use streams, pipes and redirects**

- Redirecting standard input, standard output and standard error
- Pipe the output of one command to the input of another command
- Use the output of one command as arguments to another command
- Send output to both stdout and a file
- The following is a partial list of the used files, terms and utilities:
  - tee
  - xargs

✓ 103.5   Create, monitor and kill processes

- Run jobs in the foreground and background
- Signal a program to continue running after logout
- Monitor active processes
- Select and sort processes for display
- Send signals to processes
- The following is a partial list of the used files, terms and utilities:
  - &
  - bg
  - fg
  - jobs
  - kill
  - nohup
  - ps
  - top
  - free
  - uptime
  - pgrep
  - pkill
  - killall
  - screen

✓ 103.6   Modify process execution priorities

- Know the default priority of a job that is created
- Run a program with higher or lower priority than the default
- Change the priority of a running process
- The following is a partial list of the used files, terms and utilities:
  - nice
  - ps
  - renice
  - top

✓ **103.7 Search text files using regular expressions**

- Create simple regular expressions containing several notational elements

- Use regular expression tools to perform searches through a filesystem or file content

- The following is a partial list of the used files, terms and utilities:

  - grep

  - egrep

  - fgrep

  - sed

  - regex(7)

✓ **103.8 Perform basic file editing operations using vi**

- Navigate a document using vi

- Use basic vi modes

- Insert, edit, delete, copy and find text

- The following is a partial list of the used files, terms and utilities:

  - vi

  - /, ?

  - h, j, k, l

  - i, o, a

  - c, d, p, y, dd, yy

  - ZZ, :w!, :q!, :e!

1. What command can be used to view the current settings for your environment when using Bash?

   A. environment

   B. env

   C. listenv

   D. echoenv

2. Assume that you're using the Bash shell and want to prevent output redirects from accidentally overwriting existing files. Which command and option can be used to invoke this behavior?

   A. setoutput -f

   B. overwrite=no

   C. overwrite -n

   D. set -C

3. Which command is used to access documentation on a Linux computer for a given command?

   A. doc

   B. heredoc

   C. man

   D. manual

4. Which of the following commands will print various information about the kernel and architecture, along with other details?

   A. info --sys

   B. man sys

   C. sysinfo

   D. uname -a

5. When using sed for a substitution operation, which option must be included so that the substitution applies to the entire line rather than just the first instance?

   A. g

   B. a

   C. r

   D. y

6. Which option for the wc command prints the number of lines given as input?

   A. -f

   B. -a

   C. -l

   D. -o

7. What is the default number of lines printed by the head and `tail` commands, respectively?

    A. 10 for head, 5 for `tail`

    B. 5 for head, 10 for `tail`

    C. 10 for both head and `tail`

    D. 3 for both head and `tail`

8. You are attempting to use `rmdir` to remove a directory, but there are still multiple files and other directories contained within it. Assuming that you're sure you want to remove the directory and all of its contents, what are the command and arguments needed to remove the directory and all of its contents?

    A. `rm -f`

    B. `rm -rf`

    C. `rmdir -a`

    D. `rmdir -m`

9. Which command will find directories with names beginning with 2014 located beneath the current directory?

    A. `find ./ -name "2014"`

    B. `find ./ -type d -name "2014"`

    C. `find / -type d "2014"`

    D. `find ./ -type d -name "2014*"`

10. Which of the following commands will provide the usernames in a sorted list gathered from the `/etc/passwd` file?

    A. `cat /etc/passwd | awk -F: '{print $1}' | sort`

    B. `sort /etc/passwd | cut`

    C. `echo /etc/passwd`

    D. `cat /etc/passwd | awk '{print $1}' | sort`

11. Which options to `ls` will produce output, including hidden (dot) files, in a list that is ordered such that the newest files are at the end of the output?

    A. `-la`

    B. `-lat`

    C. `-latr`

    D. `-ltr`

12. What will be the result if the `touch` command is executed on a file that already exists?

    A. The access timestamp of the file will change to the current time when the touch command is executed.

    B. The file will be overwritten.

    C. There will be no change.

    D. The file will be appended to.

13. Which option to both mv and cp will cause the command to prompt before overwriting files that already exist?

   A. -f

   B. -Z

   C. -r

   D. -i

14. Which of the following commands will send the contents of /etc/passwd to both stdout and a file called passwordfile?

   A. cat /etc/passwd > passwordfile

   B. var /etc/passwd | passwordfile

   C. cat /etc/passwd | tee passwordfile

   D. echo /etc/passwd | stdout > passwordfile

15. The current hierarchy on the server contains a directory called /usr/local. You need to create additional directories below that called /usr/local/test/october. Which command will accomplish this task?

   A. mkdir -p /usr/local/test/october

   B. mkdir /usr/local/test/october

   C. mkdir -r /usr/local/test/october

   D. mkdir -f /usr/local/test/october

16. Which option to the cp command will copy directories in a recursive manner?

   A. -v

   B. -R

   C. -Z

   D. -i

17. You have received a file that does not have a file extension. Which command can you run to help determine what type of file it might be?

   A. grep

   B. telnet

   C. file

   D. export

18. Which command will create an image of the /dev/sda1 disk partition and place that image into a file called output.img?

   A. dd if=sda of=/dev/sda1

   B. dd if=output.img of=/dev/sda1

   C. dd if=/dev/sda1 of=output.img

   D. echo /dev/sda1 > output.img

19. What is the default delimiter used by the `cut` command?
    - **A.** Colon
    - **B.** Tab
    - **C.** Space
    - **D.** Comma

20. Which of the following will unzip and extract the contents of a file that has been tarred and gzipped?
    - **A.** `tar -zxf <file.tgz>`
    - **B.** `tar -xf <file.tgz>`
    - **C.** `tar -vz <file.tgz>`
    - **D.** `tar -fd <file.tgz>`

21. What command is used to bring a command to foreground processing after it has been backgrounded with an &?
    - **A.** `bg`
    - **B.** `fore`
    - **C.** `4g`
    - **D.** `fg`

22. You need to write a script that gathers all of the process IDs for all instances of Apache running on the system. Which of the following commands will accomplish this task?
    - **A.** `ps auwx | grep apache`
    - **B.** `pgrep apache`
    - **C.** `processlist apache`
    - **D.** `ls -p apache`

23. Which of the following command lines would monitor a single process called `nagios` in a continuous manner?
    - **A.** `top -n 1`
    - **B.** `top -p 23`
    - **C.** `ps -nagios`
    - **D.** `top -p`pidof nagios``

24. Users are reporting that various programs are crashing on the server. When examining logs, you see that certain processes are reporting out-of-memory conditions. Which command can you use to see the overall memory usage, including available swap space?
    - **A.** `tree`
    - **B.** `pgrep`
    - **C.** `uptime`
    - **D.** `free`

25. You are using the vi editor for changing a file and need to exit. You receive a notice indicating "No write since last change." Assuming that you want to save your work, which of the following commands will save your work and exit vi?

   A. :wq

   B. :q!

   C. dd

   D. x

26. What option is used to change the number of lines of output for the head and tail commands?

   A. -l

   B. -f

   C. -g

   D. -n

27. Which command can be used to determine the current load average along with information on the amount of time since the last boot of the system?

   A. uptime

   B. sysinfo

   C. bash

   D. ls -u

28. You need to start a long-running process that requires a terminal and foreground processing. However, you cannot leave your terminal window open due to security restrictions. Which command will enable you to start the process and return at a later time to continue the session?

   A. fg

   B. bg

   C. kill

   D. screen

29. You have attempted to stop a process using its service command and also using the kill command. Which signal can be sent to the process using the kill command in order to force the process to end?

   A. -15

   B. -f

   C. -9

   D. -stop

30. When working in the Bash shell, you need to redirect both stdout and stderr. Which of the following commands will redirect both stdout and stderr?

   A. 1>2

   B. >2

    C. 2>&1

    D. >>

31. Which command can be run to determine the default priority for processes spawned by the current user?

    A. prio

    B. nice

    C. renice

    D. defpriority

32. Which of the following egrep commands will examine /etc/passwd to find users who are using either /bin/bash or /usr/bin/zsh for their shell environment?

    A. grep sh /etc/passwd

    B. egrep '/*/.sh$' /etc/passwd

    C. grep '/*/.=sh$' /etc/passwd

    D. egrep '/*/.?sh$' /etc/passwd

33. Which option to the man command accesses a different level of documentation, for example, system call documentation?

    A. man 2 <argument>

    B. progman <argument>

    C. man --sys <argument>

    D. man --list sys

34. When editing with vi, which command changes into insert mode and opens a new line below the current cursor location?

    A. f

    B. a

    C. o

    D. i

35. Which kill signal can be sent in order to restart a process?

    A. -HUP

    B. -RESTART

    C. -9

    D. -SIG

36. Which of the following commands will display the last 50 lines of your command history when using Bash, including commands from the current session?

    A. bashhist 50

    B. history 50

    C. cat .bash_history

    D. tail -f .bash_history

37. You have backgrounded several tasks using &. Which command can be used to view the current list of running tasks that have been backgrounded?

   A. procs

   B. plist

   C. jobs

   D. free

38. Which of the following commands searches each user's .bash_history file to determine if the user has invoked the sudo command?

   A. find /home -name "bash_history" | grep sudo

   B. find /home -name ".bash_history" | xargs grep sudo

   C. find /home/.bash_history | xargs grep sudo

   D. find /home -type history | xargs grep sudo

39. Which command will watch the Apache log at /var/log/httpd/access.log and continually scroll as new log entries are created?

   A. watch /var/log/httpd/access.log

   B. tail /var/log/httpd/access.log

   C. tail -f /var/log/httpd/access.log

   D. mon /var/log/httpd/access.log

40. You are debugging a configuration file and the daemon indicates there is a problem on line 932. Which of the following commands will prepend line numbers onto the file?

   A. lines

   B. wc -l

   C. newline

   D. nl

41. You receive a file with a .lzma extension. Which command can you use to decompress this file?

   A. xz

   B. lz

   C. gz

   D. bzip

42. Which find command will locate files within the current directory that have been modified within the last 24 hours?

   A. find ./ -type f -mtime 1

   B. find ./ -type f -mtime 24

   C. find ./ -type f -mtime +1

   D. find ./ type -f time 24

43. Which command will move all files with a .txt extension to the /tmp directory?

   A. mv txt* tmp

   B. move *txt /temp

   C. mv *.txt /tmp

   D. mv *.txt tmp

44. Which command prints your current directory?

   A. cwd

   B. curdur

   C. cd

   D. pwd

45. Assume that you have a file called zips.txt that contains several postal zip codes, and you need to determine how many unique zip codes there are in the file. Which of the following commands can be used for that purpose?

   A. sort zips.txt | uniq -c

   B. uniq zips.txt

   C. count zips.txt

   D. cat zips.txt | uniq -c

46. When using Bash, how would you execute the last command starting with a certain string, even if that command was not the last one that you typed?

   A. Precede the command with ! and then the string to search for.

   B. Search for the command in history.

   C. Precede the command with ? and then the string to search for.

   D. This is not possible with Bash.

47. Which command can be used to kill all processes by using their name?

   A. killproc

   B. killname

   C. killall

   D. kill -f

48. You're working with a large file in vi, and you need to search for instances of a string earlier in the file. Which key will search backward in the file?

   A. /

   B. h

   C. ?

   D. x

Chapter

4

Devices, Linux Filesystems, and the Filesystem Hierarchy Standard (Domain 104)

THE FOLLOWING COMPTIA LINUX+/LPIC-1 EXAM OBJECTIVES ARE COVERED IN THIS CHAPTER:

✓ **104.1 Create partitions and filesystems**

- Manage MBR partition tables
- Use various mkfs commands to create various filesystems such as:
  - ext2
  - ext3
  - ext4
  - XFS
  - VFAT
- Awareness of ReiserFS and Btrfs
- Basic knowledge of gdisk and parted with GPT
- The following is a partial list of the used files, terms and utilities:
  - fdisk
  - gdisk
  - parted
  - mkfs
  - mkswap

✓ **104.2 Maintain the integrity of filesystems**

- Verify the integrity of filesystems
- Monitor free space and inodes
- Repair simple filesystem problems
- The following is a partial list of the used files, terms and utilities:
    - du
    - df
    - fsck
    - e2fsck
    - mke2fs
    - debugfs
    - dumpe2fs
    - tune2fs
    - xfs tools (such as xfs_metadump and xfs_info)

✓ **104.3 Control mounting and unmounting of filesystems**

- Manually mount and unmount filesystems
- Configure filesystem mounting on bootup
- Configure user mountable removeable filesystems
- The following is a partial list of the used files, terms and utilities:
    - /etc/fstab
    - /media
    - mount
    - umount

✓ **104.4 Manage disk quotas**

- Set up a disk quota for a filesystem
- Edit, check and generate user quota reports

- The following is a partial list of the used files, terms and utilities:
  - quota
  - edquota
  - repquota
  - quotaon

✓ **104.5 Manage file permissions and ownership.**

- Manage access permissions on regular and special files as well as directories
- Use access modes such as suid, sgid and the sticky bit to maintain security
- Know how to change the file creation mask
- Use the group field to grant file access to group members
- The following is a partial list of the used files, terms and utilities:
  - chmod
  - umask
  - chown
  - chgrp

✓ **104.6 Create and change hard and symbolic links**

- Create links
- Identify hard and/or softlinks
- Copying versus linking files
- Use links to support system administration tasks
- The following is a partial list of the used files, terms and utilities:
  - ln
  - ls

✓ **104.7 Find system files and place files in the correct location.**

- Understand the correct locations of files under the FHS
- Find files and commands on a Linux system

- Know the location and purpose of important files and directories as defined in the FHS
- The following is a partial list of the used files, terms and utilities:
    - find
    - locate
    - updatedb
    - whereis
    - which
    - type
    - /etc/updatedb.conf

1. Which command can be used to determine the location of a given executable that would be run if typed from your current environment and location?

   A. which

   B. what

   C. whatis

   D. when

2. Which of the following commands will correctly change the group ownership of the file called a.out to users?

   A. chgrp users a.out

   B. chgrp a.out users

   C. groupchg a.out users

   D. grpchg users a.out

3. Another administrator made a change to one of the local scripts used for administrative purposes. The change was also immediately reflected in your copy of the script. However, when examining the file with ls, it appears to be a normal file. What is the likely cause of such a scenario?

   A. The file was executed after edit.

   B. The administrator copied the file to yours.

   C. Your file is a hard link to the original.

   D. The file has been restored from backup.

4. Which of the following commands shows the usage of inodes across all filesystems?

   A. df -i

   B. ls -i

   C. du -i

   D. dm -i

5. When running fsck on an ext3 filesystem, the process is taking longer than expected and requiring input from the administrator to fix issues. What option could be added to fsck next time so that the command will automatically attempt to fix errors without intervention?

   A. -o

   B. -V

   C. -y

   D. -f

6. After you insert a new hard drive into the system, what is the correct order to make the drive ready for use within Linux?

   A. Use fdisk to create partitions and then mount the partitions.

   B. Mount the partitions.

   C. Use fdisk to create partitions and mount -a to mount all of the newly created partitions.

   D. Use fdisk to create partitions, then format the partitions with something like mkfs, and then mount the partitions.

7. You are using a SAN (storage area network) that keeps causing errors on your Linux system due to an improper kernel module created by the SAN vendor. When the SAN sends updates, it causes the filesystem to be mounted as read-only. Which command and option can you use to change the behavior of the filesystem to account for the SAN bug?

    A. `mount- --continue`

    B. `tune2fs -e continue`

    C. `mkfs --no-remount`

    D. `mount -o remount`

8. Which of the following describes a primary difference between ext2 and ext3 filesystems?

    A. ext3 was primarily a bugfix update to ext2.

    B. ext3 includes journaling for the filesystem.

    C. ext3 completely changed the tools needed for management of the disks.

    D. ext3 has no significant differences.

9. Which option to umask will display the permissions to be used in a POSIX format?

    A. `-P`

    B. `-p`

    C. `-S`

    D. `-v`

10. Which option to `ln` creates a symlink to another file?

    A. `-sl`

    B. `-s`

    C. `-l`

    D. `--ln`

11. Which of the following commands can be used if you need to locate various elements of a given command, such as its binaries and man pages?

    A. `whatis`

    B. `find`

    C. `whereis`

    D. `ls`

12. Which option in `/etc/updatedb.conf` will remove a path from inclusion in the results?

    A. PRUNEPATHS

    B. EXCLUDEPATHS

    C. INCLUDEEXCLUDE

    D. SEPARATEPATH

13. According to the FHS, what is the correct location for site-specific data for a server?

　　A. /etc

　　B. /var

　　C. /tmp

　　D. /srv

14. Which of the following commands enables the sticky bit for a user on a file called homescript.sh?

　　A. chmod +sticky homescript.sh

　　B. chmod 755 homescript.sh

　　C. chmod u+s homescript.sh

　　D. chown u+sticky homescript.sh

15. Which option to the mount command will mount all filesystems that are currently available in /etc/fstab?

　　A. -f

　　B. -d

　　C. -a

　　D. -m

16. Which command is used to format a swap partition?

　　A. fdisk

　　B. mkswap

　　C. formatswap

　　D. format -s

17. Which command and option are used to display the number of times that a filesystem has been mounted?

　　A. tune2fs -h

　　B. cat /etc/fstab

　　C. mount -a

　　D. less /etc/fsmnt

18. Which option to xfs_metadump displays a progress indicator?

　　A. -g

　　B. -p

　　C. -f

　　D. -v

19. Which command is used to execute a check of user quotas on the filesystem?

   A. quota -u

   B. runquota -u

   C. qcheck -u

   D. quotacheck -u

20. The system is running out of disk space within the home directory partition and quotas have not been enabled. Which command can you use to determine the directories that might contain large files?

   A. du

   B. df

   C. ls

   D. locate

21. Which file contains information about the filesystems to mount, their partitions, and the options that should be used to mount them?

   A. /etc/filesystems

   B. /etc/mounts

   C. /etc/fstab

   D. /srv/mounts

22. According to the FHS, what is the proper mount point for removable media?

   A. /etc

   B. /srv

   C. /tmp

   D. /media

23. Which file contains information on currently mounted filesystems, including their mount options?

   A. /etc/mtab

   B. /etc/fstab

   C. /tmp/files

   D. /etc/filesystems

24. Which option to umount will cause the command to attempt to remount the filesystem in read-only mode if the unmounting process fails?

   A. -o

   B. -r

   C. -f

   D. -v

25. The umask command reports the mask as 022. What is the permission that will be in effect for a newly non-executable created file?

   A. u+rw, g+r, w+r

   B. 755

   C. 022

   D. a+r

26. When using ls -la to obtain a directory listing, you see an object with permissions of lrwxrwxrwx. What type of object is this?

   A. It is a directory.

   B. It is a symlink.

   C. It is a temporary file.

   D. It is a local file.

27. Which command and option will output a summary of quota usage across all filesystems that are currently read-write with quotas enabled?

   A. repq -a

   B. repquota -a

   C. quotarun -a

   D. quota -u

28. The locate command is reporting out-of-date information. Which command should be run in order to have the locate command update its database?

   A. locatedb -u

   B. locate -u

   C. updatedb

   D. updatelocate

29. Which shell built-in command can be used to determine what command will be run?

   A. type

   B. when

   C. find

   D. help

30. Which option to chown recursively changes the ownership?

   A. -f

   B. -R

   C. -a

   D. -m

31. Which of the following represents the correct format for the /etc/fstab file?

    A. `<directory> <device> <type> <options>`

    B. `<device> <type> <options>`

    C. `<device> <type> <options> <directory> <dump> <fsck>`

    D. `<device> <directory> <type> <options> <dump> <fsck>`

32. Which of the following commands is used to identify the UUID for partitions?

    A. `blkid`

    B. `ls`

    C. `find`

    D. `cat`

33. The `xfs_info` command is functionally equivalent to which command and option?

    A. `xfs_test -n`

    B. `xfs_list`

    C. `tunexfs -i`

    D. `xfs_growfs -n`

34. Which of the following commands will create a btrfs filesystem on the first SATA drive?

    A. `mkfs /dev/sda1`

    B. `mkfs.btrfs /dev/sda`

    C. `mkfs.btr2fs /dev/sda1`

    D. `mkfs -b /dev/sda`

35. Which option is set on a filesystem in order to enable user-level quotas?

    A. `quotaon`

    B. `enquota=user`

    C. `usrquota`

    D. `userquota`

36. You need to enable the web server (running as the www-data user and group) to write into a directory called /home/webfiles. Which commands will accomplish this task in the most secure manner?

    A. `chgrp www-data /home/webfiles; chmod 775 /home/webfiles`

    B. `chmod 777 /home/webfiles`

    C. `chgrp www-data /home/webfiles; chmod 711 /home/webfiles`

    D. `chmod 707 /home/webfiles`

37. Which command and option are used to set the maximum number of times that a filesystem can be mounted between running `fsck`?

A. `tune2fs -c`

B. `tune2fs -f`

C. `tune2fs -m`

D. `setmount`

38. Which command can be used to change the partitioning scheme for a disk, such as to change the size of existing partitions without deleting them?

A. `resize2fs`

B. `parted`

C. `mkfs`

D. `rfdisk`

39. Which of the following commands will mount a USB device at /dev/sdb1 into the /media/usb directory, assuming a VFAT filesystem for the USB drive?

A. `mount -t vfat /dev/sdb1 /mnt`

B. `usbmount /dev/sdb1 /mnt/usb`

C. `mount -t vfat /dev/sdb1 /media/usb`

D. `mount -t usb /dev/sdb1 /mnt/usb`

40. Which option within `gdisk` will change the partition name?

A. n

B. b

C. v

D. c

41. Which option to the `dumpe2fs` command can be used to display blocks that are reserved because of being marked as bad?

A. `-v`

B. `-f`

C. `-b`

D. `-m`

42. Which options to `fsck` can be used to check all filesystems listed in /etc/fstab while excluding the root partition?

A. `-NR`

B. `-AM`

C. `-X`

D. `-C`

43. Which command is used to enable quotas on a filesystem that has been previously set up for quota usage?

   A. quotaenable

   B. quotaon

   C. quotau

   D. enquota

44. Which option in /etc/fstab sets the order in which the device is checked at boot time?

   A. options

   B. dump

   C. fsck

   D. checkorder

45. Which option to quotacheck is used to create the files for the first time?

   A. -f

   B. -u

   C. -m

   D. -c

46. The SAN has crashed and one of the filesystems in a Linux server has become significantly corrupt as a result. Which command and option can be used to attempt to examine the contents of the drive without causing more damage?

   A. fdisk -f

   B. mke2fs -c

   C. debugfs -c

   D. ls -a

47. Which option to the find command will search for files by their inode number?

   A. -inode

   B. -type

   C. -in

   D. -inum

48. Which option to chgrp will change group ownership of all files within a given directory?

   A. -directory

   B. -d

   C. -R

   D. -V

Chapter 5

Working with Shells, Scripting, and Data Management (Domain 105)

THE FOLLOWING COMPTIA LINUX+/LPIC-1 EXAM OBJECTIVES ARE COVERED IN THIS CHAPTER:

✓ **105.1 Customize and use the shell environment**

- Set environment variables (e.g., PATH) at login or when spawning a new shell
- Write Bash functions for frequently used sequences of commands
- Maintain skeleton directories for new user accounts
- Set command search path with the proper directory
- The following is a partial list of the used files, terms and utilities:
    - source
    - /etc/bash.bashrc
    - /etc/profile
    - env
    - export
    - set
    - unset
    - ~/.bash_profile
    - ~/.bash_login
    - ~/.profile

- ~/.bashrc
- ~/.bash_logout
- function
- alias
- lists

✓ 105.2 Customize or write simple scripts

- Use standard sh syntax (loops, tests)
- Use command substitution
- Test return values for success or failure or other information provided by a command
- Perform conditional mailing to the superuser
- Correctly select the script interpreter through the shebang (#!) line
- Manage the location, ownership, execution and suid-rights of scripts
- The following is a partial list of the used files, terms and utilities:
  - for
  - while
  - test
  - if
  - read
  - seq
  - exec

✓ 105.3 SQL data management

- Use of basic SQL commands
- Perform basic data manipulation
- The following is a partial list of the used files, terms and utilities:
  - insert
  - update

- select

- delete

- from

- where

- group by

- order by

- join

1. Which command is used to read and execute commands from a file in the Bash shell?

    A. run

    B. execute

    C. source

    D. func

2. You need a command to be executed on logout for all users. Within which file should this be placed (assume that all users are using Bash)?

    A. `~/.bash_logout`

    B. `/etc/bash.bash_logout`

    C. `/home/.bash_logout`

    D. `/etc/bash_logout`

3. Which of the following commands removes an environment variable that has been set?

    A. `profile --unset`

    B. `env -u`

    C. `set -u`

    D. `import`

4. When setting the shebang line of a shell script, which of the following commands will help to determine the location of the interpreter automatically?

    A. `#!/usr/bin/env bash`

    B. `#!/bin/bash`

    C. `#!env`

    D. `/bin/int bash`

5. When querying a database, which of the following SQL statements retrieves all data from a table called users?

    A. `SELECT ALL_DATA FROM users;`

    B. `QUERY ALL FROM users;`

    C. `SELECT * Table: Users;`

    D. `SELECT * FROM users;`

6. Which of the following best describes the PS1 environment variable?

    A. PS1 is used to set the location of the PostScript command.

    B. PS1 is used to define the default shell prompt for Bash.

    C. PS1 is used as a per-system variable.

    D. PS1 is user defined and does not have a default value or setting.

7. Which of the following commands ensures that the `-la` options are used when the `ls` command is executed without other options?

- **A.** `alias ls="ls -la"`
- **B.** `ln -s ls ls -la`
- **C.** `alias "ls -la" = ls`
- **D.** `set ls`

8. What is the order in which user configuration files are located on login to a Bash shell?

- **A.** `.bash_login, .profile, /etc/profile`
- **B.** `.bash_profile, .bash_login, .profile`
- **C.** `.profile, .bash_login, .bash_profile`
- **D.** `.bash_login, .bash_profile, .profile`

9. Which variable within a Bash script is used to access the first command-line parameter?

- **A.** `$ARG`
- **B.** `$0`
- **C.** `$1`
- **D.** `$ARG0`

10. Which of the following provides the end for an `if` conditional in a Bash script?

- **A.** `ex`
- **B.** `}`
- **C.** `]`
- **D.** `fi`

11. Which of the following commands will delete all data from a table called `virtualusers` in MySQL on Linux?

- **A.** `DELETE FROM VIRTUALUSERS;`
- **B.** `DELETE FROM virtualusers;`
- **C.** `DELETE * FROM virtualusers;`
- **D.** `DELETE ALL FROM virtualusers;`

12. Which of the following commands displays the columns and column types within a given table?

- **A.** `DESC`
- **B.** `ASK`
- **C.** `SELECT`
- **D.** `DISPLAY`

13. Which of the following commands will print a list of six numbers beginning at 0?

   A. `list 0-5`

   B. `seq 0 1 5`

   C. `echo 0-5`

   D. `seq 0 1 6`

14. When creating a shell script, which of the following commands is used to display the contents of variables?

   A. `var_dump`

   B. `echo`

   C. `ls`

   D. `env`

15. A command has the following listing obtained with `ls -la`:

   `-rwsr-xr-x 1 suehring suehring 21 Nov 2 13:53 script.sh`

   What does the `s` denote within the user permissions in the listing?

   A. The SUID bit has been set for this program.

   B. This is a symlink.

   C. The file will not be executable.

   D. The file is a special system file.

16. Which of the following commands will execute a script and then exit the shell?

   A. `run`

   B. `source`

   C. `./`

   D. `exec`

17. Which sequence of characters will execute two commands but only if the first command exits successfully?

   A. `--`

   B. `&*`

   C. `&&`

   D. `&`

18. Which command within a shell script awaits user input and places that input into a variable?

   A. `exec`

   B. `get`

   C. `read`

   D. `prompt`

19. What characters are used to mark a sequence of commands as a function within a shell script?

    A. Parentheses to declare the function (optional) and curly braces to contain the commands

    B. Curly braces to declare the function and parentheses to contain the commands

    C. Square brackets to declare the function and curly braces to contain the commands

    D. Run quotes to denote the function

20. Assume that you are retrieving data from a MySQL database and need the data to be displayed in ascending numeric order based on a column called "id." Which of the following commands added to the SELECT statement accomplishes this task?

    A. ORDER BY id ASC;

    B. ORDER BY id;

    C. GROUP BY id;

    D. GROUP BY id ASC;

21. Which character sequence denotes an alternate command to execute if the preceding command does not exit successfully?

    A. &&

    B. --

    C. ||

    D. EL

22. Which keyword(s) is/are used to begin an alternate condition within a Bash script?

    A. if

    B. else if

    C. elif

    D. elsif

23. Which of the following commands removes a currently defined aliased command?

    A. remove

    B. rm

    C. unalias

    D. delete

24. When sourcing a file in Bash, which chmod command would be necessary to provide the minimum privileges in order for the file to be sourced correctly, assuming that your current user owns the file?

    A. chmod 600

    B. chmod 755

    C. chmod 777

    D. chmod 400

25. Assuming that a space-separated list of values has been defined as such
`LIST="one two three four"`, which of the following `for` loop constructs
will iterate through the elements in the list?

   A. `for LIST`

   B. `for VAR in LIST`

   C. `for VAR in $LIST`

   D. `for $LIST -> $VAR`

26. Which type of join will be used in SQL when you see a statement such as
`table1.id = table2.id`?

   A. Inner

   B. Outer

   C. Left outer

   D. Right outer

27. Which test within a shell script `while` loop will examine one value to see if it is less than
another?

   A. `-less`

   B. `-lessThan`

   C. `-lt`

   D. `-lthan`

28. Which of the following tests will determine if a file exists in the context of a shell script?

   A. `-a`

   B. `-e`

   C. `-m`

   D. `-i`

29. Within which directory should you place files to have them automatically copied to a user's
home directory when the user is created?

   A. `/etc/userhome`

   B. `/etc/templateuser`

   C. `/etc/skel`

   D. `/home/skel`

30. Which of the following represents the correct syntax for a SQL UPDATE statement?

   A. `UPDATE <table> SET <column> = <newvalue> WHERE <column> = <value>`

   B. `UPDATE <table> WHERE <column> = <newvalue>`

   C. `UPDATE WHERE <column> = <newvalue>`

   D. `UPDATE FROM <table> VALUE (<value>)`

31. Assume a MySQL table called AUTHENTICATION has three columns (id, username, password). Which of the following statements inserts a row into the table?

A. INSERT id,username,password INTO AUTHENTICATION;

B. INSERT INTO AUTHENTICATION VALUES ('user','pass');

C. INSERT AUTHENTICATION ('', 'user','pass');

D. INSERT INTO AUTHENTICATION (username,password) VALUES ('user','pass');

32. Which option to Bash will cause the shell to be executed without reading the initialization files?

A. --no-rc

B. --no-init

C. --norc

D. --rc-none

33. Which of the following creates an array in a bash script?

A. ARRAY=(val1 val2)

B. ARRAY = "val1 val2"

C. ARRAY_PUSH($ARRAY,"val1","val2");

D. ARRAY{0} = "val1"

34. Which option to declare statements displays output in a way that could then be used as input to another command?

A. -o

B. -n

C. -p

D. -m

35. You need to create a function that will be available each time that you log in to the system. Within which file should this function be placed?

A. .bash_profile

B. .rc0

C. /etc/profile

D. .bash_run

36. Which shell built-in command is used to display a list of read-only variables?

A. ro

B. readonly

C. env-ro

D. ro-env

37. Which of the following SQL keywords can be used with a GROUP BY clause?

   A. SELECT

   B. INSERT

   C. UPDATE

   D. DELETE

38. Which characters are used to denote the beginning and end of the test portion of a while loop in a shell script?

   A. Parentheses ( )

   B. Curly braces { }

   C. Square brackets [ ]

   D. Double-quotes " "

39. When using the test built-in with one argument, what will be the return if its argument is not null?

   A. false

   B. true

   C. unknown

   D. -1

40. Which environment variable is used when changing directory with the tilde character, such as cd ~ ?

   A. HOMEDIR

   B. HOMEPATH

   C. HOME

   D. MAILPATH

41. Which environment variable can be set if you wish to log users out of their shell automatically after a certain period of inactivity?

   A. TIMEOUT

   B. TMOUT

   C. TO

   D. IDLETIME

42. When using a case statement within a shell script, which sequence denotes the ending of the case/switch statement?

   A. caseend

   B. esac

   C. endcase

   D. }

43. Which of the following commands will obtain the date in seconds since the epoch and place it into a variable called DATE within a shell script?

A. DATE="$(date +%s)"

B. DATE="date"

C. DATE="$(date)";

D. DATE="$date %s"

44. Assume that you have a variable called $FILEPATH within a Bash shell script. Which characters can be used to ensure that the variable will be interpolated correctly regardless of where the variable appears within the script?

A. Dollar sign $FILEPATH

B. Curly braces ${FILEPATH}

C. Parentheses $(FILEPATH)

D. Square brackets $[FILEPATH]

45. Which sequence is used to mark the beginning and end of the commands to execute within a for loop in a shell script?

A. Curly braces { }

B. The keywords do and done

C. Semicolons ;

D. Tabs

46. Which of the following tests will determine if a file exists and can be read by the user executing the test?

A. -e

B. -s

C. -a

D. -r

47. Which option to the declare command will create a variable that is read-only?

A. -r

B. -ro

C. -p

D. -x

48. Which character sequence is used to provide a default case when used within a case statement in a shell script?

A. default:

B. =)

C. -->

D. *)

Chapter 6

Understanding User Interfaces and Desktops (Domain 106)

THE FOLLOWING COMPTIA LINUX+/LPIC-1 EXAM OBJECTIVES ARE COVERED IN THIS CHAPTER:

✓ **106.1 Install and configure X11.**

- Verify that the video card and monitor are supported by an X server
- Awareness of the X font server
- Basic understanding and knowledge of the X Window configuration file
- The following is a partial list of the used files, terms and utilities:
  - /etc/X11/xorg.conf
  - xhost
  - DISPLAY
  - xwininfo
  - xdpyinfo
  - X

✓ **106.2 Set up a display manager.**

- Basic configuration of LightDM
- Turn the display manager on or off
- Change the display manager greeting
- Awareness of XDM, KDM and GDM

- The following is a partial list of the used files, terms and utilities:
  - lightdm
  - /etc/lightdm/

✓ 106.3 Accessibility.

- Basic knowledge of keyboard accessibility settings (AccessX)
- Basic knowledge of visual settings and themes
- Basic knowledge of assistive technology (AT)
- The following is a partial list of the used files, terms and utilities:
  - Sticky/repeat keys
  - Slow/bounce/toggle keys
  - Mouse keys
  - High contrast/large print desktop themes
  - Screen reader
  - Braille display
  - Screen magnifier
  - On-screen keyboard
  - Gestures (used at login, for example gdm)
  - Orca
  - GOK
  - Emacspeak

1. Within which configuration file is the greeter configured for `lightdm`?

   A. `/etc/lightdm/lightdm.conf`

   B. `/etc/lightdm/greeter.conf`

   C. `/etc/lightdm.conf`

   D. `/var/lib/lightdm/lightdm.conf`

2. Which section in `/etc/X11/xorg.conf` is used to describe configurations for a given graphics card and monitor pair?

   A. Server

   B. Screen

   C. VidMode

   D. Video

3. When setting the frequency options for a given monitor, which of the following is not an available frequency unit?

   A. uHz

   B. MHz

   C. kHz

   D. M

4. Which command on a `systemd`-based system is used to disable booting into a GUI?

   A. `systemctl gui-boot disable`

   B. `systemctl set-default boot-gui false`

   C. `systemctl set-default multi-user.target`

   D. `systemctl set-default-multi false`

5. Assuming X forwarding has been enabled on the ssh server, which environment variable is used to set the location for newly spawned windows from within an ssh session?

   A. `DISPLAY`

   B. `XTERMINAL`

   C. `XTERM`

   D. `XDISP`

6. Within the greeter section of a display manager such as GDM, which option sets the welcome message for users logging in locally?

   A. `LoginMessage`

   B. `Login`

   C. `WinGreet`

   D. `Welcome`

7. Within GNOME, enabling sticky keys can be done by pressing which key five times in a row?

A. Ctrl

B. Enter

C. Shift

D. Tab

8. Which option in the Module section of the `xorg.conf` configuration file causes a default module to be unloaded or not loaded by default?

A. Disable

B. Unload

C. LoadDisable

D. DisableLoad

9. Which program is used in a GNOME environment as a screen reader?

A. Orca

B. Screed

C. Screen

D. Reader

10. Assuming a monitor currently set at 1024×768, which command will change the screen resolution such that icons and other elements appear larger?

A. xterm -r 0

B. xset res 1024x768

C. xrandr -s 800x600

D. xVGA

11. LightDM typically allows guest login by default. Which configuration option within SeatDefaults changes this to disallow guests?

A. guest-login=false

B. guest=false

C. allowg=false

D. allow-guest=false

12. When using XFree86 as the X server, which command will cause the X server to query for hardware and create a new configuration file?

A. XFree86 --newconfig

B. XFree86 --query

C. XFree86 -configure

D. xf -config

13. Which configuration option for X is used to configure the keyboard model?

    A. XkbLayout

    B. XkbModel

    C. XkbType

    D. XkbInput

14. Which configuration line within a Monitor section of an X server configuration file will set the vertical refresh rate between 55 and 75 hertz?

    A. Vert 55-75

    B. VertRefresh 55.0–75.0

    C. VertSync 55.0–75.0

    D. RefreshMode 55.0–75.0

15. From within an X session, which of the following commands shows information about the display, including resolution and color depth?

    A. xinfo

    B. xterm

    C. xwin

    D. xdpyinfo

16. Which AccelerationProfile for an input device such as a mouse enables linear acceleration (more speed and more acceleration)?

    A. 0

    B. -1

    C. 6

    D. 7

17. Which of the following directories is used by an X.org-based server for storage of fonts?

    A. /usr/share/fonts

    B. /usr/X11/fonts

    C. /etc/fonts

    D. /var/font/xorg

18. Native support for a Braille display requires a minimum of which kernel version?

    A. 2.2.0

    B. 2.4.22

    C. 2.6.26

    D. 3.2.1

19. Which configuration option in an `xorg.conf` file can be set to prevent a user from changing video modes using the Ctrl+Alt+Keypad Plus and Ctrl+Alt+Keypad Minus?

  A. `DontZoom`

  B. `Modes=No`

  C. `NoModeSwitch`

  D. `DontZap`

20. GNOME includes native on-screen keyboard functionality. Which of the following commands starts the on-screen keyboard?

  A. `gok`

  B. `osk`

  C. `kb`

  D. `oskb`

21. When using GDM as the display manager, which GUI program can be used to set options for the login window?

  A. `gdmlogin`

  B. `gdmconfig`

  C. `gdmsetup`

  D. `gdm`

22. When using KDE, which program provides magnification functionality?

  A. `xmag`

  B. `mag`

  C. `pmag`

  D. `kmag`

23. Which option in the SeatDefaults section of the `lightdm.conf` configuration file is used to disable the display of usernames for login?

  A. `greeter-disable-user`

  B. `greeter-enable-login`

  C. `greeter-show-manual-login`

  D. `greeter-disable-auto-login`

24. Within GNOME, which section of the GNOME Control Center is used to choose a high-contrast theme?

  A. Display

  B. Appearance

  C. Locale

  D. Contrast

25. Which of the following best describes the concept of a mouse gesture?

   A. A mouse gesture enables special clicks, such as right-click context menu.

   B. A mouse gesture facilitates use of programs by moving the mouse in a certain way.

   C. A mouse gesture is used for login purposes.

   D. A mouse gesture is used to capture screenshots.

26. In GNOME 3.9 or later, which keyboard shortcut activates the screen reader?

   A. Super+R

   B. Super+S

   C. Ctrl+Super+S

   D. Alt+Super+S

27. Assume that the display manager has been disabled on boot. Which command can be used after login to start the X server?

   A. xs

   B. xstart

   C. X -start

   D. startx

28. Which option in an `xorg.conf` configuration file configures the amount of time before the screen goes into blank mode but does not go into standby and is available on non-DPMS capable monitors?

   A. StandbyTime

   B. BlankTime

   C. SuspendTime

   D. OffTime

29. Which of the following commands helps you to determine information about a given window within an X session, including information on the window size and its position?

   A. xkbinfo

   B. xdspy

   C. xwininfo

   D. xver

30. Which option/button within GOK is used to show the keys that would be used in place of a mouse?

   A. Mouse

   B. MouseKeys

   C. Movement

   D. Compose

31. Which of the following commands allows a host named cwa to connect to the X server?

   A. `xconnect cwa`

   B. `xterm +cwa`

   C. `xhost +cwa`

   D. `xf cwa`

32. Which of the following options in the ssh configuration file needs to be enabled so that X sessions can be sent over an ssh connection?

   A. `X11Connect yes`

   B. `ForwardX11 yes`

   C. `ForwardX yes`

   D. `XForward yes`

33. Which configuration option in a Files section of an `xorg.conf` configuration file can be used to add a path in which the server will search for fonts?

   A. `FontSection`

   B. `Fonts`

   C. `FontLoc`

   D. `FontPath`

34. Which assistive technology is used to provide an input method for users who cannot type but can use a pointer, such as a mouse?

   A. Keyboard

   B. Sticky keys

   C. Mouse keys

   D. On-screen keyboard

35. Which assistive technology will ignore keys that are pressed in succession or held down?

   A. Sticky keys

   B. Mouse keys

   C. Bounce keys

   D. On-screen keyboard

36. When using LightDM, which key combination is used to revert to a terminal?

   A. Alt+Ctrl+F2

   B. Alt+Ctrl+F1

   C. Ctrl+F1

   D. Ctrl+Esc

37. Which option in the LightDM configuration enables automatic login for a specific user?

   A. `auto-login`

   B. `autologin-user`

C. autologin

D. auto-login-user

38. Which of the following is a legacy utility that can be used to set accessibility options on older systems?

A. Xaccessibility

B. Xas

C. AccessX

D. setX

39. Which command, when executed on a remote host, will send the display of X programs to the local client? (Assume the use of Bash for the shell.)

A. export DISPLAY

B. env DISPLAY

C. setx HOST

D. export XHOST

40. Which option in GOK is used to display the keys that correspond to a given application's menu?

A. Menus

B. Activate

C. MenuKeys

D. Keys

41. Which directory is used to store individual configuration files related to LightDM?

A. /etc/light

B. /etc/lightdm/lightdm.conf.d

C. /usr/lightdm

D. /etc/lightdm.conf

42. Which command will switch the system into an init in which the X server is not typically executed?

A. telinit 6

B. telinit 1

C. telinit 3

D. telinit 5

43. Which option within the Device section for a video card will set the amount of RAM available on the card?

A. VRAM

B. RAM

C. VideoRam

D. vRam

44. When configuring a Screen section in an X configuration file, the Display subsection can contain the color depth. What is the name of the option to set the color depth of the given display?

   A. `ColorDepth`

   B. `Depth`

   C. `CDepth`

   D. `colorDep`

45. Multiple server layouts can be created within an X configuration file. Which option is used to differentiate between the different server layout options?

   A. `ID`

   B. `Identifier`

   C. `LayoutName`

   D. `Layout`

46. Which command can be used to create a `fonts.scale` file definition when executed against the current directory?

   A. `mkfontscale`

   B. `mk.fonts`

   C. `mkfontfile`

   D. `fontmk`

47. What is the abbreviation used in X to signify a display that utilizes additional features such as extended power-saving capabilities?

   A. DPMS

   B. XPMS

   C. DISPPWR

   D. PWRD

48. What is the name of the accessibility function that provides an alternative to the Orca program to assist users that have visual impairments?

   A. Viz

   B. Emacspeak

   C. Ahleah

   D. vAssist

Chapter

7

Administrative Tasks (Domain 107)

THE FOLLOWING COMPTIA LINUX+/LPIC-1 EXAM OBJECTIVES ARE COVERED IN THIS CHAPTER:

✓ **107.1 Manage user and group accounts and related system files**

- Add, modify and remove users and groups

- Manage user/group info in password/group databases

- Create and manage special purpose and limited accounts

- The following is a partial list of the used files, terms and utilities:

  - /etc/passwd

  - /etc/shadow

  - /etc/group

  - /etc/skel

  - chage

  - getent

  - groupadd

  - groupdel

  - groupmod

  - passwd

  - useradd

  - userdel

  - usermod

✓ **107.2 Automate system administration tasks by scheduling jobs**

- Manage cron and at jobs

- Configure user access to cron and at services

- Configure anacron
- The following is a partial list of the used files, terms and utilities:
  - /etc/cron.{d,daily,hourly,monthly,weekly}
  - /etc/at.deny
  - /etc/at.allow
  - /etc/crontab
  - /etc/cron.allow
  - /etc/cron.deny
  - /var/spool/cron/*
  - crontab
  - at
  - atq
  - atrm
  - anacron
  - /etc/anacrontab

✓ **107.3 Localization and internationalization**

- Configure local settings and environment variables
- Configure timezone settings and environment variables
- The following is a partial list of the used files, terms and utilities:
  - /etc/timezone
  - /etc/localtime
  - /usr/share/zoneinfo
  - Environment variables:
    - LC_*
    - LC_ALL
    - LANG
    - TZ
  - /usr/bin/locale
  - tzselect

- tzconfig
- date
- iconv
- UTF-8
- ISO-8859
- ASCII
- Unicode

1. Which file contains user information, such as username and real name, and is readable by all users of the system?

    A. /etc/pass

    B. /etc/shadow

    C. /etc/passwd

    D. /etc/userinfo

2. Which of the following will execute a job through cron at 12:15 a.m. and 12:15 p.m. every day?

    A. 0,12 15 * * *

    B. 15 0,12 * * *

    C. 15 * * * 0/12

    D. */12 * * * 15

3. Which file is used to indicate the local time zone on a Linux server?

    A. /etc/timez

    B. /etc/timezoneconfig

    C. /etc/localtime

    D. /etc/localtz

4. Which file is used to provide a list of users that can add and delete cron jobs?

    A. /etc/cron.job

    B. /etc/cron.allow

    C. /etc/cron.users

    D. /etc/crontab

5. Which of the following commands removes an expiration from an account?

    A. sudo chage -l username

    B. sudo chage -E -1 username

    C. sudo chage -E now username

    D. sudo chage --noexpire username

6. Within which directory will you find files related to the time zone for various regions?

    A. /etc/timezoneinfo

    B. /etc/zoneinfo

    C. /var/zoneinfo

    D. /usr/share/zoneinfo

7. Which of the following commands schedules a series of commands to execute one hour from now?

    A. atq +1hr

    B. at now + 1 hour

    C. atq

    D. at -1

8. You need to delete a user from the system, including their home directory. Which of the following commands accomplishes this task?

    A. userdel

    B. userdel -r

    C. userdel -R

    D. deluser

9. Within which directory should you place files in order for the files to be copied to a user's home directory when the user is created?

    A. /etc/skel

    B. /etc/homedir

    C. /home/usertemplate

    D. /etc/template

10. Which job scheduler should you use if the computer on which you need to schedule the job is powered down at various times?

    A. cron.d

    B. cron.hourly

    C. anacron

    D. at

11. Which of the following commands provides the current date and time in a format of seconds since the epoch?

    A. date +%seconds

    B. date +%s

    C. date --seconds

    D. date --now

12. Which option to the iconv command shows the available character sets on a given system?

    A. --showchar

    B. --show

    C. --list

    D. --all

13. Which environment variable controls the format of dates and times, such as a 12-hour or 24-hour formatted clock?

    A.   LOCALE_DATE

    B.   DATE_FORMAT

    C.   LC_TIME

    D.   LC_DATE

14. Which command displays a list of jobs currently scheduled with at?

    A.   atlist

    B.   atq

    C.   atl

    D.   at --jobs

15. To which shell should a user be set if they are not allowed to log in interactively to the computer?

    A.   /bin/bash

    B.   /bin/tcsh

    C.   /bin/zsh

    D.   /bin/false

16. Which of the following encodings provides a multibyte representation of characters?

    A.   ISO-8859

    B.   UTF-8

    C.   ISO-L

    D.   UFTMulti

17. Which of the following commands changes a group called DomainAdmins to DomainUsers?

    A.   groupmod -n DomainAdmins DomainUsers

    B.   groupchg DomainAdmins DomainUsers

    C.   chgroup DomainAdmins DomainUsers

    D.   group -N DomainAdmins DomainUsers

18. Within which directory would you find a list of files corresponding to the users who have current cron jobs on the system?

    A.   /var/spool/cron/crontabs

    B.   /var/spool/jobs

    C.   /etc/cron

    D.   /etc/cron.users

19. Which command deletes an at job with an ID of 3?

  A. atq

  B. at -l

  C. atrm 3

  D. rmat 3

20. Which command can be used to view the available time zones on a system and obtain output that can be used in scripts for setting the time zone?

  A. tzd

  B. /etc/locale

  C. tzdata

  D. tzselect

21. You need to determine if LDAP integration is working correctly. In order to do so, you would like to obtain a list of users, as read by /etc/nsswitch.conf. Which command can be used for this purpose?

  A. getuser

  B. getent

  C. usermod

  D. userlist

22. What is the name of the configuration file that contains information about group and user addition, such as the maximum and minimum user and group IDs to be used when adding users and groups?

  A. /etc/groupinfo

  B. /etc/login.defs

  C. /etc/login.info

  D. /etc/loginlist

23. Which of the following is used as a system-wide cron file?

  A. /etc/cron.d

  B. /etc/cron.sys

  C. /etc/crontab

  D. /etc/cron.tab

24. Which of the following lines added to .profile in a user's home directory will set their time zone to Central time?

  A. TZ=/Central; export TZ

  B. TIMEZONE='America/Chicago'; export TIMEZONE

  C. set TZ=/Central

  D. TZ='America/Chicago'; export TZ

25. Within which directory will you find scripts that are scheduled to run through cron every 24 hours?

    A. /etc/cron.daily

    B. /etc/cron.weekly

    C. /etc/cron.hourly24

    D. /etc/crontab

26. Which of the following values for the LANG variable will configure the system to bypass locale translations where possible?

    A. LANG=COMPAT

    B. LANG=NONE

    C. LANG=C

    D. LANG=END

27. When running useradd, which option needs to be specified in order for the user's home directory to be created?

    A. -h

    B. -m

    C. -x

    D. -a

28. Which of the following commands locks out password-based login for a user but does not prevent other forms of login?

    A. usermod -L

    B. userdel -r

    C. useradd -h

    D. userlock

29. If you need to reconfigure all locale variables and settings temporarily for a given session, which environment variable can be used?

    A. LC_LIST

    B. LC_GLOBAL

    C. LC_ALL

    D. ALL_LOCALE

30. Which of the following will run a command called /usr/local/bin/changehome.sh as the www-data user when placed in /etc/crontab?

    A. 1 1 * * * www-data /usr/local/bin/changehome.sh

    B. www-data changehome.sh

    C. */1 www-data changehome.sh

    D. * * */www-data /usr/local/bin/changehome.sh

31. Which of the following commands produces a report listing the last password change date for all users on the system?

    A. passwd -a

    B. passwd -S

    C. passwd -a -S

    D. passwd --all

32. Assume that passwords must be changed every 60 days. Which command will change the date of the user's last password change without the user actually changing the account password?

    A. chage -f

    B. chage -W

    C. chage -l

    D. chage -d

33. Which of the following files is used by anacron for reading configuration information related to jobs?

    A. /etc/anacron.d

    B. /etc/anacrontab

    C. /etc/anacron.config

    D. /etc/anacron.conf

34. Which of the following commands will set the system-wide time zone to America/Los_Angeles?

    A. ln -sf /usr/share/zoneinfo/America/Los_Angeles /etc/localtime

    B. ln -sf America/Los_Angeles; /etc/localtime

    C. ln -sd /etc/localtime /usr/share/timezone/America/Los_Angeles

    D. ln -sf /etc/localtime /usr/share/zoneinfo/America/Los_Angeles

35. Which file contains a list of users who are not allowed to create cron scheduled tasks?

    A. /etc/cron.users

    B. /etc/cron.deny

    C. /etc/cron.allow

    D. /etc/cron.userlist

36. Which file contains a list of usernames, UIDs, and encrypted passwords?

    A. /etc/passwd

    B. /etc/shadow

    C. /etc/encpass

    D. /etc/grouppass

37. Which of the following best describes the relationship between UIDs and GIDs on a Linux system?

    A. The UID and GID are the same across the system for a given user.

    B. Each user has a UID and GID that are the same and are created when the user is created.

    C. The UID represents the user, whereas the GID is a globally unique user id.

    D. There is no direct relationship between UIDs and GIDs.

38. Which command on a Debian-based system can be used to change the time zone using the package-based tools?

    A. `dpkg-reconfigure time`

    B. `dpkg-reconfigure tzdata`

    C. `apt-select tzdata`

    D. `apt-config timezone`

39. Which command is used to change a user's home directory to `/srv/data/username` and move the contents at the same time?

    A. `usermod -d /srv/data/username -m`

    B. `homedir -m /srv/data/username`

    C. `userex -m /srv/data/username`

    D. `userchg /m /srv/data/username -d`

40. Which option to `useradd` will add additional groups for a user?

    A. `-g`

    B. `-x`

    C. `-l`

    D. `-G`

41. Which command will list the cron entries for a given user as denoted by `<username>`?

    A. `crontab -l -u <username>`

    B. `crontab -u <username>`

    C. `cron -u <username>`

    D. `cronent -u <username>`

42. Which option to `useradd` creates a system user rather than a normal user?

    A. `-r`

    B. `-s`

    C. `-a`

    D. `-S`

43. Which file contains encrypted password information for groups?

   A. /etc/group

   B. /etc/gshadow

   C. /etc/gsecure

   D. /etc/group.conf

44. Which locale-related variable is used for currency-related localization?

   A. LC_MONE

   B. LC_CURRENCY

   C. LC_MONETARY

   D. LC_CURR

45. Which of the following best describes the use of the groupdel command?

   A. You may force group deletion with the -f option.

   B. If a user's primary group is to be deleted, that user must be deleted first or have their primary group changed.

   C. groupdel can be run at any time, regardless of group membership.

   D. The -r option for groupdel will recursively change a user's GIDs after group deletion.

46. Which of the following commands displays the UID, primary group, and supplemental groups for a given user?

   A. id

   B. getid

   C. passwd

   D. chage

47. Which option to the usermod command is used to change a given user's real name?

   A. -R

   B. -n

   C. -d

   D. -c

48. Assume that you have deleted a user account with UID 1501, including the -r option. Which command should you also run to look for other files that might have been owned by the user?

   A. find -id 1501

   B. grep 1501 *

   C. grep -u 1501 *

   D. find / -uid 1501

Chapter 8

Essential System Services (Domain 108)

THE FOLLOWING COMPTIA LINUX+/LPIC-1 EXAM OBJECTIVES ARE COVERED IN THIS CHAPTER:

✓ **108.1 Maintain system time**

- Set the system date and time
- Set the hardware clock to the correct time in UTC
- Configure the correct timezone
- Basic NTP configuration
- Knowledge of using the pool.ntp.org service
- Awareness of the ntpq command
- The following is a partial list of the used files, terms and utilities:
  - /usr/share/zoneinfo
  - /etc/timezone
  - /etc/localtime
  - /etc/ntp.conf
  - date
  - hwclock
  - ntpd
  - ntpdate
  - pool.ntp.org

✓ **108.2 System logging**

- Configuration of the syslog daemon
- Understanding of standard facilities, priorities and actions
- Configuration of logrotate

- Awareness of rsyslog and syslog-ng
- The following is a partial list of the used files, terms and utilities:
  - syslog.conf
  - syslogd
  - klogd
  - /var/log/
  - logger
  - logrotate
  - /etc/logrotate.conf
  - /etc/logrotate.d/
  - Journalctl
  - /etc/systemd/journald.conf
  - /var/log/journal/

✓ **108.3   Mail Transfer Agent (MTA) basics**

- Create email aliases
- Configure email forwarding
- Knowledge of commonly available MTA programs (postfix, sendmail, qmail, exim) (no configuration)
- The following is a partial list of the used files, terms and utilities:
  - ~/.forward
  - sendmail emulation layer commands
  - newaliases
  - mail
  - mailq
  - postfix
  - sendmail
  - exim
  - qmail

✓ 108.4   Manage printers and printing

- Basic CUPS configuration (for local and remote printers)
- Manage user print queues
- Troubleshoot general printing problems
- Add and remove jobs from configured printer queues
- The following is a partial list of the used files, terms and utilities:
  - CUPS configuration files, tools and utilities
  - /etc/cups
  - lpd legacy interface (lpr, lprm, lpq)

1. Which of the following commands is used to examine the systemd journal or log file?

   A. journallist

   B. ctlj

   C. journalctl

   D. jctl

2. Which system logging facility is used for messages from the kernel?

   A. syslog

   B. kernel

   C. kern

   D. system

3. To what server address can you set an NTP client in order to receive time from a regionally local server?

   A. 127.0.0.1

   B. 192.168.1.100

   C. ntp.example.com

   D. pool.ntp.org

4. What is the name of the systemd service that provides logging facilities?

   A. systemd-journald

   B. systemd-loggingd

   C. systemd-syslog

   D. systemd-logger

5. Which command must you run after making a change to email aliases on a server running Postfix?

   A. service postfix restart

   B. newaliases

   C. alias -n

   D. postfix -e

6. Within which directory hierarchy will you find configuration files related to printing with the CUPS printing system?

   A. /etc/cupsd

   B. /etc/cups.d

   C. /etc/CUPS

   D. /etc/cups

7. Which access control directive in a CUPS configuration file configures the system to accept connections from the local network with addresses from 192.168.1.1 through 192.168.1.127?

   A. Allow 192.168.1.0/25

   B. Allow 192.168.1.0/24

   C. Allow 127.0.0.0/8

   D. AllowHosts 192.168.1.0

8. Which of the following commands will set the date immediately and can be used from the command line in a script?

   A. ntpd

   B. ntpdate pool.ntp.org

   C. settime

   D. time

9. When executing the ntpq command, you receive a message like "read: Connection refused." What would this typically indicate?

   A. The network is down.

   B. The NTP daemon is not running.

   C. The use of NTP is administratively prohibited.

   D. The current user does not have permission to execute ntpq.

10. Which command is used to query and work with the hardware clock on the system?

    A. hwc

    B. ntpdate

    C. systime

    D. hwclock

11. Within which directory will you find the mail queue on a qmail server?

    A. /var/spool/qmail

    B. /var/qmail/queue

    C. /var/spool/mailq

    D. /var/spool/qmail/queue

12. Which syslog level is used to provide informational messages?

    A. kern

    B. emerg

    C. debug

    D. info

13. Within /etc/ntp.conf, which of the following configuration lines sets the location of the drift file?

    A. drift /var/lib/ntp/drift

    B. driftfile /var/lib/ntp/drift

    C. drift-file /var/lib/ntp/drift

    D. driftconfig /var/lib/ntp/drift

14. Which configuration option in /etc/logrotate.conf will cause the log to be emailed to admin@example.com when the logrotation process runs for the selected log?

    A. mail admin@example.com

    B. sendmail admin@example.com

    C. maillog admin@example.com

    D. logmail admin@example.com

15. Which of the following commands is used to determine the amount of disk space used by systemd journal log files?

    A. journalctl --disk

    B. journalctl -du

    C. journalctl --disk-usage

    D. journalctl -ls

16. Which of the following commands displays the current mail queue on a Postfix server?

    A. qmail

    B. mailqueue

    C. mail -q

    D. mailq

17. When running the NTP daemon, which command can you execute to work with the NTP server in an interactive mode?

    A. ntpd

    B. ntpdate

    C. ntpq

    D. ntp-interactive

18. Assume that you want all email for the root user to be sent to admin@example.com. Which of the following lines in /etc/aliases will accomplish this task?

    A. admin@example.com -> root

    B. root -> admin@example.com

    C. root, admin@example.com

    D. root: admin@example.com

19. When working with `klogd`, which option can be used to control the file to which messages are logged?

   A. `-d`

   B. `-f`

   C. `-v`

   D. `-l`

20. Within which directory will you find configuration files for various logs that are to be rotated with `logrotate`?

   A. `/etc/logrotate`

   B. `/etc/logs`

   C. `/etc/logrotate.d`

   D. `/var/spool/logrotate`

21. Which of the following commands places a file into the print queue?

   A. `lpr`

   B. `lpd`

   C. `lpq`

   D. `lpx`

22. Which of the following options to the `sendmail` command will print information about the mail queue?

   A. `-bi`

   B. `-queue`

   C. `-bp`

   D. `-f`

23. Which function of the `hwclock` command will set the hardware clock to the current system time?

   A. `-w`

   B. `-s`

   C. `-a`

   D. `-m`

24. What is the default port for the CUPS administrative web interface?

   A. `tcp/53`

   B. `tcp/8080`

   C. `udp/456`

   D. `tcp/631`

25. Which of the following commands causes sendmail to attempt to deliver the messages in its queue?

   A. `sendmail -q`

   B. `sendmail -b`

   C. `sendmail -f`

   D. `sendmail -v`

26. You need to create an email address to accept email for abuse@example.com. However, you would like to have abuse reports sent to multiple email addresses within your organization. Which of the following will send email destined for the abuse account to admin@example .com and security@example.com?

   A. Create a `.forward` file in the home directory for the abuse user and forward email accordingly.

   B. Within /etc/aliases, add this: abuse: admin@example.com,security@example.com.

   C. Create a `.forward` file for root and forward email accordingly.

   D. Within /etc/aliases, add this: abuse: admin@example.com\tsecurity@example.com.

27. Which of the following commands sets the hardware clock to UTC based on the current system time?

   A. `hwclock --systohc --utc`

   B. `hwclock --systohc --localtime`

   C. `hwclock --systohc`

   D. `hwclock --systoutc`

28. You need to delete all of the messages from the queue on a postfix server. Which of the following commands will perform this action?

   A. `postqueue -remove`

   B. `rm -rf`

   C. `postfix -f`

   D. `postsuper -d ALL`

29. Which of the following URLs can be used to view a list of completed print jobs in CUPS?

   A. `http://localhost:631/jobs?which_jobs=completed`

   B. `http://localhost:631?completed`

   C. `http://localhost:631/?completed`

   D. `http://cups/jobs=completed`

30. Which option to the `journalctl` command will continuously update the display as new log entries are created?

   A. `-tail`

   B. `-t`

   C. `-f`

   D. `-l`

31. Assuming that the `$ModLoad imudp` configuration option has been set in the configuration for `rsyslogd`, which of the following additional options is necessary to configure the port on which the server will listen?

    A. `$Port 514`

    B. `$UDPServerRun 514`

    C. `$Listen 514`

    D. `$UDPListen 514`

32. Which of the following commands causes the mail queue to be processed on a Postfix server?

    A. `postqueue -f`

    B. `postqueue -D`

    C. `postfix -q`

    D. `postsuper -q`

33. When running `ntpd`, the server will not adjust or synchronize if the time is skewed from the NTP server by a significant amount of time. Which option to `ntpd` disables this and causes the synchronization process to continue even if there is large skew?

    A. `ntpd -noskew`

    B. `ntpd -skewcheck=off`

    C. `ntpd -g 0`

    D. `ntpd -s 0`

34. Which option in `journald.conf` controls the maximum file size for individual journal logs?

    A. `SystemMaxFileSize`

    B. `MaxFile`

    C. `LogFileSize`

    D. `LogSize`

35. Which command can be executed to view completed print jobs?

    A. `lpstat -q`

    B. `lpq`

    C. `lpstat -W completed`

    D. `lpqueue -c`

36. When configuring a log file for rotation, you need to execute a command to run a script after log file rotation. Which option within the configuration can be used to facilitate this behavior?

    A. `after-rotate`

    B. `run-script`

    C. `rotatecomplete`

    D. `postrotate`

37. You are deploying an Exim server and need to work with the firewall to ensure that the proper incoming ports are open. Which protocol and port should you allow inbound for normal SMTP traffic?

    A. TCP/23

    B. TCP/25

    C. TCP/110

    D. TCP/143

38. Which command should be executed after making a change to the sendmail access database /etc/access?

    A. makemap

    B. makedb

    C. newaccess

    D. rebuilddb

39. When working with syslog-ng, which of the following is the correct path and filename for the primary configuration file?

    A. /etc/syslog-ng/syslog-ng.conf

    B. /etc/syslog/syslog-ng.conf

    C. /etc/syslog-ng/ng.conf

    D. /etc/syslog-ng/ngd.conf

40. A developer has created an application and wants to take advantage of syslog for logging to a custom log file. Which facility should be used for an application such as this?

    A. syslog

    B. kern

    C. local#

    D. user

41. A user needs to work with printer-related items. Which of the following commands adds the user (called username in the options) to the appropriate group for this purpose?

    A. usermod -aG printerusers username

    B. usermod -aG lpadmin username

    C. usermod -gA lpadm username

    D. usermod -a lpadm username

42. Which option within a logrotate configuration file disables compression of the log file?

    A. compressoff

    B. limitcompress

    C. nocompression

    D. nocompress

43. Which option to the date command can be used to set the date and time?

   A. `date -f`

   B. `date -t`

   C. `date --change`

   D. `date -s`

44. Which command can be used to gather and display statistics about mail processed on a server running sendmail?

   A. `mailq`

   B. `mailstats`

   C. `statmail`

   D. `sendmailstats`

45. When running from a shell script, which command enables logging to syslog?

   A. `logd`

   B. `login`

   C. `logit`

   D. `logger`

46. Which of the following commands can be used to restart CUPS on a server running systemd?

   A. `systemctl restart cups.service`

   B. `systemctl restart cups`

   C. `systemctl reboot cups.target`

   D. `systemctl restart cups.target`

47. When viewing the syslog configuration, you notice a minus sign (-) preceding several log files. What is the significance of the - in the configuration?

   A. The use of - indicates that the log may be rotated any time.

   B. The use of - indicates that the system can utilize other logging facilities when appropriate.

   C. The use of - omits the disk sync process for every entry into the log.

   D. The use of - comments out the line.

48. Which option in a CUPS configuration file causes the daemon to listen on all interfaces on port 631?

   A. `Port 631`

   B. `Listen All:631`

   C. `Listen 127.0.0.1:631`

   D. `Port All:631`

Chapter

9

Networking Fundamentals (Domain 109)

THE FOLLOWING COMPTIA LINUX+/LPIC-1 EXAM OBJECTIVES ARE COVERED IN THIS CHAPTER:

✓ **109.1 Fundamentals of Internet protocols**

- Demonstrate an understanding of network masks and CIDR notation

- Knowledge of the differences between private and public "dotted quad" IP addresses

- Knowledge about common TCP and UDP ports (20, 21, 22, 23, 25, 53, 80, 110, 123, 139, 143, 161, 162, 389, 443, 465, 514, 636, 993, 995)

- Knowledge about the differences and major features of UDP, TCP and ICMP

- Knowledge of the major differences between IPv4 and IPv6

- Knowledge of the basic features of IPv6

- The following is a partial list of the used files, terms and utilities:

    - /etc/services

    - IPv4, IPv6

    - Subnetting

    - TCP, UDP, ICMP

✓ **109.2 Basic network configuration**

- Manually and automatically configure network interfaces

- Basic TCP/IP host configuration

- Setting a default route
- The following is a partial list of the used files, terms and utilities:
  - /etc/hostname
  - /etc/hosts
  - /etc/nsswitch.conf
  - ifconfig
  - ifup
  - ifdown
  - ip
  - route
  - ping

✓ 109.3 Basic network troubleshooting

- Manually and automatically configure network interfaces and routing tables to include adding, starting, stopping, restarting, deleting or reconfiguring network interfaces
- Change, view or configure the routing table and correct an improperly set default route manually
- Debug problems associated with the network configuration
- The following is a partial list of the used files, terms and utilities:
  - ifconfig
  - ip
  - ifup
  - ifdown
  - route
  - host
  - hostname
  - dig
  - netstat
  - ping

- ping6
- traceroute
- traceroute6
- tracepath
- tracepath6
- netcat

✓ **109.4 Configure client side DNS**

- Query remote DNS servers
- Configure local name resolution and use remote DNS servers
- Modify the order in which name resolution is done
- The following is a partial list of the used files, terms and utilities:
  - /etc/hosts
  - /etc/resolv.conf
  - /etc/nsswitch.conf
  - Host
  - Dig
  - getent

1. Which of the following commands shows the current default route without performing DNS lookups on the IP address(es) involved?

    A. `netstat -rn`

    B. `netstat -n`

    C. `netstat -r`

    D. `netstat -f`

2. You are having difficulty with an interface on the server, and it is currently down. Assuming that there is not a hardware failure on the device itself, which command and option can you use to display information about the interface?

    A. `ifconfig -a`

    B. `ifup`

    C. `netstat -n`

    D. `ifconfig`

3. Which of the following is not used as a private address for internal, non-Internet, use?

    A. `172.16.4.2`

    B. `192.168.40.3`

    C. `10.74.5.244`

    D. `143.236.32.231`

4. Which of the following commands adds a default gateway of `192.168.1.1` for interface eth0?

    A. `route add default gateway 192.168.1.1 eth0`

    B. `eth0 --dg 192.168.1.1`

    C. `route add default gw 192.168.1.1 eth0`

    D. `route define eth0 192.168.1.1`

5. Which option for the `host` command will query for the authoritative nameservers for a given domain?

    A. `-t ns`

    B. `-t all`

    C. `-ns`

    D. `-named`

6. Which port(s) and protocol(s) should be opened in a firewall in order for the primary and secondary name servers to communicate for a given domain?

    A. UDP/53

    B. Both TCP/53 and UDP/53

    C. TCP/53

    D. UDP/53 and TCP/503

7. Which option for the `ping` command enables you to choose the interface from which the ICMP packets will be generated?

   A. `-i`

   B. `-I`

   C. `-t`

   D. `-a`

8. You need to split a subnet to enable four subnets with up to 30 hosts each. Which subnet mask, in CIDR notation, facilitates this scenario?

   A. `/25`

   B. `/24`

   C. `/32`

   D. `/27`

9. Which of the following commands queries the mail servers for the domain example.com?

   A. `dig example.com mx`

   B. `dig example.com`

   C. `host -t smtp example.com`

   D. `dig example.com smtp`

10. Which of the following addresses represents the localhost in IPv6?

   A. `0:1`

   B. `::1`

   C. `127:0:1`

   D. `:127:0:0:1`

11. Which option to the `traceroute` command will use TCP SYN packets for the path trace?

   A. `-T`

   B. `-t`

   C. `-s`

   D. `-i`

12. Which of the following commands will attempt to bring online all interfaces marked as auto within the networking configuration?

   A. `ifconfig -a`

   B. `ifup auto`

   C. `ifup -a`

   D. `ifstat`

13. In a scripting scenario, which command will return the domain name configured for the server?

   A. dnsname

   B. fqdn

   C. hostname

   D. hostname -d

14. Which command can be used to listen for netlink messages on a network?

   A. ip monitor

   B. netlink -a

   C. ip netlink

   D. route

15. If the traceroute6 command is not available, which option to the traceroute command can be used for an IPv6 traceroute?

   A. -ipv6

   B. -net6

   C. -v6

   D. -6

16. Which of the following configuration lines in /etc/nsswitch.conf causes a lookup for group information to use local files first and then to use LDAP?

   A. group: files ldap

   B. lookup: group [local ldap]

   C. group: [local ldap]

   D. group: localfiles ldap

17. Which of the following dig commands sends the query for example.com directly to the server at 192.168.2.5 rather than to a locally configured resolver?

   A. dig example.com @192.168.2.5

   B. dig -t 192.168.2.5 example.com

   C. dig -s 192.168.2.5 example.com

   D. dig server=192.168.2.5 example.com

18. Which ports need to be allowed through the firewall for SNMP traffic?

   A. Ports 23 and 25

   B. Ports 110 and 143

   C. Ports 80 and 443

   D. Ports 161 and 162

19. Which of the following commands will enumerate the hosts database?

A. `getent hosts`

B. `gethosts`

C. `nslookup`

D. `host`

20. Which of the following netmasks is used for a subnet described with a /25 in CIDR notation?

A. `255.255.255.0`

B. `255.255.0.0`

C. `255.255.255.192`

D. `255.255.255.128`

21. Which of the following configuration lines will set the DNS server to `192.168.1.4` using `/etc/resolv.conf`?

A. `dns 192.168.1.4`

B. `dns-server 192.168.1.4`

C. `nameserver 192.168.1.4`

D. `name-server 192.168.1.4`

22. When examining open ports on the server, you see that TCP port 3000 is listed with no corresponding protocol name, such as smtp, imaps, and so on. In which file would you find a list of port-to-protocol translations that could be customized to add this new port?

A. `/etc/ports`

B. `/etc/p2p`

C. `/etc/ppp`

D. `/etc/services`

23. Which of the following commands adds a route to the server for the network `192.168.51.0/24` through its gateway of `192.168.51.1`?

A. `route add -net 192.168.51.0 netmask 255.255.255.0 gw 192.168.51.1`

B. `route add -net 192.168.51/24 gw 192.168.1.51`

C. `route -net 192.168.51.0/24 192.168.51.1`

D. `route add 192.168.51.1 -n 192.168.51.0//255.255.255.0`

24. Which of the following commands shows network services or sockets that are currently along with sockets that are not listening?

A. `netstat -a`

B. `netlink -a`

C. `sockets -f`

D. `opensock -l`

25. Which of the following represents a correct configuration line for /etc/hosts?

    A. 192.168.1.4 cwa.braingia.org cwa

    B. cwa.braingia.org cwa 192.168.1.4

    C. cwa.braingia.org 192.168.1.8 alias cwa

    D. alias cwa.braingia.org cwa 192.168.1.4

26. Which of the following commands configures the eth0 device with an IP address of 192.168.1.1 in a /24 network?

    A. ifconfig eth0 192.168.1.1/24

    B. ifconfig eth0 192.168.1.1/255.255.255.0

    C. ifconfig eth0 192.168.1.1 netmask 255.255.255.0

    D. ifconfig 192.168.1.1 netmask 255.255.255.0 eth0

27. Which of the following describes a primary difference between IPv4 and IPv6?

    A. IPv4 is for internal networks only, while IPv6 is for public networks.

    B. IPv4 is for public networks, while IPv6 is for internal networks.

    C. IPv4 uses a 32-bit address, while IPv6 uses a 128-bit address.

    D. With IPv6, there is no subnetting necessary.

28. On which port does ICMP operate?

    A. TCP/43

    B. UDP/111

    C. UDP/69

    D. ICMP does not use ports.

29. Which of the following commands will change the default gateway to 192.168.1.1 using eth0?

    A. ip route default gw 192.168.1.1

    B. ip route change default via 192.168.1.1 dev eth0

    C. ip route default gw update 192.168.1.1

    D. ip route update default 192.168.1.1 eth0

30. Which of the following ports is used for Secure Shell communication?

    A. TCP/23

    B. TCP/25

    C. TCP/22

    D. TCP/2200

31. Which options for netcat will create a server listening on port 8080?

    A. netcat -p 8080

    B. nc -l -p 8080

    C. nc -p 8080

    D. nc -s 8080

32. Which of the following commands displays the Start of Authority information for the domain `example.com`?

   A. `dig example.com soa`

   B. `dig example.com authority`

   C. `dig example.com -auth`

   D. `dig -t auth example.com`

33. Assume that you want to enable local client services to go to hosts on the network without needing to qualify the name fully by adding the domain for either `example.com` or `example.org`. Which option in `/etc/resolv.conf` will provide this functionality?

   A. `search`

   B. `domain`

   C. `local-domain`

   D. `local-order`

34. Which of the following commands sends an IPv6 ping to a unique local address?

   A. `ping -6 127.0.0.1`

   B. `ping6 fddi/128`

   C. `ping6 fdd6:551:b09f::`

   D. `ping -6 fdd6:551:b09f::`

35. Which of the following commands prevents traffic from reaching the host `192.168.1.3`?

   A. `route add -host 192.168.1.3 reject`

   B. `route -nullroute 192.168.1.3`

   C. `route add -null 192.168.1.3`

   D. `route add -block 192.168.1.3`

36. Which of the following describes a primary difference between `traceroute` and `tracepath`?

   A. The `traceroute` command requires root privileges.

   B. The `tracepath` command provides the MTU for each hop whereas `traceroute` does not.

   C. The `tracepath` command cannot be used for tracing a path on an external network.

   D. The `traceroute` command is not compatible with IPv6.

37. Which of the following commands will emulate the `ping` command in Microsoft Windows, where the `ping` is sent for four packets and then exits?

   A. `ping -n 4`

   B. `ping -t 4`

   C. `ping -p 4`

   D. `ping -c 4`

38. You are troubleshooting a DNS problem using the dig command, and you receive a "status: NXDOMAIN" message. Which of the following best describes what NXDOMAIN means?

    A. NXDOMAIN means that you have received a non-authoritative answer for the query.

    B. NXDOMAIN means that the domain or host is not found.

    C. NXDOMAIN indicates a successful query.

    D. NXDOMAIN signifies a new domain record has been added.

39. Which of the following commands configures eth1 with an additional IPv6 address of fdd6:551:b09e::?

    A. ifconfig eth1 inet6 add fdd6:551:b09e::/128

    B. ifconfig add fdd6:551:b09e::

    C. ifconfig fdd6:551:b09e:: eth1

    D. ifconfig eth1 fdd6:551:b09e

40. On which port does LDAP over SSL operate?

    A. Port 53

    B. Port 389

    C. Port 636

    D. Port 443

41. You need to prevent local clients from going to a certain host, www.example.com, and instead redirect them to a localhost. Which of the following is a method to override DNS lookups for the specified host?

    A. Add a firewall entry for the IP address of www.example.com to prevent traffic from passing through it.

    B. Delete www.example.com from the route table using the route command.

    C. Add a null route to prevent access to the IP address for www.example.com.

    D. Add an entry for www.example.com in /etc/hosts to point to 127.0.0.1.

42. Which of the following commands should be executed after running ip route change?

    A. ip route flush cache

    B. ip route reload

    C. ip route cache reload

    D. ip route restart

43. Which option should be used to send a DNS query for an SPF record with dig?

    A. -t txt

    B. -t spf

    C. -t mx

    D. -t mailspf

44. Which of the following protocols uses a three-way handshake?

    A. ICMP

    B. TCP

    C. UDP

    D. IP

45. How many IP addresses are available in the `172.16.0.0` private range in IPv4?

    A. /32

    B. 16,777,216

    C. 65,536

    D. 1,048,576

46. When troubleshooting a connectivity issue, you have found that you can reach a server via the web but cannot ping it. Which of the following best describes a possible cause for this scenario?

    A. TCP traffic has been blocked at the firewall.

    B. The DNS lookup is failing.

    C. ICMP traffic has been blocked.

    D. There is a reject route in place.

47. When viewing the available routes using the `route` command, one route contains flags UG while the others contain U. What do the letters UG signify in the route table?

    A. The G signifies that the route is good.

    B. The G signifies that the route is unavailable.

    C. The G signifies that this is a gateway.

    D. The G signifies that the route is an aggregate.

48. Which of the following commands requests a zone transfer of `example.org` from the server at `192.168.1.4`?

    A. `dig example.org @192.168.1.4 axfr`

    B. `dig example.org @192.168.1.4`

    C. `dig example.org @192.168.1.4 xfer`

    D. `dig example.org #192.168.1.4 xfer`

Chapter

10

Security (Domain 110)

THE FOLLOWING COMPTIA LINUX+/LPIC-1 EXAM OBJECTIVES ARE COVERED IN THIS CHAPTER:

✓ **110.1 Perform security administration tasks**

- Audit a system to find files with the suid/sgid bit set
- Set or change user passwords and password aging information
- Being able to use nmap and netstat to discover open ports on a system
- Set up limits on user logins, processes and memory usage
- Determine which users have logged in to the system or are currently logged in
- Basic sudo configuration and usage
- The following is a partial list of the used files, terms and utilities:
    - find
    - passwd
    - fuser
    - lsof
    - nmap
    - chage
    - netstat
    - sudo
    - /etc/sudoers
    - su
    - usermod
    - ulimit
    - who, w, last

1. You need to prevent users temporarily from logging into the system using ssh or another means. Which of the following describes one method for accomplishing this task?

    A. Use the command `touch /etc/nologin`.

    B. Disable sshd.

    C. Remove `/etc/login`.

    D. Add a shadow file.

2. Which of the following commands searches the entire filesystem for files with the `setuid` bit set?

    A. `find ./ -perm suid`

    B. `find / -perm 4000`

    C. `find / -type suid`

    D. `find / -type f -perm setuid`

3. Which of the following commands displays the currently open ports and the process that is using the port?

    A. `netstat -a`

    B. `lsof -i`

    C. `ps auwx`

    D. `netlist`

4. You are attempting to unmount a filesystem using the `umount` command. However, when you do so, you receive a message indicating that the filesystem is in use. Which of the following commands can be used to determine what process is keeping a filesystem open?

    A. `fuser`

    B. `ls`

    C. `find`

    D. `ps`

5. Which of the following commands displays account information such as expiration date, last password change, and other related details?

    A. `usermod -l`

    B. `userinfo -a`

    C. `chageuser -l`

    D. `chage -l`

6. Which of the following commands scans the IP address `192.168.1.154` for open ports?

    A. `nmap 192.168.1.154`

    B. `lsof 192.168.1.154`

    C. `netstat 192.168.1.154`

    D. `netmap 192.168.1.154`

7. Which command is used to create a public/private key pair for use with ssh?

    A. ssh -k

    B. ssh-keygen

    C. ssh-genkey

    D. ssh -key

8. Which of the following configuration options sets a hard limit of 25 processes for a user called suehring in /etc/security/limits.conf?

    A. suehring hard proc 25

    B. suehring hard nproc 25

    C. suehring proc 25 hard-limit

    D. proc 25 suehring hard

9. Within which file should you place public keys for servers from which you will accept key-based ssh authentication?

    A. ~/.ssh/authorized_keys

    B. ~/.ssh/keys

    C. ~/.ssh/keyauth

    D. ~/.sshd/authkeys

10. The system on which you are working does not have the lsof command installed, and you are not allowed to install software without going through four levels of approval and scheduling the installation weeks in advance. However, the netstat command is available. Which option to netstat will show the process ID to which a given network port is connected?

    A. -a

    B. -n

    C. -p

    D. -l

11. You need to look at information on logins beyond that which is captured by the current log file for the last command. Which option to the last command can be used to load information from an alternate file?

    A. -a

    B. -t

    C. -e

    D. -f

12. You need to examine who is currently logged in to the system. Which of the following commands will display this information?

    A. listuser

    B. fuser

    C. ls -u

    D. w

13. You need to execute a command as a specific user. Which of the following commands enables this to occur?

   A. sudo -u

   B. sudo -U

   C. sudo -s

   D. sudo -H

14. Which option in /etc/sudoers will cause the specified command to not prompt for a password?

   A. PASSWORD=NO

   B. NOPASSWD

   C. NOPASSWORD

   D. NOPROMPT

15. Which of the following commands will display the cputime, memory, and other limits for the currently logged-in user?

   A. reslimit

   B. limitres -a

   C. ulimit -a

   D. proclimit -n

16. Which line within the /etc/hosts.deny file will prevent any host within the 192.168.1.0/24 network from accessing services that operate from xinetd?

   A. BLOCK: 192.168.1.0/24

   B. REJECT: 192.168.1.0

   C. ALL: 192.168.1.0/255.255.255.0

   D. NONE: 192.168.1/255.255.255.0

17. When expiring a user account with usermod -e, which of the following represents the correct date format?

   A. YYYY-MM-DD

   B. MM/DD/YYYY

   C. DD/MM/YY

   D. MM/DD/YY HH:MM:SS

18. Which of the following directives in a configuration file found within /etc/xinetd.d will prevent the service from starting?

   A. enable no

   B. start no

   C. disable yes

   D. boot no

19. You are using an RSA-based key pair for SSH. By default, what is the name of the private key file in ~/.ssh?

    A. id_rsa

    B. id_rsa.priv

    C. id_rsa.key

    D. rsa_key.priv

20. Which option to the su command will execute a single command with a non-interactive session?

    A. -s

    B. -u

    C. -c

    D. -e

21. After specifying the keyserver, which option to gpg is used to specify the key to send to the key server?

    A. key-name

    B. keyname

    C. send-key

    D. sendkey

22. Which of the following best describes the method to use with ssh in order to execute a single command on a remote server?

    A. Use the -e option followed by the command.

    B. Send the command after the other options as part of the command line.

    C. Use the --execute option followed by the command.

    D. Use the -s option followed by the command.

23. When using ssh-agent, which command and option lists the currently loaded keys?

    A. ssh-agent -l

    B. ssh -l

    C. ssh-list-keys

    D. ssh-add -l

24. Which of the following commands should be used to edit the /etc/sudoers file?

    A. Any text editor such as vi or emacs

    B. editsudo

    C. visudo

    D. visudoers

25. Which of the following commands can be used to stop a given service, such as `httpd.service`, from starting on boot with a systemd-based system?

    A. `systemctl disable httpdservice`

    B. `systemctl stop httpd.service`

    C. `systemd disable httpd.service`

    D. `systemd enable httpd.service boot=no`

26. Which of the following commands will set an account to expire based on the number of days elapsed since January 1, 1970?

    A. `passwd -e`

    B. `chage -E`

    C. `usermod -l`

    D. `chguser`

27. You are using `nmap` to scan a host for open ports. However, the server is blocking ICMP echo requests. Which option to `nmap` can you set in order to continue the scan?

    A. `-P0`

    B. `-no-ping`

    C. `-s0`

    D. `-ping-0`

28. Which option within `/etc/security/limits.conf` is used to control the number of times that a given account can log in simultaneously?

    A. `nlogins`

    B. `loginmax`

    C. `maxlogins`

    D. `loginlimit`

29. Which file can be used to store a server-wide cache of hosts whose keys are known for ssh?

    A. `/etc/sshd_known_hosts`

    B. `/etc/ssh_known_hosts`

    C. `~/.ssh/known_hosts`

    D. `/root/ssh_known_hosts`

30. Within the following entry in `/etc/shadow`, to what does the number 15853 refer?

`mail:*:15853:0:99999:7:::`

    A. The UID of the mail user

    B. The number of files owned by mail

    C. The date of the last password change (since 1/1/1970)

    D. The number of days until the account expires

31. Which of the following commands sets up a local port forwarding session on local port 5150 to remote port 80 of www.example.com?

   A. `ssh -L 5150:www.example.com:80`

   B. `ssh 5150:www.example.com`

   C. `ssh -p 5150 www.example.com`

   D. `ssh -e 5150 www.example.com:80`

32. Which option must be enabled in `/etc/sshd_config` on the destination server in order for X11 forwarding to work?

   A. `XForward yes`

   B. `Xenable yes`

   C. `X11Forwarding yes`

   D. `Xconnection yes`

33. Which of the following commands generates a GnuPG key pair?

   A. `gpg --gen-key`

   B. `gpg --key`

   C. `gpg --send-key`

   D. `gpg --create-key`

34. Which of the following represents a group called `admins` within `/etc/sudoers`?

   A. `@admins`

   B. `admins`

   C. `-admins`

   D. `%admins`

35. Which option to ssh is used to set the port for the remote host?

   A. `-p`

   B. `-P`

   C. `-l`

   D. `@`

36. Which option to nmap sets the scan to use TCP SYN packets for finding open ports?

   A. `-sS`

   B. `-sT`

   C. `-sY`

   D. `-type SYN`

37. Which of the following logs is used by the last command for detailing recent logins?

   A. /var/log/last

   B. /var/log/all.log

   C. /var/log/wtmp

   D. /var/log/logins

38. Which option to ssh enables the use of a key for authentication?

   A. -i

   B. -k

   C. -f

   D. --key

39. In a scripting scenario, you need to prevent sudo from prompting for credentials or for any other reason. Which option to sudo is used to indicate this?

   A. -n

   B. --noprompt

   C. -i

   D. -q

40. Which of the following commands generates an RSA key for use with ssh?

   A. ssh -key rsa

   B. ssh --gen-key rsa

   C. ssh-keygen -t rsa

   D. ssh-keygen rsa

41. You need to disable a service found in /etc/inetd.conf. Which of the following is used as a comment character in that file?

   A. -

   B. #

   C. /

   D. %

42. Which of the following commands can be used to lock an account?

   A. usermod -L

   B. usermod -l

   C. passwdlock

   D. lockacct

43. Which file is used as the default storage for public keyrings for gpg?

    A.   publickeys.gpg

    B.   pubring.gpg

    C.   public.gpg

    D.   pubkeys.gpg

44. Which file in ~/.gnupg, if present, indicates that files have been migrated to gpg version 2.1 or later?

    A.   .gpg-v21

    B.   .gpg-updated

    C.   .gpg-v21-migrated

    D.   .gpg-files-v21

45. Which of the following commands searches a server for files with the setgid bit enabled?

    A.   find / -perm 4000

    B.   find ./ -perm setgid

    C.   grep setgid *

    D.   find / -perm 2000

46. Which of the following commands creates links within /etc/rc.d/* for starting and stopping services on a Debian system?

    A.   createsym

    B.   startstop-service

    C.   update-rc.d

    D.   createconfig

47. Which runlevel is typically used for single-user mode, as indicated in /etc/inittab?

    A.   1

    B.   2

    C.   5

    D.   6

48. Which option to the su command is used to obtain the normal login environment?

    A.   -u

    B.   -U

    C.   -

    D.   -login

LPIC-2

Chapter

11

Capacity Planning (Topic 200)

THE FOLLOWING LPIC-2 EXAM TOPICS ARE COVERED IN THIS CHAPTER:

✓ **200.1   Measure and troubleshoot resource usage**

- Measure CPU usage.

- Measure memory usage.

- Measure disk I/O.

- Measure network I/O.

- Measure firewalling and routing throughput.

- Map client bandwidth usage.

- Match / correlate system symptoms with likely problems.

- Estimate throughput and identify bottlenecks in a system including networking.

- The following is a partial list of the used files, terms and utilities:

  - iostat

  - iotop

  - vmstat

  - netstat

  - ss

  - iptraf

  - pstree, ps

  - w

  - lsof

  - top

- htop
- uptime
- sar
- swap
- processes blocked on I/O
- blocks in
- blocks out

✓ 200.2 Predict future resource needs

- Use monitoring and measurement tools to monitor IT infrastructure usage.
- Predict capacity break point of a configuration.
- Observe growth rate of capacity usage.
- Graph the trend of capacity usage.
- Awareness of monitoring solutions such as Icinga2, Nagios, collectd, MRTG and Cacti
- The following is a partial list of the used files, terms and utilities:
  - diagnose
  - predict growth
  - resource exhaustion

1. When using `iostat` to assess performance, which option displays information on a per-partition basis for block devices?

    A. `-a`

    B. `-c`

    C. `-d`

    D. `-p`

2. When using `iptraf` for monitoring over an ssh connection, all of the traffic from your ssh session is showing up within the monitor. Which of the following is used to exclude and/or include traffic from the `iptraf` monitor?

    A. Area

    B. Filter

    C. Exclusion

    D. Selector

3. Which of the following commands displays blocks in and blocks out as related to I/O?

    A. `iorpt`

    B. `iptraf`

    C. `vmswap`

    D. `vmstat`

4. Which of the following commands can be used to display real-time information about disk usage on a per-process basis?

    A. `iostat`

    B. `top`

    C. `iotop`

    D. `free`

5. You need to deploy a monitoring solution that enables alerts along with advanced scripted responses based on configurable performance conditions. Which of the following software packages performs these tasks?

    A. MySQL

    B. ntop

    C. mrtg

    D. Nagios

6. Which of the following commands can be used to display a list of currently logged-in users along with the current load average and time since last reboot?

    A. `uptime`

    B. `w`

    C. `swap`

    D. `sysinfo`

7. Which of the following commands provides an overview of current memory usage along with swap space and its current utilization?

    A. `mem`

    B. `free`

    C. `pstat`

    D. `swap`

8. Which of the following describes a method for changing the sort order when using the `top` command such that the highest memory utilizers will be shown at the top of the list?

    A. Within `top`, type **o** and then select mem.

    B. Within `top`, press Shift+F, scroll to %MEM, press **s** to select, and then press **q** to quit.

    C. Within `top`, press **S** and then select %MEM.

    D. Within `top`, press Shift+S, select %MEM, then press **q** to quit.

9. Which of the following commands can be used to display the current disk utilization?

    A. `df`

    B. `du`

    C. `diskutil`

    D. `diskuse`

10. Which of the following monitoring tools can use SNMP and scripts to collect data for performance-related graphing?

    A. `ptop`

    B. `pstree`

    C. `Cacti`

    D. `Grafr`

11. Which tool can be used to measure the memory usage of individual processes in order to aid in capacity planning?

    A. `ps`

    B. `iotop`

    C. `iostat`

    D. `ifconfig`

12. Which option to `htop` enables monitoring of a single process ID?

    A. `-p`

    B. `-a`

    C. `-e`

    D. `-s`

13. Which of the following `netstat` options displays the send and receive queues for each socket?

    A. `-r`

    B. `-M`

C. -a

D. -v

14. Which of the following tools provides an ncurses-based graphical tool for network monitoring that can be used over an ssh connection?

   A. ipmon

   B. iptraf

   C. ipconfig

   D. netmon

15. Which of the following commands enables a sorted and grouped list of processes, grouped into a parent/child display?

   A. ps

   B. psdisp

   C. pstree

   D. ptree

16. Which of the following commands displays CPU-related performance information a total of 10 times gathered every two seconds?

   A. sar -u 2 10

   B. sar -u 10 2

   C. sar -u 2

   D. uptime -t

17. Which of the following tools provides an ncurses-based interface for working with processes, including viewing, changing priority, and killing the processes?

   A. htop

   B. ptop

   C. libtop

   D. restop

18. When viewing statistics with vmstat, which statistic represents the time that the CPU spent waiting for I/O?

   A. sy

   B. us

   C. wa

   D. io

19. Which option to the pstree command displays process IDs along with the normal output?

   A. -i

   B. -b

   C. -p

   D. -a

20. When viewing information with ps, what does the RSS column indicate?

   A. Real Swap Size

   B. Remaining Swap Space

   C. Resident Set Size

   D. Recommended Set Space

21. Which of the following commands displays a list of currently open files along with their sizes?

   A. ls

   B. lsof

   C. lsio

   D. ls -o

22. When using htop to monitor a process interactively, which key can be used to display open files for the selected process?

   A. L

   B. l

   C. f

   D. o

23. When working in a virtual server environment, which column within iostat output shows the amount (percentage) of time spent in an involuntary wait scenario due to the hypervisor?

   A. proc

   B. wait

   C. user

   D. steal

24. Which of the following performance-monitoring commands is available by default in most modern Linux installs and does not need to be installed as a separate package?

   A. Icinga2

   B. top

   C. sar

   D. Nagios

25. What time intervals are represented by the three numbers in the load average output obtained with the uptime command?

   A. 1, 5, and 15 minutes

   B. 5, 10, and 15 minutes

   C. 10, 30, and 60 seconds

   D. 1, 3, and 5 minutes

26. Which of the following files contains information about the swap space including the currently used amount of swap and the disk partitions used for the swap space?

   A. `/proc/swapinfo`

   B. `/proc/swaps`

   C. `/proc/swap`

   D. `/etc/swap.conf`

27. Which of the following tools provides a web interface for network-related statistics such as bandwidth usage per protocol and host?

   A. `mrtg`

   B. `Nagios`

   C. `ntop`

   D. `htop`

28. Which option to the `ps` command displays information in a wide format?

   A. z

   B. w

   C. a

   D. o

29. When no interval or count is provided for the `sar` command, what information is used as output?

   A. Statistics gathered since last restart

   B. Current load average

   C. Statistics on current utilization

   D. Average I/O

30. Which of the following `lsof` commands will display all open connections for port 80?

   A. `lsof -i 80`

   B. `lsof 80`

   C. `lsof -i :80`

   D. `lsof -i -80`

31. Which option to `iostat` causes the display to output in megabytes?

   A. `-k`

   B. `-l`

   C. `-m`

   D. `-o m`

32. When viewing information with vmstat, you notice that there are two processes in the b column, indicating uninterruptible sleep. How do you find which specific processes are currently in uninterruptible sleep mode?

    A. Add the -n option to vmstat.

    B. Use ps and look for D in the Stat column.

    C. Use ps and look for Sl in the Stat column.

    D. Reboot the server.

33. When working with htop, which of the following options sets the delay between updates to 10 seconds?

    A. -d 10

    B. -d 100

    C. -f 10

    D. -f 100

34. Which of the following commands and options displays performance information including memory and CPU usage every second for 10 seconds?

    A. vmstat 1 10

    B. iostat 10 1

    C. vmstat 10 1

    D. iostat 1 10

35. Which of the following commands displays the number of packets forwarded by the kernel?

    A. ls

    B. ipstat

    C. ifconfig -a

    D. netstat -s

36. You are using a two-processor system and notice that the one-minute load average is 1.00. What does this mean for performance?

    A. One of the processors was idle 50% of the time.

    B. The system is constrained by the CPUs because it is at 100% capacity.

    C. The CPU utilization cannot be determined from this information.

    D. One of the processors was idle 25% of the time.

37. What is the expected output when providing a 0-increment value to the sar command with no count value provided?

    A. Statistics from the beginning of time

    B. Average utilization since last restart

    C. Continuously updated statistics

    D. An error will occur.

Chapter

12

Linux Kernel (Topic 201)

THE FOLLOWING LPIC-2 EXAM TOPICS ARE COVERED IN THIS CHAPTER:

✓ **201.1   Kernel components**

- Kernel 2.6.x, 3.x and 4.x documentation
- The following is a partial list of the used files, terms and utilities:
    - /usr/src/linux/
    - /usr/src/linux/Documentation/
    - zImage
    - bzImage
    - xz compression

✓ **201.2   Compiling a Linux kernel**

- /usr/src/linux/
- Kernel Makefiles
- Kernel 2.6.x, 3.x and 4.x make targets
- Customize the current kernel configuration.
- Build a new kernel and appropriate kernel modules.
- Install a new kernel and any modules.
- Ensure that the boot manager can locate the new kernel and associated files.
- Module configuration files
- Use DKMS to compile kernel modules.
- Awareness of dracut

- The following is a partial list of the used files, terms and utilities:

  - mkinitrd

  - mkinitramfs

  - make

  - make targets (all, config, xconfig, menuconfig, gconfig, oldconfig, mrproper, zImage, bzImage, modules, modules_install, rpm-pkg, binrpm-pkg, deb-pkg)

  - gzip

  - bzip2

  - module tools

  - /usr/src/linux/.config

  - /lib/modules/kernel-version/

  - depmod

  - dkms

✓ 201.3 Kernel runtime management and troubleshooting

- Use command-line utilities to get information about the currently running kernel and kernel modules.

- Manually load and unload kernel modules.

- Determine when modules can be unloaded.

- Determine what parameters a module accepts.

- Configure the system to load modules by names other than their file name.

- /proc filesystem

- Content of /, /boot/, and /lib/modules/

- Tools and utilities to analyse information about the available hardware

- udev rules

- The following is a partial list of the used files, terms and utilities:

  - /lib/modules/kernel-version/modules.dep

  - module configuration files in /etc/

- /proc/sys/kernel/
- /sbin/depmod
- /sbin/rmmod
- /sbin/modinfo
- /bin/dmesg
- /sbin/lspci
- /usr/bin/lsdev
- /sbin/lsmod
- /sbin/modprobe
- /sbin/insmod
- /bin/uname
- /usr/bin/lsusb
- /etc/sysctl.conf, /etc/sysctl.d/
- /sbin/sysctl
- udevmonitor
- udevadm monitor
- /etc/udev/

1. You are upgrading the kernel that has been previously compiled on the same server. Which of the following commands incorporates the contents of the existing kernel configuration into the new kernel?

   A. config --merge

   B. make oldconfig

   C. merge config

   D. int configs

2. Within which directory is the kernel source typically kept?

   A. /usr/src/linux

   B. /usr/linux/kernel

   C. /usr/source/kernel

   D. /etc/kernelsrc

3. Which of the following commands unzips a kernel source file that has been compressed with xz compression?

   A. xz -c

   B. xz -u

   C. xz -f

   D. xz -d

4. Which of the following compressed kernel images is limited to a maximum size of 512 KB?

   A. zImage

   B. bzImage

   C. kImage

   D. lImage

5. Which make target provides a curses-based interface into kernel compilation to help select options within the kernel?

   A. config

   B. menuconfig

   C. cursesconfig

   D. cleanconfig

6. You are working with a legacy CentOS 5 system and need to re-create the initial RAM disk. Which of the following commands is used for this purpose?

   A. mkinitrd

   B. mkramdisk

   C. mkdisk --init

   D. mkfs.init

7. Which compression method is used for creation of a bzImage?

  A. zip

  B. lzip

  C. bzip2

  D. bzip3

8. When compiling a kernel, the final configuration is placed into which of the following files?

  A. `/usr/src/linux/.kernelcfg`

  B. `/usr/src/linux/.config`

  C. `/usr/src/linux/.kconfig`

  D. `/usr/src/linux/kernel.cfg`

9. Which of the following commands is used to display the currently loaded modules on a running system?

  A. `ls -mod`

  B. `lsmod`

  C. `listmod`

  D. `mod --list`

10. Which of the following make targets should be used in order to ensure that most compiled files from a previous compile are removed?

  A. `config`

  B. `clean`

  C. `proper`

  D. `mrproper`

11. Which kernel configuration option enables you to add information such as a custom version number to the kernel version?

  A. CUSTVER

  B. LOCALVERSION

  C. CUSTOMVERSION

  D. APPENDVER

12. Which of the following tools is used to create kernel modules, even if the source is outside the kernel source tree?

  A. `kbuild`

  B. `mkmod`

  C. `dkms`

  D. `modbuild`

13. Which of the following commands creates a list of modules and their dependencies?

    A. lsmod

    B. depmod

    C. modlist

    D. listmod

14. Which of the following commands is used to view kernel-related udev events in real time?

    A. udevls all

    B. lsudev -f

    C. udevmon -a

    D. udevadm monitor

15. Which of the following commands displays USB-related information from the kernel in a tree-like structure?

    A. lsusb -t

    B. usblist --tree

    C. usbtree

    D. usblist -t

16. Which option to sysctl displays all values and their current settings?

    A. -a

    B. -b

    C. -d

    D. -c

17. Which of the following commands installs a kernel module, including dependencies?

    A. lsmod

    B. modprobe

    C. modinst

    D. instmod

18. Which of the following make targets can be used to create a Debian package of a kernel image and related files?

    A. kpkg

    B. deb-pkg

    C. bin-deb

    D. deb-bin

19. Which of the following commands displays the current kernel version?

   A. kver

   B. uname -r

   C. uptime -k

   D. kerver

20. Within which directory hierarchy are the names and values for sysctl gathered?

   A. /sysctl

   B. /etc/sysctl.info

   C. /proc/sys

   D. /proc/sysctl

21. Within which directory are rules related to udev stored?

   A. /etc/udev.conf

   B. /etc/udev.conf.d

   C. /etc/udev/rules.d

   D. /etc/udev.d

22. Which command is used to determine the modules on which another module depends?

   A. modinfo

   B. modlist

   C. modprobe

   D. tracemod

23. Within which directory will you typically find the documentation related to kernel source?

   A. /usr/src/Documentation

   B. /usr/share/kerneldocs

   C. /usr/src/linux/Documentation

   D. /usr/share/kernel/Documentation

24. Which option to lspci displays the kernel driver in use for the given PCI device?

   A. -t

   B. -k

   C. -n

   D. -a

25. Which of the following commands inserts a module into the running kernel but does not resolve dependencies?

   A. lsmod

   B. modinstall

   C. insmod

   D. moduleinst

26. Which option to modprobe will remove a module and attempt to remove any unused modules on which it depends?

    A. -v

    B. -r

    C. -d

    D. -f

27. Which of the following make targets is used to install previously compiled modules?

    A. modules

    B. modules_install

    C. instmod

    D. modinst

28. Within which of the following directories will you find blacklist information for modules loaded with modprobe?

    A. /etc/blacklist

    B. /etc/modprobe.d

    C. /etc/blacklist.mod

    D. /etc/modprobe

29. Which of the following commands displays a list of currently loaded modules?

    A. depmod

    B. depmod -a

    C. lsmod

    D. listmod

30. When working with a CentOS 6 system, which command is used to create the initial RAM disk?

    A. mkinit

    B. dracut

    C. mkraminit

    D. mkinitfs

31. Which command is used to remove a kernel module from a running system?

    A. modrm

    B. rmmod

    C. modremove

    D. removemod

32. If you'd like a value set with the `sysctl` command to take effect on boot, within which file should you place the variable and its value?

    A. `/etc/sysctl.cfg`

    B. `/etc/sysctl.conf`

    C. `/lib/sysctl`

    D. `/var/sysctl.conf`

33. Within which file will you find a list of the currently available kernel symbols?

    A. `/proc/kernelsyms`

    B. `/etc/kernel.conf`

    C. `/etc/lsyms`

    D. `/proc/kallsyms`

34. Which of the following options to `modprobe` will show the dependencies for a module?

    A. `--show-deps`

    B. `--show-depends`

    C. `--deps`

    D. `--list-depends`

35. Which of the following commands can be used to show the various pieces of information related to a currently loaded module, including core size and settings for options?

    A. `systool -v -m <module>`

    B. `modinfo -r <module>`

    C. `lsmod <module>`

    D. `infmod <module>`

36. Which directory contains various elements and configuration information about the kernel, such as the release number, domain name, location of `modprobe`, and other settings?

    A. `/proc/sys/kmod`

    B. `/proc/sys/kernel`

    C. `/proc/kernel`

    D. `/proc/kernel/sys`

37. Which of the following commands displays messages in the kernel ring buffer?

    A. `kring`

    B. `ringbuf`

    C. `dmesg`

    D. `kmesg`

Chapter

13

System Startup (Topic 202)

THE FOLLOWING LPIC-2 EXAM TOPICS ARE COVERED IN THIS CHAPTER:

✓ **202.1 Customising system startup**

- Systemd
- SysV init
- Linux Standard Base Specification (LSB)
- The following is a partial list of the used files, terms and utilities:
  - /usr/lib/systemd/
  - /etc/systemd/
  - /run/systemd/
  - systemctl
  - systemd-delta
  - /etc/inittab
  - /etc/init.d/
  - /etc/rc.d/
  - chkconfig
  - update-rc.d
  - init and telinit

✓ **202.2 System recovery**

- BIOS and UEFI
- NVMe booting
- GRUB version 2 and Legacy

- grub shell
- boot loader start and hand off to kernel
- kernel loading
- hardware initialisation and setup
- daemon/service initialisation and setup
- Know the different boot loader install locations on a hard disk or removable device.
- Overwrite standard boot loader options and using boot loader shells.
- Use systemd rescue and emergency modes.
- The following is a partial list of the used files, terms and utilities:
  - mount
  - fsck
  - inittab, telinit and init with SysV init
  - The contents of /boot/, /boot/grub/ and /boot/efi/
  - EFI System Partition (ESP)
  - GRUB
  - grub-install
  - efibootmgr
  - UEFI shell
  - initrd, initramfs
  - Master boot record
  - systemctl

✓ 202.3 **Alternate bootloaders**

- SYSLINUX, ISOLINUX, PXELINUX
- Understanding of PXE for both BIOS and UEFI
- Awareness of systemd-boot and U-Boot

- The following is a partial list of the used files, terms and utilities:

  - syslinux

  - extlinux

  - isolinux.bin

  - isolinux.cfg

  - isohdpfx.bin

  - efiboot.img

  - pxelinux.0

  - pxelinux.cfg/

  - uefi/shim.efi

  - uefi/grubx64.efi

1. Within which directory should systemd unit files that you create be stored?

    A. /etc/system

    B. /etc/systemd/system

    C. /usr/share/systemd

    D. /usr/share/system

2. Which of the following commands should you execute after making changes to systemd service configurations in order for those changes to take effect?

    A. systemd reload

    B. reboot

    C. systemctl daemon-reload

    D. systemctl reboot

3. Which of the following files contains the runlevels for the system along with a reference to the corresponding rc file?

    A. /etc/runlevels

    B. /etc/inittab

    C. /etc/rc

    D. /etc/runlevel

4. Which bootloader can be used for FAT filesystems and might be used for a rescue disk?

    A. SYSBOOT

    B. SYSLINUX

    C. TIELINUX

    D. FATLINUX

5. Which filesystem format type is used for the EFI System Partition (ESP)?

    A. FAT

    B. EXT4

    C. NTFS

    D. EXT3

6. Which of the following is used to provide an early filesystem-based loading process for key drivers needed to continue the boot process?

    A. bootrd

    B. driverload

    C. initrd

    D. initdrv

7. When booting a system, you receive an error similar to "No init found" and are then placed at an `initramfs` prompt. You need to check the hard drive for errors. Which of the following commands performs an error check on a hard drive partition in Linux?

    A. `defrag`

    B. `fsck`

    C. `checkfs`

    D. `chkfs`

8. Which of the following commands places the system in single-user mode?

    A. `tellinit 1`

    B. `chginit 1`

    C. `telinet 1`

    D. `telinit 1`

9. Which of the following commands installs `extlinux` into the `/boot` partition?

    A. `extlinux --install /boot`

    B. `extlinux --inst /boot`

    C. `extlinux -boot`

    D. `extlinux /boot install`

10. Which of the following commands mounts `/dev/sda1` in the `/boot` partition?

    A. `mount /dev/sda /boot`

    B. `mount /boot /dev/sda1`

    C. `mount /dev/sda1 /boot`

    D. `mount -dev sda1 /boot`

11. Which of the following commands installs GRUB into the master boot record (MBR) of the first SATA drive?

    A. `grub-install /dev/hda`

    B. `grub-install /dev/sda`

    C. `grub-install /dev/hd0,0`

    D. `grub -i /dev/hda`

12. Which of the following commands changes the boot order for the next boot?

    A. `efibootmgr -c`

    B. `efibootmgr -b -B`

    C. `efibootmgr -o`

    D. `efibootmgr -n`

13. Which bootloader can be used with ISO9660 CD-ROMs?

   A. ISOLINUX

   B. EFIBOOT

   C. ISOFS

   D. BOOTISO

14. Within which directory are `systemd` user unit files placed by installed packages?

   A. `/usr/lib/systemd/user`

   B. `/usr/lib/systemd/system`

   C. `/usr/systemd`

   D. `/usr/system`

15. When using UEFI, which of the following files can be used as a bootloader?

   A. `shim.uefi`

   B. `shim.efi`

   C. `shim.fx`

   D. `efi.shim`

16. Which of the following describes the priority order for configuration files with `systemd`?

   A. Files in `/etc`, files in `/run`, and then files in `/lib`

   B. Files in `/run`, files in `/etc`, and then files in `/lib`

   C. Files in `/lib`, files in `/run`, and then files in `/etc`

   D. Files in `/lib`, files in `/etc`, and then files in `/run`

17. Which directory on a SysV init-based system contains scripts that are used for starting and stopping services?

   A. `/etc/rc.int`

   B. `/etc/boot`

   C. `/etc/bootscripts`

   D. `/etc/init.d`

18. Which of the following commands is used to find overriding configuration files on a systemd-based system?

   A. `diff`

   B. `systemctl -diff`

   C. `systemd-delta`

   D. `systemctl configoverride`

19. Which of the following commands on a Red Hat system lists all of the files set to be executed on boot along with their setting for each runlevel?

   A. `rlevel`

   B. `chkconfig --list`

    C. `bootldr --list`

    D. `init --bootlist`

20. Which of the following commands, executed from within the UEFI shell, controls the boot configuration?

    A. `bootcfg`

    B. `bcfg`

    C. `grub-install`

    D. `grcfg`

21. Which of the following can be identified as an initial sector on a disk that stores information about the disk partitioning and operating system location?

    A. Minimal Boot Record (MBR)

    B. Master Boot Record (MBR)

    C. Init sector

    D. Master Partition Table (MPT)

22. Once booted, within which directory is the EFI bootloader mounted?

    A. `/boot/efi`

    B. `/etc/boot/efi`

    C. `/etc/efi`

    D. `/boot/loader`

23. To which target can a `systemd`-based system be set in order to assist with recovery?

    A. `recovery.target`

    B. `recover.target`

    C. `target.recover`

    D. `rescue.target`

24. Which of the following configuration files is used for ISOLINUX?

    A. `isolinux.cfg`

    B. `isolinux.conf`

    C. `isolin.cfg`

    D. `isolinux.conf.d`

25. Which file must exist within `/tftpboot` on the TFTP server for a system that will use PXELINUX for its bootloader?

    A. `pxelinux.tftp`

    B. `pxelinux.boot`

    C. `pxelinux.conf`

    D. `pxelinux.0`

26. Which utility can you use on a Debian or Ubuntu system to manage SysV init scripts, such as setting them to run on boot?

   A. bootorder

   B. bootloader

   C. configchk

   D. update-rc.d

27. Which key when pressed during the operating system selection menu is used to enable editing of the parameters related to boot with GRUB?

   A. v

   B. e

   C. r

   D. y

28. Which of the following commands displays the default target for a systemd-based system?

   A. systemctl list-unit-default

   B. systemctl get-default

   C. systemctl get-unit-default

   D. systemctl get-default-unit

29. Which options to the fsck command will find errors and automatically assume that it should repair the errors that it finds?

   A. -ry

   B. -vy

   C. -my

   D. -xy

30. Which option to grub-install will place the GRUB images into an alternate directory?

   A. --boot-dir

   B. -b

   C. -boot

   D. --boot-directory

31. Which systemctl subcommand is used to switch runlevels?

   A. switch

   B. move

   C. runlevel

   D. isolate

32. When examining the /etc/inittab file, which option signifies the default run level to which the system will boot?

A. default

B. defaultboot

C. initdefault

D. defaultlvl

33. Which of the following is used instead of initrd to provide an early filesystem for essential drivers?

A. initnext

B. initramfs

C. initialize

D. initfs

34. Which of the following commands sets the default systemd target to multi-user?

A. systemctl set-default multi-user.target

B. systemd set-default multi-user.target

C. systemctl set-def muser.target

D. systemd set-def muser.target

35. Using a shim for booting a UEFI-based system, which of the following files is loaded after shim.efi?

A. grubx64.cfg

B. grub.conf

C. grubx64.efi

D. efi.boot

36. Within which hierarchy are files from /etc/init.d linked so that the files are executed during the various runlevels of a SysV system?

A. /etc/rc.S

B. /etc/rc

C. /etc/boot/rc

D. /etc/rc.d

37. What is the name of the unit to which a systemd system is booted in order to start other levels?

A. default.target

B. init.target

C. initial.target

D. load.target

Chapter

14

Filesystems and Devices (Topic 203)

THE FOLLOWING LPIC-2 EXAM TOPICS ARE COVERED IN THIS CHAPTER:

✓ **203.1 Operating the Linux filesystem**

- The concept of the fstab configuration
- Tools and utilities for handling swap partitions and files
- Use of UUIDs for identifying and mounting file systems
- Understanding of systemd mount units
- The following is a partial list of the used files, terms and utilities:
  - /etc/fstab
  - /etc/mtab
  - /proc/mounts
  - mount and umount
  - blkid
  - sync
  - swapon
  - swapoff

✓ **203.2 Maintaining a Linux filesystem**

- Tools and utilities to manipulate and ext2, ext3 and ext4
- Tools and utilities to perform basic Btrfs operations, including subvolumes and snapshots
- Tools and utilities to manipulate XFS
- Awareness of ZFS

- The following is a partial list of the used files, terms and utilities:

  - mkfs (mkfs.*)

  - mkswap

  - fsck (fsck.*)

  - tune2fs, dumpe2fs and debugfs

  - btrfs, btrfs-convert

  - xfs_info, xfs_check, xfs_repair, xfsdump and xfsrestore

  - smartd, smartctl

✓ 203.3 Creating and configuring filesystem options

- autofs configuration files

- Understanding of automount units

- UDF and ISO9660 tools and utilities

- Awareness of other CD-ROM filesystems (HFS)

- Awareness of CD-ROM filesystem extensions (Joliet, Rock Ridge, El Torito)

- Basic feature knowledge of data encryption (dm-crypt / LUKS)

- The following is a partial list of the used files, terms and utilities:

  - /etc/auto.master

  - /etc/auto.[dir]

  - mkisofs

  - cryptsetup

1. Within which file is a list of the currently mounted filesystems stored?

   A. /etc/fstab

   B. /etc/curmount

   C. /var/spool/files

   D. /etc/mtab

2. Which option to mke2fs sets the type of filesystem to be created?

   A. -f

   B. -a

   C. -t

   D. -e

3. Which of the following files is the default configuration file for the autofs automounter?

   A. /etc/autofs

   B. /etc/auto.master

   C. /etc/autofs.conf

   D. /etc/automounter.conf

4. Which of the following commands is used to create an ISO filesystem?

   A. mkiso

   B. mkfsiso

   C. mkisofs

   D. isofs-mk

5. Which of the following commands is used to configure dm-crypt volumes?

   A. cryptsetup

   B. dm-cryptsetup

   C. dm-setup

   D. dm-crypts

6. Which command is used to format a swap partition?

   A. mkfs -swap

   B. mkswap

   C. format -swap

   D. mksw

7. Which option to the tune2fs command sets the maximum mount count before the system will automatically run fsck on the partition on boot?

   A. -b

   B. -c

   C. -C

   D. -a

8. Which option to the mount command can be used to simulate the mount process without actually mounting the filesystem?

   A. -q

   B. -v

   C. -l

   D. -f

9. When viewing /proc/mounts, you see a filesystem with the letters ro in the fourth column. To what do the letters ro refer?

   A. relative option

   B. realtime option

   C. read only

   D. relative only

10. Which option to dumpe2fs displays the bad blocks for a given partition?

   A. -bb

   B. -C

   C. -b

   D. -f

11. Which of the following filesystem types features copy-on-write?

   A. ext3

   B. ext4

   C. FAT

   D. btrfs

12. Which of the following commands displays filesystem geometry for an XFS filesystem?

   A. xfsinfo

   B. xfs_info

   C. xfs -info

   D. xfs --info

13. Which of the following commands can be used to display information such as the UUID for partitions on a system?

   A. blkid

   B. blockdev

   C. devinfo

   D. uuidinfo

14. Which option to the umount command will cause it to unmount only filesystems of the specified type?

    A. -v

    B. -f

    C. -t

    D. -a

15. Which command causes unwritten data to be written to disk immediately?

    A. write

    B. wrnow

    C. connwrite

    D. sync

16. Which command is used to activate swap space on a system?

    A. mkswap

    B. swapon

    C. swapact

    D. actswap

17. Which option to xfs_check is used to verify a filesystem that is stored in a file?

    A. -v

    B. -a

    C. -f

    D. -d

18. Which option to debugfs causes the filesystem to be opened in read-write mode rather than the default read-only?

    A. -rw

    B. -w

    C. -r

    D. -n

19. Which daemon is responsible for monitoring Self-Monitoring, Analysis, and Reporting Technology–compatible hard drives?

    A. smartmon

    B. smarty

    C. sartd

    D. smartd

20. Which option to the `fsck` command causes it to run the check even if the filesystem is apparently marked as clean?

    A. `-f`

    B. `-m`

    C. `-a`

    D. `-c`

21. You are performing an `xfsrestore`. The `xfsdump` was executed with a block size of 4M. Which option do you need to invoke on `xfsrestore` in order for it to use this dump successfully?

    A. `-b 4M`

    B. `-g 1M`

    C. `-i 1M`

    D. `-k 1028K`

22. You see the word `defaults` within `/etc/fstab`. Which options are encompassed within the `defaults`?

    A. `ro, exec, auto`

    B. `rw, suid, dev, exec, auto, nouser, async`

    C. `rw, exec, auto, nouser, async`

    D. `rw, exec, nouser, async, noauto, suid`

23. Which of the following commands is used to administer and configure how SMART monitoring is done?

    A. `smartmon`

    B. `smartconf`

    C. `smartd`

    D. `smartctl`

24. Which of the following is the correct format for a filesystem in `/etc/fstab`?

    A. `<filesystem> <mountpoint> <type> <options> <dump> <pass>`

    B. `<mountpoint> <filesystem> <type> <options> <dump> <pass>`

    C. `<mountpoint> <filesystem> <type> <options> <pass> <dump>`

    D. `<filesystem> <mountpoint> <type> <dump> <pass> <options>`

25. Which key derivation function is used by LUKS?

    A. PBKDF2

    B. SSL

    C. RSA

    D. DSA

26. Which of the following commands creates a btrfs subvolume?

A. `btrfs create subvolume`

B. `btrfs subvolume create`

C. `btrfs sv create`

D. `btrfs svcreate`

27. Which of the following options to `xfsdump` sets the maximum size for files to be included in the dump?

A. `-p`

B. `-s`

C. `-z`

D. `-b`

28. Which option to the `tune2fs` command sets the behavior when a filesystem error occurs?

A. `-f`

B. `-d`

C. `-e`

D. `-k`

29. The `/etc` filesystem has been mounted as read-only for a recovery process. You need to mount another partition. Which option to the `mount` command causes it not to write to `/etc/mtab`?

A. `-a`

B. `-m`

C. `-b`

D. `-n`

30. Which of the following commands deactivates swap space?

A. `swapoff`

B. `swap -off`

C. `unmountswap`

D. `uswap`

31. Within the [mount] section of a `systemd` mount unit, which directive specifies the location for mounting the chosen filesystem?

A. `Where=`

B. `Location=`

C. `List=`

D. `Dest=`

32. Which of the following swapon options displays information on the size of swap space along with its used space?

    A. `--list`

    B. `-a`

    C. `--show`

    D. `-h`

33. Which of the following commands can be used to format a FAT filesystem?

    A. `mkfs.fat`

    B. `mkfs -f`

    C. `mkfs --fat`

    D. `mkfat`

34. Which of the following commands adds a journal to an existing ext3 filesystem?

    A. `tune2fs -jrn`

    B. `e2fs -x`

    C. `tune3fs`

    D. `tune2fs -j`

35. Which of the following commands creates a snapshot of a btrfs subvolume?

    A. `btrfs subvolume snapshot`

    B. `btrfs snapshot --create`

    C. `btrfs create snapshot`

    D. `btrfs --create`

36. Which option to xfs_repair will force log zeroing, even if there may be metadata within the log?

    A. `-L`

    B. `-v`

    C. `-d`

    D. `-V`

37. Which of the following commands mounts a filesystem in read-only mode?

    A. `mount read-only`

    B. `mount --read`

    C. `mount -o ro`

    D. `mount -or`

Chapter

15

Advanced Storage Device Administration (Topic 204)

THE FOLLOWING LPIC-2 EXAM TOPICS ARE COVERED IN THIS CHAPTER:

✓ **204.1   Configuring RAID**

- Software RAID configuration files and utilities
- The following is a partial list of the used files, terms and utilities:
  - mdadm.conf
  - mdadm
  - /proc/mdstat
  - partition type 0xFD

✓ **204.2   Adjusting Storage Device Access**

- Tools and utilities to configure DMA for IDE devices including ATAPI and SATA
- Tools and utilities to configure Solid State Drives including AHCI and NVMe
- Tools and utilities to manipulate or analyse system resources (e.g. interrupts)
- Awareness of sdparm command and its uses
- Tools and utilities for iSCSI
- Awareness of SAN, including relevant protocols (AoE, FCoE)

- The following is a partial list of the used files, terms and utilities:
- hdparm, sdparm
  - nvme
  - tune2fs
  - fstrim
  - sysctl
  - /dev/hd*, /dev/sd*, /dev/nvme*
  - iscsiadm, scsi_id, iscsid and iscsid.conf
  - WWID, WWN, LUN numbers

✓ 204.3   Logical Volume Manager

- Tools in the LVM suite
- Resizing, renaming, creating, and removing logical volumes, volume groups, and physical volumes
- Creating and maintaining snapshots
- Activating volume groups
- The following is a partial list of the used files, terms and utilities:
  - /sbin/pv*
  - /sbin/lv*
  - /sbin/vg*
  - mount
  - /dev/mapper/
  - lvm.conf

1. Which file is used as a configuration file for RAID devices that use the md driver?

   A. `/etc/md.conf`

   B. `/etc/mdadm.conf`

   C. `/etc/md.cfg`

   D. `/etc/md/md.conf`

2. Which partition type is used to indicate a software RAID array, such as that built with mdadm?

   A. 0xmd

   B. -x-

   C. 0xRD

   D. 0xFD

3. When working with World Wide Identifiers (WWIDs), within which directory on a Red Hat server will you find symlinks to the current /dev/sd device names?

   A. `/dev/disk/wwid`

   B. `/dev/wwid`

   C. `/dev/disk/by-id`

   D. `/dev/sd.wwid`

4. Which of the following commands is used to perform administration related to iSCSI on a Linux server?

   A. `iscsiadm`

   B. `iscsiadmin`

   C. `iscsi`

   D. `scsiadm`

5. Which of the following commands displays information about a given physical volume in an LVM setup?

   A. `pvdisp`

   B. `pvlist`

   C. `pvdisplay`

   D. `pvl`

6. Which of the following configuration lines informs the md program that the first partition on both sda and sdb are eligible for use in a RAID array?

   A. `DEV sda1 sdb1`

   B. `DEV /dev/sda1 /dev/sdb1`

   C. `DEVICE sda0 sdb0`

   D. `DEVICE /dev/sda1 /dev/sdb1`

7. When viewing information in /dev/disk/by-path using the command ls -l, which of the following filenames represents a LUN from Fibre Channel?

   A. /dev/fc0

   B. pci-0000:1a:00.0-fc-0x500601653ee0025f:0x0000000000000000

   C. pci-0000:1a:00.0-scsi-0x500601653ee0025f:0x0000000000000000

   D. /dev/fibre0

8. Which of the following commands displays path information for LUNs?

   A. luninfo -a

   B. ls -lun

   C. multipath -l

   D. dm-multi

9. Which command is used to remove unused filesystem blocks from thinly provisioned storage?

   A. thintrim

   B. thtrim

   C. fstrim

   D. fsclean

10. You have purchased new SSD hardware that uses the NVMe protocol, but you cannot find the disks in the normal /dev/sd* location in which you have traditionally found such storage. In which location should you look for these drives?

   A. /dev/nd*

   B. /dev/nvme*

   C. /dev/nv*

   D. /dev/nvme/*

11. Which of the following commands can be used to generate a unique SCSI identifier?

   A. scsi_id

   B. scsi_identifier

   C. id_scsi

   D. lsid

12. Which storage protocol features the ability to send ATA commands over Ethernet?

   A. iSCSI

   B. PXE

   C. POE

   D. AOE

13. Which command can be used to set parameters for IDE and SATA devices on Linux?

    A. hdparam

    B. hdparm

    C. hdc

    D. hdcontrol

14. After creating the physical volumes for an md RAID setup, what is the typical next step?

    A. Create one or more volume groups with vgcreate.

    B. Reboot the server.

    C. Start the array.

    D. Link the physical volumes to virtual groups with vgcreate.

15. When using tune2fs to set an extended option such as stripe_width, which command-line option is needed to signify that an extended option follows?

    A. -extend

    B. -E

    C. -e

    D. -f

16. Which file contains information about the current md RAID configuration such as the personalities?

    A. /proc/raidinfo

    B. /proc/rhyinfo

    C. /proc/mdraid

    D. /proc/mdstat

17. Which of the following daemons is in charge of maintaining connections to iSCSI targets?

    A. iscsid

    B. iscsiadm

    C. iscsimgr

    D. iscsim

18. Which module can be examined with modinfo for information related to the NVMe driver?

    A. nvmeid

    B. sata

    C. nvme

    D. nvmemod

19. Which of the following directory hierarchies contains information such as the WWN for Fibre Channel?

    A. `/sys/class/wwn`

    B. `/sys/class/fc_host`

    C. `/sys/class/fclist`

    D. `/sys/class/fc/wwn`

20. Which option to mdadm is used to create a new array?

    A. `--create`

    B. `--start`

    C. `--begin`

    D. `--construct`

21. Which of the following files is used as a configuration file for iscsid?

    A. `iscsid.cfg`

    B. `iscsid.conf`

    C. `iscsidaemon.conf`

    D. `iscsi.cfg`

22. Information about logical volumes can be found in which of the following directories?

    A. `/dev/lvinfo`

    B. `/dev/map`

    C. `/dev/mapper`

    D. `/dev/lvmap`

23. Which option to mdadm watches a RAID array for anomalies?

    A. `--mon`

    B. `--watch`

    C. `--monitor`

    D. `--examine`

24. When troubleshooting a failed md RAID array, you need to mount one of the drives in read-only mode. Which option will mount the drive in read-only?

    A. `-o ro`

    B. `read-only`

    C. `-o rw`

    D. `-op ro`

25. Which of the following commands creates a logical volume with LVM?

- **A.** lvc
- **B.** lvcreate
- **C.** lvlist
- **D.** lvmake

26. When running mdadm in monitor mode, which option within /etc/mdadm.conf sets the destination for email if an issue is discovered?

- **A.** MAILTO
- **B.** MAILADDR
- **C.** MAILFROM
- **D.** MAILDEST

27. Which of the following commands looks for LVM physical volumes and volume groups involved in an LVM configuration?

- **A.** vgscan
- **B.** lvmscan
- **C.** lvlist
- **D.** pvlist

28. Which partition type is used to indicate a software RAID array, such as that built with mdadm?

- **A.** 0xmd
- **B.** -x-
- **C.** 0xRD
- **D.** 0xFD

29. Which of the following commands is used to display a list of physical volumes involved in LVM?

- **A.** pvdisp
- **B.** pvlist
- **C.** pvscan
- **D.** pvmm

30. Which of the following options to the multipathd command will enter the interactive console?

- **A.** -c
- **B.** -k
- **C.** -f
- **D.** -n

31. Which option to lvchange sets whether the logical volume is available?

 A. -a

 B. -b

 C. -c

 D. -d

32. Within which file can you configure a filter for devices when using vgscan?

 A. lvm.conf

 B. vg.conf

 C. vgscan.conf

 D. lv.cfg

33. Which option to lvcreate will create a snapshot of a logical volume?

 A. snap

 B. snapshot

 C. ss

 D. Snapshots are not created with lvcreate.

34. Which option is given to sysctl to change one of the kernel parameters?

 A. -a

 B. -k

 C. -w

 D. -A

35. Which of the following commands is used to access and change values for SCSI devices?

 A. scsiparm

 B. scsiparam

 C. sdlist

 D. sdparm

36. Which of the following directories contains configuration information for Fibre Channel over Ethernet (FCoE) on Linux?

 A. /etc/fcoe

 B. /etc/fibrecoe

 C. /etc/fibredev

 D. /etc/fc

37. Which of the following commands will examine the PCI subsystem for NVMe-based devices?

 A. psnvme

 B. lsnvme

 C. lspci | grep scsi

 D. lspci | grep -i nvme

Chapter 16

Networking Configuration (Topic 205)

THE FOLLOWING LPIC-2 EXAM TOPICS ARE COVERED IN THIS CHAPTER:

✓ **205.1 Basic networking configuration**

- Utilities to configure and manipulate Ethernet network interfaces
- Configuring basic access to wireless networks
- The following is a partial list of the used files, terms and utilities:
  - ip
  - ifconfig
  - route
  - arp
  - iw
  - iwconfig
  - iwlist

✓ **205.2 Advanced network configuration**

- Utilities to manipulate routing tables
- Utilities to configure and manipulate Ethernet network interfaces
- Utilities to analyse the status of the network devices

- Utilities to monitor and analyse the TCP/IP traffic

- The following is a partial list of the used files, terms and utilities:

  - ip

  - ifconfig

  - route

  - arp

  - ss

  - netstat

  - lsof

  - ping, ping6

  - nc

  - tcpdump

  - nmap

✓ 205.3   Troubleshooting network issues

- Location and content of access restriction files

- Utilities to configure and manipulate Ethernet network interfaces

- Utilities to manage routing tables

- Utilities to list network states.

- Utilities to gain information about the network configuration

- Methods of information about the recognised and used hardware devices

- System initialisation files and their contents (Systemd and SysV init)

- Awareness of NetworkManager and its impact on network configuration

- The following is a partial list of the used files, terms and utilities:

  - ip
  - ifconfig
  - route
  - ss
  - netstat
  - /etc/network/, /etc/sysconfig/network-scripts/
  - ping, ping6
  - traceroute, traceroute6
  - mtr
  - hostname
  - System log files such as /var/log/syslog, /var/log/messages and the systemd journal
  - dmesg
  - /etc/resolv.conf
  - /etc/hosts
  - /etc/hostname, /etc/HOSTNAME
  - /etc/hosts.allow, /etc/hosts.deny

1. When using the `ip` command, which protocol family is used as the default if not otherwise specified?

   A. TCPIP

   B. IP

   C. INET

   D. ARP

2. Which of the following commands changes the MAC address of eth0?

   A. `ifmac eth0`

   B. `ifconfig eth0 hw ether`

   C. `ifconfig eth0 mac`

   D. `ifconfig eth0 hw mac`

3. You are using the `route` command to view routes. However, name resolution is taking a long time and causing a delay in the response from the `route` command. Which option to `route` can be added to cause it to not perform name resolution?

   A. `-d`

   B. `-e`

   C. `-f`

   D. `-n`

4. You have replaced a device on the network but used the IP address from another active device. Which command can be run to remove the MAC address entry from your computer so that it performs the address resolution again?

   A. `arp -d`

   B. `netstat -rn`

   C. `hostname`

   D. `dig`

5. Which of the following commands displays information such as link status about the wireless device wlan0?

   A. `iw dev wlan0 link`

   B. `wlan0 list`

   C. `iw wlan0 -l`

   D. `iw dev link`

6. Which command is used for setting parameters such as the essid, channel, and other related options for a wireless device?

   A. `ifconfig`

   B. `iwconfig`

   C. `wlancfg`

   D. `iconf`

7. Which of the following commands can be used to scan for available wireless networks?

   A. iwlist get

   B. iwconfig scan

   C. iwlist scan

   D. iw-scan

8. When looking to parse the output of the ip command, which option can be set to remove newlines such that the output could be piped to the grep command?

   A. -n

   B. -o

   C. -l

   D. -f

9. You need to set the MTU to a specific value for a network interface. Which option to ifconfig facilitates this?

   A. -mtu

   B. mtu

   C. metric

   D. addrmtu

10. Which of the following commands creates a reject route for the network 172.16.3.0/24?

   A. route del 172.16.3.0/24

   B. route add -net 172.16.3.0 netmask 255.255.255.0 reject

   C. route del -net 172.16.3.0 netmask 255.255.255.0

   D. route del default

11. Which option to the arp command creates a new entry for a given IP address to a MAC address pair?

   A. -s

   B. -c

   C. -d

   D. --add

12. Which of the following commands shows network sockets and their allocated memory?

   A. ss -m

   B. mpas

   C. mem

   D. free

13. Which options to netstat shows both active and listening TCP sockets and connections?

    A. -tu

    B. -f

    C. -an

    D. -ta

14. Which of the following commands lists open files belonging to all processes except those owned by the user bind?

    A. lsof -i

    B. lsof -u bind

    C. lsof -u ^bind

    D. lsof | grep bind

15. When troubleshooting a potential hardware problem, you need to determine which physical interface is being used for a certain address. One way to accomplish this is with the ping command in order to monitor the activity lights on the device. Which of the following options to ping will flood the interface with ECHO_REQUEST packets?

    A. -e

    B. -a

    C. -c

    D. -f

16. Which of the following commands can be used to test network connectivity at the TCP level instead of Telnet?

    A. netstat

    B. nc

    C. nettest

    D. ping

17. Which option to tcpdump displays a list of available interfaces on which tcpdump can operate?

    A. -a

    B. -d

    C. -D

    D. -i

18. Which option to nmap will cause it always to perform name resolution?

    A. -n

    B. -R

    C. -b

    D. -a

19. Which command provides a method for sending ICMP requests for IPv6?

    A. `ping6`

    B. `pingv6`

    C. `tracert`

    D. `6ping`

20. Which of the following commands displays information about addresses, specifically only IPv6 addresses, currently in use on the computer?

    A. `ip addr`

    B. `ip -6 addr`

    C. `ip6add`

    D. `ipv6addr`

21. Which of the following commands will disable ARP on the interface eth0?

    A. `ifconfig eth0 -arp`

    B. `ip eth0 noarp`

    C. `ifconfig eth0 noarp`

    D. `if eth0 disable arp`

22. Which option to the `route` command forces the kernel to use the specified device for the route rather than attempting to determine the correct device?

    A. `inet`

    B. `addr`

    C. `dev`

    D. `device`

23. Which option to the `ss` command shows the process IDs associated with the socket?

    A. `-l`

    B. `-a`

    C. `-p`

    D. `-f`

24. Which option to `netstat` displays interface information in a table-like format that might be suitable for use with scripting?

    A. `-i`

    B. `-r`

    C. `-t`

    D. `-l`

25. On a Debian system, within which directory hierarchy will you find configuration information and directories to hold scripts to be run when an interface is brought up or taken down?

   A. `/etc/netconf`

   B. `/etc/netconfig`

   C. `/etc/net.conf.d`

   D. `/etc/network`

26. Which option to `traceroute` causes the command to use ICMP for requests?

   A. `-T`

   B. `-A`

   C. `-I`

   D. `-i`

27. Which of the following commands provides a live traceroute of the route between two hosts, updating the information for each hop in near real time?

   A. `traceroute --live`

   B. `mtr`

   C. `route -update`

   D. `liveroute`

28. Which programmatic function is used by the `hostname` command internally?

   A. `getaddr`

   B. `gethost`

   C. `gethostname`

   D. `getname`

29. Which of the following commands will examine the system log for information regarding DHCP activity?

   A. `grep -i dhcp /var/log/syslog`

   B. `grep -v dhcp /var/log/syslog`

   C. `grep -vi dhcp /var/log/kern.log`

   D. `dmesg | grep dhcp`

30. Which of the following characters are valid for hostnames in `/etc/hosts`?

   A. Alphanumerics, minus, underscore, and dot

   B. Alphanumerics, minus, and dot

   C. Alphanumerics and dot

   D. Alphanumerics

31. Which of the following configuration lines in `/etc/resolv.conf` enables debugging?

   A. `debug`

   B. `options debug`

    C. `option debug`

    D. `enable-debug`

32. Which option to `dmesg` clears the contents after they have been read once?

    A. `-C`

    B. `-c`

    C. `-a`

    D. `-e`

33. Which of the following commands views `systemd` journal entries for the NetworkManager unit?

    A. `systemd NetworkManager`

    B. `systemd NetworkCtl`

    C. `systemctl NetworkManager`

    D. `systemctl -u NetworkManager`

34. Which file is read at boot to set the local computer's hostname?

    A. `/etc/hostname`

    B. `/etc/hosts`

    C. `/etc/localhost`

    D. `/etc/networkhost`

35. Which of the following directories on a Red Hat system contains network interface configuration information?

    A. `/etc/network-scripts`

    B. `/etc/system/network`

    C. `/etc/sysconfig/network-scripts`

    D. `/etc/sysconfig/net.d`

36. Which `traceroute` command is used exclusively for IPv6 route traces?

    A. `trace6`

    B. `traceroute6`

    C. `tracert6`

    D. `6trace`

37. Which wildcard can be used in `/etc/hosts.allow` to specify a match for a host whose name does not match its IP address?

    A. `*`

    B. `ALL`

    C. `PARANOID`

    D. `NAMEMATCH`

Chapter 17

System Maintenance (Topic 206)

THE FOLLOWING LPIC-2 EXAM TOPICS ARE COVERED IN THIS CHAPTER:

✓ **206.1 Make and install programs from source**

- Unpack source code using common compression and archive utilities.

- Understand basics of invoking make to compile programs.

- Apply parameters to a configure script.

- Know where sources are stored by default.

- The following is a partial list of the used files, terms and utilities:

    - /usr/src/

    - gunzip

    - gzip

    - bzip2

    - xz

    - tar

    - configure

    - make

    - uname

    - install

    - patch

✓ 206.2 Backup operations

- Knowledge about directories that have to be include in backups
- Awareness of network backup solutions such as Amanda, Bacula, Bareos and BackupPC
- Knowledge of the benefits and drawbacks of tapes, CDR, disk or other backup media
- Perform partial and manual backups.
- Verify the integrity of backup files.
- Partially or fully restore backups.
- The following is a partial list of the used files, terms and utilities:
  - /bin/sh
  - dd
  - tar
  - /dev/st* and /dev/nst*
  - mt
  - rsync

✓ 206.3 Notify users on system-related issues

- Automate communication with users through logon messages.
- Inform active users of system maintenance
- The following is a partial list of the used files, terms and utilities:
  - /etc/issue
  - /etc/issue.net
  - /etc/motd
  - wall
  - shutdown
  - systemctl

1. Which of the following compression programs is used for compression of the official kernel source code?

   A. gzip2

   B. bzip2

   C. xz

   D. xy

2. Which option to the `rsync` command provides archive mode?

   A. -r

   B. -o

   C. -a

   D. -f

3. Which option to the `tar` command creates a tar file?

   A. -c

   B. -b

   C. -f

   D. -d

4. Which option to tar removes files after adding them to the archive?

   A. -r

   B. -d

   C. --remove-files

   D. -f

5. Which of the following `patch` commands strips the leading slash from the path for files to patch?

   A. patch -p0

   B. patch -strip 1

   C. patch -s0

   D. patch -p1

6. Which of the following is the recommended name for a file containing commands and relationships used with the `make` command?

   A. Makefile

   B. makefile

   C. make.file

   D. Makefile.txt

7. Which make target is commonly used as a standard convention for removing extraneous files from a previous make process?

   A. cleanup

   B. next

   C. netbuild

   D. clean

8. Which script, typically included with source code, is used to check dependencies and prepare the Makefile with customizations based on the system?

   A. config

   B. installer

   C. prep

   D. configure

9. According to the Filesystem Hierarchy Standard (FHS), within which directory should source code be placed?

   A. /usr/local/src

   B. /usr/src

   C. /src

   D. /home/source

10. You have downloaded a source file with the extension .gz. Which of the following commands will uncompress the file?

    A. unzip

    B. gunzip

    C. dezip

    D. uncomp

11. Which of the following dd commands reads and writes bytes one megabyte at a time?

    A. dd bsl=1024M

    B. dd size=1M

    C. dd bs=1M

    D. dd rw=1M

12. Which configuration directive for Amanda defines a name for the type of tape (or device) to be used as a backup destination?

    A. dest

    B. index

    C. tapetype

    D. desttype

13. Which of the following devices is the location of the first SCSI tape device detected at boot?

   A. `/dev/st`

   B. `/dev/sd0`

   C. `/dev/sd1`

   D. `/dev/st0`

14. Which of the following files should be used to display a message to users prior to logging in locally?

   A. `/etc/loginmesg`

   B. `/etc/logmessage.txt`

   C. `/etc/issue`

   D. `/etc/banner`

15. Which option to the `rsync` command, when used in archive mode, will remove files that no longer exist on the host?

   A. `--delete`

   B. `--remove`

   C. `-del`

   D. `-rem`

16. Which of the following commands broadcasts a message to all logged-in users?

   A. `bcast`

   B. `broadcast`

   C. `show`

   D. `wall`

17. When creating a tar archive, you need to exclude certain files from the archive. Which option facilitates this scenario?

   A. `-x`

   B. `--exclude`

   C. `--ex`

   D. `--remove`

18. Which file contains a message that is then displayed after a successful login?

   A. `/etc/loginbanner`

   B. `/etc/issue`

   C. `/etc/motd`

   D. `/etc/message`

19. Which of the following `tar` commands is used to extract from a file named `archive.tar` in such a manner that the contents are printed to STDOUT during extraction?

   A. `tar -cvf archive.tar`

   B. `tar -xvf archive.tar`

   C. `tar -zf archive.tar`

   D. `tar -yvf archive.tar`

20. Which of the following commands will properly execute the `configure` script for a source code package, assuming that you have already changed into the source code directory?

   A. `configure./`

   B. `./config`

   C. `./configure`

   D. `exec config`

21. Which of the following options to the `tar` command can be used to uncompress a file that has been compressed using gzip?

   A. `-z`

   B. `-x`

   C. `-c`

   D. `-f`

22. Which of the following files can be used to provide a message to users logging in remotely with a protocol such as Telnet?

   A. `/etc/telnet.msg`

   B. `/etc/issue.net`

   C. `/etc/login.msg`

   D. `/etc/telnet.login`

23. Which of the following commands turns **off** the computer, including removing power, if possible?

   A. `systemctl halt`

   B. `systemctl reboot`

   C. `systemctl stop`

   D. `systemctl poweroff`

24. Which of the following commands outputs information about the kernel version and processor architecture?

   A. `uname -a`

   B. `lskern`

   C. `kern -v`

   D. `proc info`

25. Which option to the rsync command changes the resolution for determining file modifications?

   A. --mod-time

   B. --modify-time

   C. --mod-res

   D. --modify-window

26. Which option to the patch command creates a backup of files being patched?

   A. -r

   B. -b

   C. -l

   D. -a

27. Which target for make, typically included in the Makefile for most projects, will place compiled files into their final destination and perform other operations such as making the appropriate files executable?

   A. list

   B. distclean

   C. run

   D. install

28. Which option to the tar command indicates xz compression?

   A. -x

   B. -c

   C. -J

   D. -j

29. Which option to the rsync command examines only the file size as a means of determining whether the file should be synchronized?

   A. --filesize

   B. --size-only

   C. --list-size

   D. --file-size

30. Which of the following xz options is used to uncompress a file and send the uncompressed contents to STDOUT?

   A. --decompress --stdout

   B. --deout

   C. --uncomp --stdout

   D. -out -u

31. Which of the following options to bzip2 sends the output to STDOUT?

    A. -s

    B. -c

    C. -d

    D. -f

32. Which of the following files is typically used as the Bacula Director configuration file?

    A. /etc/bacula/bacula.cfg

    B. /etc/bacula.cfg

    C. /etc/bacula-dir.conf

    D. /etc/bacula/bacula-dir.conf

33. Which of the following commands rewinds a tape when using the mt command?

    A. mt reverse

    B. mt rewind

    C. mt goback

    D. mt operation=back

34. Which of the following shutdown commands reboots the system in 15 minutes?

    A. shutdown -r +15

    B. shutdown +15

    C. shutdown -15

    D. shutdown -r 00:15

35. Which option to the gzip command will suppress all warning messages and might be useful in a situation where output is not appropriate?

    A. -v

    B. -q

    C. -L

    D. -r

36. Which option to rsync specifies that the remote shell or transport for the synchronization process should use SSH?

    A. -t ssh

    B. --overssh

    C. -e ssh

    D. -F ssh

37. Which option to a configure script will typically produce a list of available options for the command?

    A. --list

    B. --help

    C. --show

    D. --get

Chapter
18

Domain Name Server (Topic 207)

THE FOLLOWING LPIC-2 EXAM TOPICS ARE COVERED IN THIS CHAPTER:

✓ **207.1 Basic DNS server configuration**

- BIND 9.x configuration files, terms and utilities
- Defining the location of the BIND zone files in BIND configuration files
- Reloading modified configuration and zone files
- Awareness of dnsmasq, djbdns, and PowerDNS as alternate name servers
- The following is a partial list of the used files, terms and utilities:
  - /etc/named.conf
  - /var/named/
  - rndc
  - named-checkconf
  - kill
  - host
  - dig

✓ **207.2 Create and maintain DNS zones**

- BIND 9 configuration files, terms and utilities
- Utilities to request information from the DNS server
- Layout, content and file location of the BIND zone files
- Various methods to add a new host in the zone files, including reverse zones

- The following is a partial list of the used files, terms and utilities:

  - /var/named/
  - zone file syntax
  - resource record formats
  - named-checkzone
  - named-compilezone
  - masterfile-format
  - dig
  - nslookup
  - host

✓ **207.3   Securing a DNS server**

- BIND 9 configuration files
- Configuring BIND to run in a chroot jail
- Split configuration of BIND using the forwarders statement
- Configuring and using transaction signatures (TSIG)
- Awareness of DNSSEC and basic tools
- Awareness of DANE and related records
- The following is a partial list of the used files, terms and utilities:

  - /etc/named.conf
  - /etc/passwd
  - DNSSEC
  - dnssec-keygen
  - dnssec-signzone

1. Which configuration file is used as the default configuration for a BIND server?

    A. `named.conf`

    B. `named.cfg`

    C. `bind.cfg`

    D. `bind.conf`

2. Which directive within a BIND configuration specifies the addresses or networks that are allowed to query the nameserver?

    A. `query-addresses`

    B. `allow-query`

    C. `query-allow`

    D. `query-auth`

3. Which signal to the `kill` command can be used to signal that BIND should reload, including its configuration?

    A. `-15`

    B. `-1`

    C. `-9`

    D. `-2`

4. What option to `dnssec-keygen` specifies the algorithm to use for the key?

    A. `-a`

    B. `-n`

    C. `-d`

    D. `-e`

5. Which of the following describes a fundamental difference between `named-compilezone` and `named-checkzone`?

    A. `named-checkzone` and `named-compilezone` do the same thing.

    B. `named-checkzone` checks a zone for syntax errors; `named-compilezone` checks a zone for syntax errors and sends output to a file.

    C. `named-checkzone` performs syntax checking, while `named-compilezone` converts the zone to a different format.

    D. `named-checkzone` performs syntax checking, while `named-compilezone` prepares the zone for usage with BIND.

6. When creating MX records for a zone, which of the following is the highest priority mail exchanger?

    A. 0

    B. 10

    C. 20

    D. 100

7. On which protocol and port are zone transfer requests sent?

   A. UDP/53

   B. ICMP/53

   C. TCP/143

   D. TCP/53

8. Within which of the following directories are zone files stored for BIND?

   A. /var/named

   B. /etc/named

   C. /var/cache/named

   D. /var/named.zones

9. Which of the following commands is used to control a BIND name server?

   A. bind-config

   B. named-config

   C. rndc

   D. rdmc

10. Which type can be used with the dig command to test a zone transfer?

   A. xfr

   B. transfer

   C. zxfr

   D. axfr

11. Which BIND configuration directive sets the IP addresses on which the daemon will listen?

   A. listeners

   B. listen-on

   C. listen-in

   D. ip-listeners

12. When configuring BIND for a chroot scenario, within which of the following files should you set the home directory for the chroot user to use with bind?

   A. /etc/bind.home

   B. /etc/bind.user

   C. /etc/passwd

   D. /etc/bindauth

13. Which command is used to sign a DNS zone for DNSSEC?

   A. dnssec-signzone

   B. signzone

   C. bind-signzone

   D. dnssec-sign

14. Which option to the host command sets the query type to ANY?

    A. -a

    B. -b

    C. -c

    D. -d

15. Which of the following correctly creates a CNAME record between the hostname www and the host web.example.com?

    A. www CNAME web.example.com

    B. web.example.com CNAME www

    C. www IN CNAME web.example.com.

    D. www IN CNAME web.example.com

16. Which option to the forward directive in BIND sets the server as a forwarding server?

    A. only

    B. first

    C. now

    D. required

17. When running a recursive nameserver, which of the following options refuses to provide answers to queries from the given addresses?

    A. deny-hosts

    B. blackhole

    C. deny-query

    D. deny-answer

18. Which of the following is a prerequisite for installing djbdns?

    A. BIND9

    B. daemontools

    C. qmail

    D. bind-tools

19. Which command can be used to verify that a BIND configuration file is valid?

    A. bind9-ver

    B. bind-check

    C. config-check

    D. named-checkconf

20. Which of the following TTL values represents eight hours?

    A. 8

    B. 480

    C. 28800

    D. 86400

21. Assuming the following portion of a BIND zone file, what does the value 1800 represent?

    ```
    @ IN SOA cwa.example.org. root.example.org. (
    2016070400
    3600
    1800
    604800
    86400 )
    ```

    A. Refresh

    B. Retry

    C. Default TTL

    D. Serial

22. Which type of resource record is used for SPF records?

    A. SPF

    B. MX

    C. TXT

    D. MAIL

23. Which of the following defines an MX record with a priority of 10?

    A. `MX 10 mail.example.com.`

    B. `10 MX mail.example.com.`

    C. `mail.example.com 10 MX`

    D. `mail.example.com MX 10`

24. Within which file can per-user default settings be created for the `dig` command?

    A. `/etc/dig.cfg`

    B. `/etc/dig.conf`

    C. `~/.digrc`

    D. `~/.dig.conf`

25. Which option to the `mount` command is helpful to facilitate running BIND in a chroot environment?

    A. `--bind`

    B. `--chroot`

C. `--lift`

D. `--secure`

26. When setting up a recursive name server, which type of zone is set up for the root hints file?

    A. Master

    B. Slave

    C. Recurse

    D. Hint

27. After making changes to a DNS zone, which of the following commands can be used to reload the zones so that the changes take effect?

    A. `rndc reload`

    B. `rndc restart-zones`

    C. `rndc zone-reload`

    D. `rndc-rel`

28. Which configuration option within a BIND zone configuration specifies the hosts that are allowed to request a zone transfer?

    A. `allow-axfr`

    B. `allow-xfr`

    C. `allow-trans`

    D. `allow-transfer`

29. Which type of DNS record is used for specifying a POP3 server?

    A. POP

    B. PO

    C. MX

    D. There is no specific type for POP3 servers.

30. Which directive within a BIND configuration enables specification of the hosts or networks that are allowed to perform a recursive lookup using the server?

    A. `allow-recurs`

    B. `allow-recursive`

    C. `allow-recursion`

    D. `allow-rec`

31. Which of the following is the correct format for a `named-checkzone` command?

    A. `named-checkzone <zone> <zonefile>`

    B. `named-checkzone -z <zone>`

    C. `named-checkzone -f <zonefile>`

    D. `named-checkzone <zonefile> <zone>`

32. Which algorithm must be used for `rndc` authentication when generating a key with `dnssec-keygen`?

   A. sha1

   B. sha256

   C. md5

   D. hmac-md5

33. Which of the following configuration directives tells BIND not to divulge its version?

   A. `allow-version { none }`

   B. `version none;`

   C. `allow-query-version { none; }`

   D. `query-version no;`

34. Which option to `named-checkconf` is used to perform a test of all master zones noted in the config file?

   A. `-l`

   B. `-f`

   C. `-z`

   D. `-d`

35. You have specified 300 as the TTL for an individual record within your zone, and the zone itself has an 86400 default TTL. When making a change to that individual record, how long will it take for the change to propagate to external resolvers after you have restarted BIND?

   A. Up to 86400 seconds

   B. Up to 300 seconds

   C. The change is immediate after restart.

   D. It is impossible to tell from the information given.

36. Which of the following packages will install the PowerDNS authoritative nameserver on Debian and Red Hat, respectively?

   A. `pdns-server` on Debian and `pdns` on Red Hat

   B. `pdns` on Debian and `pdns-server` on Red Hat

   C. `pdns` on both Debian and Red Hat

   D. `pdns-server` on both Debian and Red Hat

37. Which of the following commands can be used to restart a BIND server so that changes to the `named.conf` file take effect?

   A. `rndc reload`

   B. `rndc reconfig`

   C. `named reboot`

   D. `restart bind`

Chapter

19

HTTP Services (Topic 208)

THE FOLLOWING LPIC-2 EXAM TOPICS ARE COVERED IN THIS CHAPTER:

✓ **208.1 Basic Apache configuration**

- Apache 2.4 configuration files, terms and utilities
- Apache log files configuration and content
- Access restriction methods and files
- mod_perl and PHP configuration
- Client user authentication files and utilities
- Configuration of maximum requests, minimum and maximum servers and clients
- Apache 2.4 virtual host implementation (with and without dedicated IP addresses)
- Using redirect statements in Apache's configuration files to customize file access
- The following is a partial list of the used files, terms and utilities:
  - access logs and error logs
  - .htaccess
  - httpd.conf
  - mod_auth_basic, mod_authz_host and mod_access_compat
  - htpasswd
  - AuthUserFile, AuthGroupFile
  - apachectl, apache2ctl
  - httpd, apache2

✓ **208.2 Apache configuration for HTTPS**

- SSL configuration files, tools and utilities
- Generate a server private key and CSR for a commercial CA

- Generate a self-signed Certificate

- Install the key and certificate, including intermediate CAs

- Configure Virtual Hosting using SNI

- Awareness of the issues with Virtual Hosting and use of SSL

- Security issues in SSL use, disable insecure protocols and ciphers

- The following is a partial list of the used files, terms and utilities:

  - Apache2 configuration files

  - /etc/ssl/, /etc/pki/

  - openssl, CA.pl

  - SSLEngine, SSLCertificateKeyFile, SSLCertificateFile

  - SSLCACertificateFile, SSLCACertificatePath

  - SSLProtocol, SSLCipherSuite, ServerTokens, ServerSignature, TraceEnable

✓ **208.3   Implementing Squid as a caching proxy**

- Squid 3.x configuration files, terms and utilities

- Access restriction methods

- Client user authentication methods

- Layout and content of ACL in the Squid configuration files

- The following is a partial list of the used files, terms and utilities:

  - squid.conf

  - acl

  - http_access

✓ **208.4   Implementing Nginx as a web server and a reverse proxy**

- Nginx

- Reverse Proxy

- Basic Web Server

- The following is a partial list of the used files, terms and utilities:

  - /etc/nginx/

  - nginx

1. Which directive within an Apache configuration file facilitates serving websites for more than one domain using a single IP address?

    A. `<VirtualServer>`

    B. `<VirtualHost>`

    C. `<VirtContainer>`

    D. `<Virtualization>`

2. Which command is used to creates or update credentials for htaccess scenarios?

    A. `passwd`

    B. `apachepasswd`

    C. `htpass`

    D. `htpasswd`

3. Which option to the `apachectl` command examines the configuration files to verify that there are no syntax errors?

    A. `verifyconfig`

    B. `configver`

    C. `configtest`

    D. `testconfig`

4. Which of the following commands generates a private key for use with SSL and places it into the file /etc/ssl/example.com.private?

    A. `openssl genrsa -out /etc/ssl/example.com.private`

    B. `openssl generate-private > /etc/ssl/example.com.private`

    C. `openssl genpriv > /etc/ssl/example.com.private`

    D. `openssh genkey -out /etc/ssl/example.com.private`

5. Which of the following configuration directives for Apache works with the `mod_auth_basic` and `mod_authn_file` modules to specify the filename for authentication?

    A. `AuthFile`

    B. `AuthUserFile`

    C. `AuthenticationFile`

    D. `AuthN_File`

6. Which directive within a `<VirtualHost>` stanza in an Apache configuration is used to specify the name of the virtual server?

    A. `Server`

    B. `VirtualServer`

    C. `ServerName`

    D. `ServerInfo`

7. Which option in an Apache configuration enables the SSL configuration for a given website or server?

   A. SSLEngine

   B. SSLDirect

   C. SSLEnable

   D. SSLConnect

8. Which option within an http section for nginx is used to configure the names of valid index files?

   A. indexFiles

   B. index_files

   C. indexfile

   D. index

9. When creating a Squid proxy configuration, you need to create an access control list for the local network. Which configuration option creates an access control list for Squid?

   A. accesscontrol

   B. acl

   C. access-control

   D. access-control-list

10. Which of the following configuration directives prevents Apache from printing version information on documents generated by the server?

   A. ServerDocs Off

   B. Signature Off

   C. ServerSignature Off

   D. ServerStatus Off

11. Which of the following technologies enables name-based virtual hosting over SSL using a single IP address?

   A. Server Naming (SN)

   B. Extended Virtual Host (EVH)

   C. Server Name Indication (SNI)

   D. Advanced Virtual Hosting (AVH)

12. Which Apache configuration directive sets the name of the PEM file containing CA certificates for clients?

   A. SSLCACertificateFile

   B. SSLCaCertFile

   C. SSLCAFile

   D. CACertificateFile

13. Which Apache2 configuration option sets the name that is displayed in the pop-up window for authentication when using Basic authentication?

 A. `AuthDisplay`

 B. `AuthName`

 C. `AuthList`

 D. `FriendlyName`

14. Which of the following Apache configuration lines enables the `php7_module` located at `modules/libphp7.so`?

 A. `Load php7_module modules/libphp7.so`

 B. `Module php7_module modules/libphp7.so`

 C. `LoadMod php7_module modules/libphp7.so`

 D. `LoadModule php7_module modules/libphp7.so`

15. Which subcommand of `openssl` is used to create a Certificate Signing Request (CSR)?

 A. `req`

 B. `csr`

 C. `gencsr`

 D. `newcsr`

16. Which Apache configuration directive sets the default directory for documents to be served for a given virtual host?

 A. `ServerRoot`

 B. `DocumentRoot`

 C. `DefaultLoc`

 D. `DefaultDocRoot`

17. Which of the following files represents the primary configuration file for PHP?

 A. `php.conf`

 B. `php.cfg`

 C. `php.config`

 D. `php.ini`

18. Which of the following lines within an Apache configuration disables the display of files in a directory for which no default document exists?

 A. `Options +Default`

 B. `Options -Default`

 C. `Options -Indexes`

 D. `Options +Indexes`

19. Which of the following `RedirectMatch` directives will provide a Page Not Found error to the user if they attempt to view the `.git` directory?
    A. `RedirectMatch 404 /\\.git(/|$)`
    B. `RedirectMatch PageNotFound /.git/`
    C. `RedirectMatch 404 .git`
    D. `RedirectMatch .git 404`

20. Which of the following directives for an Apache configuration tells the server the location of the SSL private key?
    A. `SSLKeyFile`
    B. `SSLCertificatePrivateKey`
    C. `SSLCertificateKeyFile`
    D. `SSLPrivateKey`

21. On which port does Squid listen by default?
    A. 3000
    B. 3128
    C. 5150
    D. 10300

22. Which of the following modules provides authorization for Apache based on a hostname or IP address?
    A. `mod_auth_ipaddress`
    B. `mod_auth_host`
    C. `mod_authz_host`
    D. `mod_auth_dns`

23. Within which log file does Apache record requests to the server?
    A. `access_log`
    B. `access-log`
    C. `access.txt`
    D. `syslog`

24. Which directive in a Squid configuration configures whether a given ACL can use the proxy?
    A. `access_allow`
    B. `http_access`
    C. `proxy_access`
    D. `enable_access`

25. Which of the following Apache configuration lines changes the name of the `.htaccess` file to `.accesslist`?
    A. `Access .accesslist`
    B. `AccessFile .accesslist`

C. `AccessFileName ".accesslist"`

D. `AuthFile ".accesslist"`

26. According to the Apache documentation, what is the preferred location for directives related to user authentication?

A. Within a `.htaccess` file

B. Within the main server configuration

C. Inside a `mod_rewrite` block

D. In a specialized module for user authentication

27. Which Apache configuration directive enables group-based authorization?

A. `AuthGroups`

B. `AuthGroupList`

C. `AuthGrouping`

D. `AuthGroupFile`

28. Which of the following commands shows the current status of the Apache server, including number of requests currently being processed and server uptime?

A. `apachectl serverstatus`

B. `apachectl status`

C. `apachectl faststatus`

D. `apachectl stats`

29. Which HTTP status code is returned when TraceEnable has been set to off within Apache?

A. 405

B. 100

C. 302

D. 200

30. Which option to `htpasswd` creates the credentials file and places a new entry into it?

A. `-f`

B. `-b`

C. `-c`

D. `-e`

31. Which Apache server log format sequence is used to log the time taken to service the request in microseconds?

A. `%D`

B. `%T`

C. `%t`

D. `-m`

32. Which of the following configuration lines makes the directory /home/web/docs available at the location /documentation/ on the server?

A. `Connect /documentation /home/web/docs`

B. `Alias /documentation/ /home/web/docs/`

C. `Connect /home/web/docs /documentation`

D. `Alias ~/docs/ /documentation/`

33. Within a valid `<Location>` stanza, which directive in Apache indicates that mod_perl will be used for resources in that location?

A. `Handler mod_perl`

B. `SetHandler perl-script`

C. `SetHandler mod_perl`

D. `LoadModule perl-script`

34. Which directive for nginx sets up a pass-through proxy for a given location?

A. `pass-through`

B. `proxy`

C. `proxy_pass`

D. `proxypass`

35. Which configuration directive determines the number of Apache child server processes to initially start?

A. `Servers`

B. `MaxServers`

C. `StartServers`

D. `ServerStarts`

36. Which Apache directive sets the format of a log file, including which elements are recorded in the log file?

A. `LogFile`

B. `Format`

C. `LoggingDirective`

D. `LogFormat`

37. Which option within a `.htaccess` file allows access only to the user ssuehring?

A. `Require ssuehring`

B. `RequireUser ssuehring`

C. `Require user ssuehring`

D. `AllowOnly ssuehring`

Chapter

20

File Sharing
(Topic 209)

THE FOLLOWING LPIC-2 EXAM TOPICS ARE COVERED IN THIS CHAPTER:

✓ **209.1   Samba Server Configuration**

- Samba 4 documentation
- Samba 4 configuration files
- Samba 4 tools and utilities and daemons
- Mounting CIFS shares on Linux
- Mapping Windows user names to Linux user names
- User-Level, Share-Level and AD security
- The following is a partial list of the used files, terms and utilities:
  - smbd, nmbd, winbindd
  - smbcontrol, smbstatus, testparm, smbpasswd, nmblookup
  - samba-tool
  - net
  - smbclient
  - mount.cifs
  - /etc/samba/
  - /var/log/samba/

✓ 209.2 NFS Server Configuration

- NFS version 3 configuration files
- NFS tools and utilities
- Access restrictions to certain hosts and/or subnets
- Mount options on server and client
- TCP Wrappers
- Awareness of NFSv4
- The following is a partial list of the used files, terms and utilities:
  - /etc/exports
  - exportfs
  - showmount
  - nfsstat
  - /proc/mounts
  - /etc/fstab
  - rpcinfo
  - mountd
  - portmapper

1. Within which directory will you find configuration files related to Samba version 4?

    A. `/etc/samba4`

    B. `/etc/samba`

    C. `/etc/smb`

    D. `/etc/filesharing/samba`

2. Which of the Samba daemons is responsible for responding to NetBIOS name service requests?

    A. `smbd`

    B. `nmbd`

    C. `winbindd`

    D. `samba`

3. You have made a configuration change to `smb.conf` and need to have the config reloaded. Which of the following commands accomplishes this task with the least disruption to users?

    A. `smbcontrol all shutdown`

    B. `smbcontrol smbd reload`

    C. `smbctrl all reload`

    D. `smbcontrol all reload-config`

4. Which of the following files is used to define the filesystems shared by NFS?

    A. `/etc/nfs.cfg`

    B. `/etc/nfs.conf`

    C. `/etc/export.nfs`

    D. `/etc/exports`

5. Which of the following NFS shares allows users from `cwa.example.com` to connect with read-write access to an NFS share at `/srv/vhosts`?

    A. `/srv/vhosts www.example.com(rw)`

    B. `www.example.com (rw) /srv/vhosts`

    C. `/srv/vhosts www.example.com (rw)`

    D. `/srv/vhosts www.example.com`

6. When using the `net` command in an Active Directory environment, which option enables authentication using Kerberos?

    A. `-b`

    B. `-k`

    C. `-l`

    D. `-a`

7. Which option within a Samba configuration enables translation of Windows to Linux usernames?

   A. usermap

   B. usernamemaps

   C. userfile

   D. username map

8. When specifying credentials on the command line with the Samba net command, which character is used to separate the username from the password?

   A. /

   B. \

   C. %

   D. !

9. Which of the following host specifications enables any host within the example.org domain to mount an NFS filesystem?

   A. all=example.org

   B. rw=*.example.org

   C. *.example.org

   D. %.example.org

10. Which filesystem type for the mount command is used for mounting Samba shares?

   A. win

   B. ext4

   C. vfat

   D. cifs

11. Which of the following commands displays the currently mounted CIFS filesystems?

   A. mount -t smb

   B. lssmbd

   C. mount -t cifs

   D. ls -cifs

12. To which setting should the security parameter be set within the Samba configuration in order for share-level security to be used?

   A. sharelevel

   B. share-level

   C. high

   D. share

13. Which option to `rpcinfo` displays statistics on `rpcbind` operations?

    A. `-s`

    B. `-m`

    C. `-l`

    D. `-e`

14. Which of the following commands displays the export list for a given NFS server?

    A. `rpcmount`

    B. `showmount -e`

    C. `mount -shownfs`

    D. `mount -listnfs`

15. Which of the following lines in `/etc/fstab` will mount an NFS filesystem shared as `/source` from the host `src.example.com` into a directory called `/srv/source` on the local server?

    A. `/source /srv/source -h src.example.com`

    B. `src.example.com/source /srv/source`

    C. `src.example.com:/source /srv/source nfs`

    D. `nfs src.example.com:/source /srv/source`

16. Which option to the `nfsstat` command shows statistics about only NFSv3?

    A. `-3`

    B. `-o3`

    C. `-v3`

    D. `-t`

17. Which of the following files shows the currently mounted filesystems?

    A. `/etc/mounts`

    B. `/proc/mounts`

    C. `/proc/mtab`

    D. `/etc/fstab`

18. Which of the following blocks access to the `portmap` service from the hosts within `example.com`'s network (`192.168.1.0/24`) when placed in `hosts.deny`?

    A. `portmap: 192.168.1.0/24`

    B. `portmap: example.com`

    C. `portmap: *.example.com`

    D. `portmap: ALL/DENY 192.168.1.0/24`

19. Which option to `smbstatus` displays a list of locks?

   A. `-l`

   B. `-L`

   C. `-o`

   D. `-m`

20. Which of the following commands creates a new user in the Samba password database?

   A. `passwd -samba`

   B. `smbpasswd -a`

   C. `smbpass`

   D. `smbuser -c`

21. Which option, defined within a share in the Samba configuration file, specifies whether users browsing for network shares will be able to see the share?

   A. `browsable`

   B. `shareconnect`

   C. `sharepoint`

   D. `browseenable`

22. Which of the `samba-tool` commands is used to verify the local Active Directory database to ensure that it is error free?

   A. `dbverify`

   B. `dblist`

   C. `verifydb`

   D. `dbcheck`

23. Within which section of the Samba configuration file is the log file specified?

   A. `[server]`

   B. `[logging]`

   C. `[global]`

   D. `[debug]`

24. Which of the following commands can be used to verify the syntax of the Samba configuration file?

   A. `testsmb`

   B. `smbtest`

   C. `testparm`

   D. `smbver`

25. Which of the following commands exports all filesystems in `/etc/exports` by reloading the file to do so?

   A. `export -a`

   B. `exportfs -ra`

C. `exportnfs -a`

D. `exportnfs -r`

26. Which option to `smbclient` enables specification of the order in which names are resolved?

A. `-R`

B. `-r`

C. `-d`

D. `-o`

27. Which option to `mountd` logs all successful requests?

A. `-n`

B. `-b`

C. `-l`

D. `-r`

28. Which option within a Samba share configures whether the share will allow read-write access?

A. `read write`

B. `read only`

C. `read/write`

D. `read-write`

29. On which port(s) does `smbd` listen by default?

A. 139

B. 443

C. 139 and 445

D. 161 and 162

30. Which option within `/etc/exports` prevents remote root users from having root privileges on the filesystem shared by the NFS server?

A. `no_root`

B. `deny_root`

C. `root_squash`

D. `disallow_root`

31. Which of the following commands shows the Windows-to-Linux group mappings?

A. `groupmap list`

B. `net groupmap list`

C. `netgroup list`

D. `net list groupmapping`

32. Which option to rpcinfo shows the current port mappings?

    A. -p

    B. -c

    C. -m

    D. -f

33. Which of the following options to the smbpasswd command deletes the specified user?

    A. -d

    B. -x

    C. -o

    D. -e

34. Which of the following commands lists the shares available on a host called fs.example.com?

    A. smblist

    B. smbshares -list

    C. smbclient -L

    D. smbshare -L

35. Which of the following log file directives creates a separate log file for each share?

    A. log file = <share>.log

    B. log file = %<share>.log

    C. log file = %S.log

    D. log file = [share].log

36. Which of the following commands can be used to test the status of Windows NetBIOS-related name services and browsing?

    A. mblookup

    B. adlookup

    C. browserl

    D. nmblookup

37. Which of the following commands stops sharing all NFS file shares?

    A. nfs stop -a

    B. nfs-stopshare

    C. stopnfs -a

    D. exportfs -ua

Chapter

21

Network Client Management (Topic 210)

THE FOLLOWING LPIC-2 EXAM TOPICS ARE COVERED IN THIS CHAPTER:

✓ **210.1 DHCP configuration**

- DHCP configuration files, terms and utilities
- Subnet and dynamically-allocated range setup
- Awareness of DHCPv6 and IPv6 Router Advertisements
- The following is a partial list of the used files, terms and utilities:
  - dhcpd.conf
  - dhcpd.leases
  - DHCP Log messages in syslog or systemd journal
  - arp
  - dhcpd
  - radvd
  - radvd.conf

✓ **210.2 PAM authentication**

- PAM configuration files, terms and utilities
- passwd and shadow passwords
- Use sssd for LDAP authentication
- The following is a partial list of the used files, terms and utilities:
  - /etc/pam.d/
  - pam.conf
  - nsswitch.conf

- pam_unix, pam_cracklib, pam_limits, pam_listfile, pam_sss
- sssd.conf

✓ 210.3 LDAP client usage

- LDAP utilities for data management and queries
- Change user passwords
- Querying the LDAP directory
- The following is a partial list of the used files, terms and utilities:
  - ldapsearch
  - ldappasswd
  - ldapadd
  - ldapdelete

✓ 210.4 Configuring an OpenLDAP server

- OpenLDAP
- Directory based configuration
- Access Control
- Distinguished Names
- Changetype Operations
- Schemas and Whitepages
- Directories
- Object IDs, Attributes and Classes
- The following is a partial list of the used files, terms and utilities:
  - slapd
  - slapd-config
  - LDIF
  - slapadd
  - slapcat
  - slapindex
  - /var/lib/ldap/
  - loglevel

1. Which option within dhcpd.conf configures how dynamic DNS updates are done?
   A. ddns-update-style
   B. ddns-updates
   C. ddns-server
   D. ddns-enable

2. Which of the following subnet definitions for DHCP can be used with private networks with at least 100 addresses?
   A. subnet 192.168.1.0 netmask 255.255.255.128
   B. subnet 192.168.1.0 size 100
   C. subnet 192.168.1.0 size 102
   D. subnet 192.168.1.0/26

3. When creating a DHCP reservation, which option within a host stanza is used to indicate the MAC address for the host?
   A. mac
   B. hardware ethernet
   C. mac address
   D. hw-address

4. Within which directory are individual configuration files stored for the Pluggable Authentication Module mechanism?
   A. /etc/pamd
   B. /etc/pam
   C. /etc/pam.d
   D. /etc/pam.conf.d

5. On which port does the slapd LDAP daemon listen for connections?
   A. 389
   B. 3389
   C. 3306
   D. 110

6. Which of the following commands is used to add entries to the OpenLDAP database?
   A. ldapd
   B. adduser
   C. addldap
   D. ldapadd

7. On which ports does DHCP traffic communicate?

    A. 50 and 51

    B. 143 and 144

    C. 67 and 68

    D. 530 and 531

8. Which of the following commands can be used to help with recovery of a corrupt OpenLDAP database?

    A. `openldap-recover`

    B. `oreco`

    C. `slapd-recover`

    D. `slapd_db_recover`

9. Which of the following configuration lines sets the domain suffix search order to example.com followed by example.org within a DHCP configuration?

    A. `open domain-search "example.com", "example.org";`

    B. `option domain-search "example.com, example.org";`

    C. `option domain-search "example.com", "example.org";`

    D. `option domain-suffix "example.com", "example.org";`

10. Within which directory are databases stored for OpenLDAP?

    A. `/var/lib/ldap`

    B. `/var/cache/openldap`

    C. `/var/share/ldap`

    D. `/usr/share/openldap`

11. Which PAM module prevents logins from accounts other than root when the file /etc/nologin exists?

    A. `pam_login.so`

    B. `pam_preventlogin.so`

    C. `pam_nologin.so`

    D. `pam_logindef.so`

12. When importing entries into the LDAP database using `ldapadd -f <filename>`, what should the format of the file be?

    A. LDAP

    B. TXT

    C. CSV

    D. LDIF

13. Which PAM module is responsible for normal or standard password authentication?

    A. pam_auth.so

    B. pam_login.so

    C. pam_unix.so

    D. pam_standardlogin.so

14. Which option within radvd.conf is used to limit the nodes to which advertisements will be sent?

    A. cnodes

    B. clients

    C. nodes

    D. lnodes

15. Which debug level for slapd is used to provide debugging of configuration file processing?

    A. 1

    B. 64

    C. 8

    D. 0

16. Which option in dhcpd.conf specifies the maximum amount of time that a client is allowed to have a DHCP lease?

    A. max-time

    B. max-lease-time

    C. lease-max

    D. maximum-lease-duration

17. When viewing DHCP-related messages through syslog or the systemd journal, you see the message DHCPDISCOVER followed by a MAC address and an interface. Which of the following best describes the DHCPDISCOVER message being logged?

    A. The server is sending out messages to discover all clients.

    B. The client is sending a message to begin the process of obtaining an IP address.

    C. The server is responding to a message from a client.

    D. The client is responding to an offer from the server.

18. Which of the following lines in /etc/nsswitch.conf uses local files followed by LDAP for authentication?

    A. passwd: files ldap

    B. passwd [files ldap]

    C. auth: local ldap

    D. auth: localfiles ldap

19. Which PAM module provides a mechanism for checking and enforcing the strength of passwords?

    A. pam_passwdstr.so

    B. pam_cracklib.so

    C. pam_libpasswd.so

    D. pam_strpass.so

20. You need to specify an alternate configuration file for sssd. Which option can be used on the sssd command line in order to point to a new configuration file?

    A. -f

    B. -c

    C. -a

    D. -m

21. On which port does DHCP failover communicate?

    A. 67

    B. 68

    C. 647

    D. 389

22. Which option with dhcpd.conf defines the default gateway that will be sent with the DHCP lease?

    A. default-gw

    B. default-gateway

    C. routers

    D. default-route

23. Which command creates an LDIF file from the current LDAP database?

    A. slapdump

    B. ldapdump

    C. slapcat

    D. catldap

24. Which PAM module is responsible for enforcing limits such as the maximum number of logins and CPU time used?

    A. pam_enforce.so

    B. pam_limittest.so

    C. pam_max.so

    D. pam_limits.so

25. Which of the following commands is used to re-create indexes based on existing slapd databases?

   A. `ldapind`

   B. `ldapindex`

   C. `slapindex`

   D. `indexldap`

26. What will be logged with the loglevel set to 0x10 in a `slapd.conf` configuration file?

   A. No debugging

   B. Trace debugging

   C. Stats logging

   D. Packets sent and received

27. When using `slapadd` for a large import, an error occurs at roughly 90 percent completion. Which option to `slapadd` enables specification of a line number from which the import will be restarted?

   A. `-l`

   B. `-f`

   C. `-q`

   D. `-j`

28. Which command is recommended for configuration of `slapd` for OpenLDAP versions 2.3 and later?

   A. `slapd-conf`

   B. `config-slapd`

   C. `openldap-config`

   D. `slapd-config`

29. When working with an LDIF file to make changes to the LDAP database, which `changetype` is used to create a new database entry?

   A. `create`

   B. `add`

   C. `addmod`

   D. `insert`

30. When working with `ldapsearch`, which of the following option sets creates output in LDIFv1 format without comments or versioning information?

   A. `-L`

   B. `-LLL`

   C. `-cal`

   D. `-e`

31. On which port does LDAP over SSL listen for connections?

   A. 389

   B. 443

   C. 636

   D. 3128

32. Which of the following PAM modules can be used for authorization and authentication scenarios using external files?

   A. pam_authfiles.so

   B. pam_listfiles.so

   C. pam_filesauth.so

   D. pam_fileauth.so

33. Which option to ldapmodify is used to perform a dry run, where no changes are made to the database?

   A. -n

   B. -d

   C. -l

   D. -e

34. What is the default filter for ldapsearch when no filter is provided?

   A. (*)

   B. (objectClass=*)

   C. (class=*)

   D. (list*)

35. Which PAM module is used for integration with the SSSD system?

   A. pam_sss.so

   B. pam_sssd.so

   C. pam_sssd_config.so

   D. pam_sss_mod.so

36. Which option within sssd.conf sets the URI for the LDAP server?

   A. ldap_server

   B. ldap_uri

   C. ldap_connect

   D. ldap_use

37. Which of the following configuration lines causes the DHCP server to refuse address requests from clients that are unknown to the server?

   A. unknown-clients: deny;

   B. deny unknown-clients;

   C. clients-deny: unknown

   D. list-clients-deny

Chapter

22

E-Mail Services (Topic 211)

THE FOLLOWING LPIC-2 EXAM TOPICS ARE COVERED IN THIS CHAPTER:

✓ **211.1   Using e-mail servers**

- Configuration files for postfix
- Basic TLS configuration for postfix
- Basic knowledge of the SMTP protocol
- Awareness of sendmail and exim
- The following is a partial list of the used files, terms and utilities:
  - Configuration files and commands for postfix
  - /etc/postfix/
  - /var/spool/postfix/
  - sendmail emulation layer commands
  - /etc/aliases
  - mail-related logs in /var/log/

✓ **211.2   Managing E-Mail Delivery**

- Understanding of Sieve functionality, syntax and operators
- Use Sieve to filter and sort mail with respect to sender, recipient(s), headers and size
- Awareness of procmail
- The following is a partial list of the used files, terms and utilities:
  - Conditions and comparison operators
  - keep, fileinto, redirect, reject, discard, stop
  - Dovecot vacation extension

✓ 211.3 Managing Mailbox Access

- Dovecot IMAP and POP3 configuration and administration
- Basic TLS configuration for Dovecot
- Awareness of Courier
- The following is a partial list of the used files, terms and utilities:
  - /etc/dovecot/
  - dovecot.conf
  - doveconf
  - doveadm

1. Which command is used to remove an e-mail from the mail queue with Postfix?

   A. `postsuper -d`

   B. `postmaster`

   C. `postfix -d`

   D. `postdel`

2. Within which directory hierarchy are queue-related messages stored for Postfix?

   A. `/var/mqueue`

   B. `/var/spool/mailq`

   C. `/var/spool/postfix`

   D. `/var/postfix`

3. Which format should the certificate and key be in for a Postfix TLS configuration?

   A. PKCS

   B. PEM

   C. TLS

   D. SSL

4. Which configuration keyword for Sieve is responsible for moving mail into the specified mailbox?

   A. `filein`

   B. `moveinto`

   C. `mailmover`

   D. `fileinto`

5. Within which directory are configuration files stored for the Postfix e-mail server?

   A. `/etc/postfix.d`

   B. `/etc/postfix.conf.d`

   C. `/etc/mail/postfix`

   D. `/etc/postfix`

6. Which of the following files is used as a user-based configuration file for Procmail?

   A. `/home/procmail.conf`

   B. `~/.procmailrc`

   C. `/etc/procmail.conf`

   D. `~/procmail.conf`

7. Which of the following definitions in `/etc/aliases` will deliver mail destined to root to two e-mail addresses, admin@example.com and webmaster@example.com?

   A. `[root] = admin@example.com, webmaster@example.com`

   B. `root: admin webmaster`

   C. `root: admin, webmaster`

   D. `root: admin@example.com, webmaster@example.com`

8. Which of the following commands displays the mail queue for a Postfix server?

  A. `mailqueue`

  B. `qmail`

  C. `mailq`

  D. `mail-queue`

9. Which of the following commands causes Postfix to process the mail queue immediately?

  A. `postqueue -f`

  B. `mailq -f`

  C. `postqueue -a`

  D. `postmailq -process`

10. Which of the following commands deletes all messages from the mail queue with Postfix?

  A. `postsuper -d mqueue`

  B. `postsuper -d ALL`

  C. `postsuper delete-all`

  D. `postsuper -D`

11. Which of the following commands can be executed in order to rebuild the /etc/aliases database?

  A. `newaliases`

  B. `realias`

  C. `rebuildaliases`

  D. `realiases`

12. Which Sieve action retains the message in the mailbox?

  A. `remain`

  B. `keep`

  C. `store`

  D. `file`

13. Which of the following commands views the contents of a message that exists in the Postfix queue?

  A. `postshow`

  B. `postless`

  C. `postmore`

  D. `postcat`

14. Which command can be used to view the currently logged-in users for the Dovecot server?

  A. `doveadm list`

  B. `dovecot list`

  C. `dovecot users`

  D. `doveadm who`

15. Which of the following deletes a message that matches on a condition with Sieve?

 A. `delete`

 B. `discard`

 C. `remove`

 D. `kill`

16. Which of the following commands is used to view the pending messages queue on a Postfix server?

 A. `postqueue -p`

 B. `postconf -pending`

 C. `postqueue -f`

 D. `postsuper pending`

17. Which of the following action lines in a Sieve configuration forwards a copy of the message to admin@example.com and keeps a copy for further processing?

 A. `redirect "admin@example.com";`

 B. `forward "admin@example.com";`

 C. `redirect :copy "admin@example.com";`

 D. `forward :duplicate "admin@example.com";`

18. Which configuration parameter within the vacation Sieve functionality is used to specify how often a vacation reply should be sent to the same sender?

 A. `:freq`

 B. `:days`

 C. `:often`

 D. `:replyfrequency`

19. Which Postfix-related command is used to provide an overview of the number of messages in the incoming and active queues arranged by age?

 A. `queuelist`

 B. `postq`

 C. `qshape`

 D. `queueshow`

20. Which of the following commands displays the current Dovecot configuration?

 A. `doveconf`

 B. `doveconfig`

 C. `dovecot --list`

 D. `doveadm conf`

21. When working with Sieve, which action is performed implicitly when no other action takes precedence?

   A. keep

   B. discard

   C. shred

   D. forward

22. Which configuration parameter for Postfix sets the networks that are allowed to relay through the server?

   A. relaynet

   B. mynetworks

   C. networkrelay

   D. relnet

23. Which of the following commands tests authentication for a user of a Dovecot server?

   A. dovecot -testauth

   B. doveadm testauth

   C. dovecot auth

   D. doveadm auth

24. Which of the following commands compiles a Sendmail configuration file in its native language to a standard Sendmail configuration file at /etc/sendmail.cf?

   A. makemap sendmail.mc > /etc/sendmail.cf

   B. m1 sendmail.mc > /etc/sendmail.cf

   C. gcc sendmail.mc > /etc/sendmail.cf

   D. m4 sendmail.mc > /etc/sendmail.cf

25. Which of the following commands views all parameters related to a Postfix configuration?

   A. postconf -d

   B. postmaster -config

   C. postfix -c

   D. postc -a

26. Within which file will you find errors related to delivery of mail on a Postfix server?

   A. /var/log/mail

   B. /var/log/postfix.log

   C. /var/log/mail.err

   D. /var/log/postfix.err

27. Which option is used to create a listening port stanza within a Dovecot configuration?

    A. `inet_port`

    B. `inet_listener`

    C. `listening_port`

    D. `listener`

28. On which port does SMTP operate by default?

    A. 25

    B. 2525

    C. 110

    D. 143

29. You need to find the mail queue path on a Postfix server. You're using `postconf -d` to view all parameters. Which configuration parameter contains the mail queue path on a Postfix server?

    A. `mqueue`

    B. `queue_dir`

    C. `mailq_path`

    D. `mqueue_path`

30. When testing SMTP communications between a client and a server, you need to begin the conversation. Which of the following lines shows the beginning of an SMTP conversation using Extended Hello syntax from `mail.example.com`?

    A. `BEGIN mail.example.com`

    B. `SMTP mail.example.com`

    C. `HELO mail.example.com`

    D. `EHLO mail.example.com`

31. Which of the following keywords defines an alternate condition when the original `if` condition fails in Sieve?

    A. `else if`

    B. `elsif`

    C. `elseif`

    D. `alt`

32. Which Sieve test examines an object such as an address to determine if there is a string within it?

    A. `:grep`

    B. `:contains`

    C. `:has`

    D. `:lookin`

33. Which configuration option specifies the maximum number of authentication processes that can be active within a Dovecot server?

   A. process_limit

   B. max_proc

   C. proc_max

   D. auth_proc_max

34. When examining an address in Sieve, which keyword attempts to look at just the domain name portion of the address?

   A. :domainname

   B. :afterat

   C. :last

   D. :domain

35. On which port does Dovecot listen for SSL/TLS-based IMAP or IMAPS?

   A. 143

   B. 993

   C. 995

   D. 110

36. Which of the following files is used as the default configuration file for Exim 4 on a Debian system?

   A. /etc/exim/exim4.conf

   B. /etc/exim.conf

   C. /etc/exim.configure

   D. /etc/exim/configure

37. Which Postfix configuration option is used with the postscreen server to set the TLS security level?

   A. postscreen_tls

   B. postscreen_tls_security_level

   C. postscreen_security_level

   D. post_tls_sec_level

Chapter

23

System Security (Topic 212)

THE FOLLOWING LPIC-2 EXAM TOPICS ARE COVERED IN THIS CHAPTER:

✓ **212.1 Configuring a router**

- iptables and ip6tables configuration files, tools and utilities
- Tools, commands and utilities to manage routing tables.
- Private address ranges (IPv4) and Unique Local Addresses as well as Link Local Addresses (IPv6)
- Port redirection and IP forwarding
- List and write filtering and rules that accept or block IP packets based on source or destination protocol, port and address
- Save and reload filtering configurations
- The following is a partial list of the used files, terms and utilities:
  - /proc/sys/net/ipv4/
  - /proc/sys/net/ipv6/
  - /etc/services
  - iptables
  - ip6tables

✓ **212.2 Managing FTP servers**

- Configuration files, tools and utilities for Pure-FTPd and vsftpd
- Awareness of ProFTPd
- Understanding of passive vs. active FTP connections
- The following is a partial list of the used files, terms and utilities:
  - vsftpd.conf
  - important Pure-FTPd command line options

✓ 212.3 Secure shell (SSH)

- OpenSSH configuration files, tools and utilities
- Login restrictions for the superuser and the normal users
- Managing and using server and client keys to login with and without password
- Usage of multiple connections from multiple hosts to guard against loss of connection to remote host following configuration changes
- The following is a partial list of the used files, terms and utilities:
  - ssh
  - sshd
  - /etc/ssh/sshd_config
  - /etc/ssh/
  - Private and public key files
  - PermitRootLogin, PubKeyAuthentication, AllowUsers, PasswordAuthentication, Protocol

✓ 212.4 Security tasks

- Tools and utilities to scan and test ports on a server
- Locations and organisations that report security alerts as Bugtraq, CERT or other sources
- Tools and utilities to implement an intrusion detection system (IDS)
- Awareness of OpenVAS and Snort
- The following is a partial list of the used files, terms and utilities:
  - telnet
  - nmap
  - fail2ban
  - nc
  - iptables

✓ 212.5 OpenVPN

- OpenVPN
- The following is a partial list of the used files, terms and utilities:
  - /etc/openvpn/
  - openvpn

1. Which of the following options within an OpenSSH server configuration is used to determine whether the root user can log in directly with an ssh client?

   A. `PermitRootLogin`

   B. `AllowRoot`

   C. `RootLogin`

   D. `PermitDirectRootLogin`

2. Which of the following files is used as the primary configuration file for `vsftpd`?

   A. `vsftp.cfg`

   B. `vsftpd.conf`

   C. `vsftpd.cfg`

   D. `vsftp.conf`

3. Which iptables chain is used to create a port redirect?

   A. REDIRECT

   B. PREROUTING

   C. PORTREDIR

   D. ROUTING

4. Which of the following files is the primary server configuration file for OpenSSH?

   A. `/etc/ssh/sshd_config`

   B. `/etc/sshserver.conf`

   C. `/etc/openssh.conf`

   D. `/etc/openssh/sshd.conf`

5. Which of the following commands saves the current set of iptables rules into a file?

   A. `save-iptables`

   B. `iptables-create`

   C. `iptables-save`

   D. `ipt-save`

6. When starting Pure FTPd, which command-line option is used to indicate that host names should not be resolved on client connection?

   A. `-n`

   B. `-H`

   C. `-r`

   D. `-z`

7. Which of the following commands can be used to generate a private and public key pair for authentication with ssh?

   A. `ssh-createkey`

   B. `sshkey`

   C. `ssh-key`

   D. `ssh-keygen`

8. Which of the following commands tests a connection to `mail.example.com` on the standard SMTP port?

 A. `telnet mail.example.com smtp`

 B. `telnet mail.example.com 25`

 C. `telnet mail.example.com`

 D. `smtptest mail.example.com`

9. Which of the following commands lists the current iptables rules while not attempting to resolve host or port names?

 A. `iptables -L`

 B. `iptables -List -no-resolve`

 C. `iptables -a`

 D. `iptables -nL`

10. Which command-line option to Pure FTPd disables anonymous upload?

 A. `-n`

 B. `-a`

 C. `-i`

 D. `-m`

11. Which option within an OpenSSH configuration is used to specify the port on which the daemon will listen?

 A. `Port`

 B. `ListenOn`

 C. `ListenPort`

 D. `PortNum`

12. Which option within an OpenVPN configuration lets a client know that it can reach the network 192.168.5.0/24?

 A. `client-route 192.168.5.0`

 B. `push "route 192.168.5.0 255.255.255.0"`

 C. `send "route 192.168.5.0/24"`

 D. `client-route "192.168.5.0/24"`

13. Which of the following commands executes a port scan using TCP Connect to the host 192.168.2.3?

 A. `portscan 192.168.2.3`

 B. `nmap -sT 192.168.2.3`

 C. `maphost 192.168.2.3`

 D. `tcpscan -C 192.168.2.3`

14. Which of the following directories contains configuration files for the fail2ban system?

    A. /etc/fail2ban.cfg

    B. /etc/fail2ban.d

    C. /etc/f2b

    D. /etc/fail2ban

15. Which option on the client side of an SSH connection is used to specify the private key for authentication?

    A. ssh -i

    B. ssh -k

    C. ssh -p

    D. ssh -l

16. Which of the following commands saves the current IPv6 iptables configuration?

    A. iptables6-save

    B. ip6tables-save

    C. iptables6save

    D. save-iptables6

17. Within an OpenSSH configuration, which option disables the use of empty passwords?

    A. DisableEmptyPass

    B. PermitEmptyPasswords

    C. EmptyPasswordAuth

    D. PermitPasswordLength

18. Which of the following commands sets the default policy for the INPUT chain to discard packets that don't have a specific rule allowing them?

    A. iptables INPUT DROP

    B. iptables chain INPUT policy DROP

    C. iptables -P INPUT DROP

    D. iptables POLICY=DROP CHAIN=INPUT

19. On which port and protocol does OpenVPN listen?

    A. ICMP/1194

    B. UDP/1194

    C. TCP/1194

    D. VPN/1194

20. Which directive in an OpenSSH configuration is used for specifying the version of the SSH protocol to use?

   A.   Proto

   B.   Protocol

   C.   ProtoVer

   D.   Version

21. Which of the following best describes the difference between the DROP and REJECT targets in iptables?

   A.   Both DROP and REJECT do the same thing.

   B.   DROP silently discards packets, while REJECT sends back an ICMP acknowledgement.

   C.   REJECT silently discards packets, while DROP sends back an ICMP acknowledgement.

   D.   DROP sends back a direct message, and REJECT sends a redirect.

22. Which file contains a list of keys that will be accepted for authentication for a given user?

   A.   ~/ssh/keys

   B.   ~/.ssh/pubkeys

   C.   ~/.ssh/keyauth

   D.   ~/.ssh/authorized_keys

23. Which of the following partial iptables rules sets up a configuration that limits log entries to three per minute?

   A.   -m limit 3 -j LOG

   B.   -m limit --limit 3/minute --limit-burst 3 -j LOG

   C.   -m limit --limit 3

   D.   -m limit --limit-minute 3 --burst 3 -j LOG

24. Which option to the ssh command is used for X11 application forwarding?

   A.   -X11

   B.   -A

   C.   -X

   D.   -F

25. The command netstat -a is reporting that port 80 is in use on the server. Which of the following commands can be used to determine what is actually using that port?

   A.   listPorts

   B.   portlist -a

   C.   lsof -i

   D.   tcpdump

26. Which of the following partial `iptables` rules allows incoming ICMP traffic?

   A. `-A INPUT -p ICMP -j ACCEPT`

   B. `-A IN -P ICMP`

   C. `-A INPUT -P ACCEPT-ICMP`

   D. `-A IN -P ICMP -j ACCEPT`

27. Which option in an OpenSSH configuration is used to determine whether port forwarding will be enabled?

   A. `AllowPortForwarding`

   B. `PortForwarding`

   C. `ForwardPort`

   D. `AllowTcpForwarding`

28. Which of the following partial iptables rules blocks all traffic from `192.168.51.50`?

   A. `-A INPUT -p ALL 192.168.51.50 -j ACCEPT`

   B. `-A INPUT -p ALL -s 192.168.51.50 -j DROP`

   C. `-A INPUT -p ALL -s 192.168.51.50 -j BLOCK`

   D. `-A INPUT -p ALL -f 192.168.51.50 -j DISCARD`

29. Which of the following partial iptables rules will allow all hosts to connect to TCP port 2222?

   A. `-A INPUT -p TCP -s 0/0 --destination-port 2222 -j ACCEPT`

   B. `-A TCP -s ALL -p 2222 -j ACCEPT`

   C. `-A INPUT -p TCP -s *.* --destination-port 2222 -j ALLOW`

   D. `-A INPUT --destination-port */* -j ACCEPT`

30. Which of the following commands enables forwarding such as would be used for NAT?

   A. `echo "1" > /proc/sys/net/ipv4/nat`

   B. `echo "1" > /proc/sys/net/ipv4/ip_forward`

   C. `iptables --enable-forwarding`

   D. `ip-forward --enable`

31. Within the `vsftpd.conf` file, which directive enables IPv6?

   A. `ipv6_enable`

   B. `ipv6`

   C. `ipv6_listen`

   D. `listen_ipv6`

32. Which configuration directive for OpenSSH determines whether key-based authentication will be used?

    A. KeyAuth

    B. PubKeyAuth

    C. PubkeyAuthentication

    D. AuthenticationKey

33. Within a jail configuration for fail2ban, which configuration option sets the name and location of the log file to monitor for failures?

    A. logpath

    B. monitor

    C. logfile_mon

    D. monitor_log

34. Which command sends a copy of the public key identity to another server for use with SSH?

    A. ssh-key

    B. ssh-copy-key

    C. ssh-sendkey

    D. ssh-copy-id

35. Which command is used for creation and maintenance of firewall rules for IPv6?

    A. iptables6

    B. ip6tables

    C. ipv6tables

    D. ipfw6

36. Which of the following OpenVPN configuration entries sends a DHCP option to a client to indicate the DNS server (192.168.2.1) to be used by the client?

    A. push "dhcp-option ns 192.168.2.1"

    B. push "dhcp-nameserver 192.168.2.1"

    C. push "dhcp-option DNS 192.168.2.1"

    D. push "dhcp-dns 192.168.2.1"

37. Which option in vsftpd.conf specifies whether users will be able to authenticate to the server?

    A. local_enable

    B. users_login

    C. user_login

    D. local_users

Chapter

24

Practice Test 1

THE FOLLOWING IS A PRACTICE TEST FOR THE COMPTIA LINUX+ EXAM 103

1. Which filesystem is used to store information about current running processes?

   A. /environment

   B. /proc

   C. /etc

   D. /dev

2. What is the default directory for configuration information related to the modprobe command?

   A. /etc/modprobe.conf

   B. /etc/modprobe

   C. /etc/modprobe.d

   D. /var/modprobe

3. Which of the following wall commands send the message "Please Log Off" to users in the operator group?

   A. wall -g operator "Please Log Off"

   B. wall "Please Log Off"

   C. wall -operator "Please Log Off"

   D. echo "Please Log Off" | group operator

4. When using systemctl to kill a process, what is the default signal sent to a process?

   A. SIGKILL

   B. SIGTERM

   C. SIGINT

   D. SIGCALL

5. Which option to dmesg displays the time in local time?

   A. -rel

   B. -e

   C. -f

   D. -t

6. Which process ID is typically associated with the init process?

   A. 0

   B. 1

   C. 5

   D. 100

7. You have been troubleshooting a system issue that may be related to the driver in use for a PCI device in the system. Which command and option will display the PCI devices and the drivers being used for those devices?

   A. `lsusb -v`

   B. `ls -pci`

   C. `lspci -k`

   D. `showpci`

8. Which option to the `telinit` command will cause the operation to not send any notice to logged-on users?

   A. `-q`

   B. `-v`

   C. `--no-wall`

   D. `-l`

9. Which file in the `sysfs` filesystem could you view in order to see the MAC address of eth0?

   A. `/sys/class/net/eth0/address`

   B. `/sys/devices/eth0`

   C. `/sysfs/devices/eth0`

   D. `/sys/net/eth0`

10. A newly added SATA disk is not showing up during the boot process. Where can you check to begin troubleshooting this issue?

    A. System logging

    B. Debugfs

    C. Within the `fdisk` utility

    D. Within the computer BIOS

11. Which command can be used to monitor communication taking place with dbus?

    A. `dbus-mon`

    B. `dbus -m`

    C. `dbus-monitor`

    D. `dbus-debug`

12. Within a systemd environment, which service manages udev?

    A. `systemd-udevd.service`

    B. `systemd-udev.service`

    C. `udevd-service`

    D. `systemd.udevd-service`

13. What is the correct syntax to indicate that the system should shut down at 8 p.m.?

    A. `shutdown 20:00`

    B. `shutdown 8pm`

    C. `shutdown +20:00`

    D. `halt 20`

14. Which option to the `systemctl kill` command will change the signal sent to the process to be killed?

    A. `-k`

    B. `-f`

    C. `-s`

    D. `-d`

15. Which systemd command and option are equivalent to the `chkconfig --list` command in a SysVinit environment?

    A. `systemctl list-unit-files`

    B. `systemctl list-service`

    C. `systemctl --list`

    D. `systemctl list-unit-files --type=service`

16. Which option to `ldconfig` is used to change the location of the cache to be updated?

    A. `-C`

    B. `-c`

    C. `--f`

    D. `-v`

17. Which of the following commands will remove all files for a package in Debian, including configuration files?

    A. `apt-get remove`

    B. `apt-cache clean`

    C. `dpkg -P`

    D. `apt-get conf-remove`

18. What is the prefix used to denote a Debian source repository in `/etc/apt/sources.list`?

    A. `deb`

    B. `source`

    C. `deb-src`

    D. `debsrc`

19. Which options to rpm will upgrade a package while displaying progress and other additional information about the operation?

    A. `-Iv`

    B. `-Uvh`

    C. `-U`

    D. `-vh`

20. Which option to a `yum install` command will cause yum to assume yes and therefore not prompt for verification when performing actions deemed critical?

    A. `-y`

    B. `-f`

    C. `-p`

    D. `-m`

21. When working with a yum-based system, you need to create a configuration to ensure that certain packages are not upgraded or installed. Which option can you set in `/etc/yum.conf` to facilitate this behavior?

    A. `exclude`

    B. `noupdate`

    C. `assumeupdate`

    D. `clearupdate`

22. You are having difficulty with shared libraries on the system. Which of the following commands will print the current directories and libraries in the cache?

    A. `ldconfig -C`

    B. `ldd -f`

    C. `ldconfig -p`

    D. `ldd -b`

23. Which option within the `.repo` file in `/etc/yum.repos.d/` is used to set the URL for the repository?

    A. `url`

    B. `repourl`

    C. `httpurl`

    D. `baseurl`

24. Which command and option are used to display basic information about each available package and its dependencies on a Debian system?

    A. `apt-get list`

    B. `apt-cache dump`

    C. `apt-get list-all`

    D. `apt-cache list`

25. When running the `lsblk` command, there is no separate partition listed for /boot. From which partition is the system likely booted?

    A. There is a /boot directory under the / partition.

    B. The /boot partition is hidden.

    C. The system has not yet built the /boot partition.

    D. The /boot partition does not show up with `lsblk`.

26. Within which hierarchy is cached data stored for both yum and `apt-style` systems?

    A. /etc

    B. /var/cache

    C. /usr/lib

    D. /tmp

27. On a BIOS-based system, within which region of the disk is the bootloader typically installed?

    A. MBR

    B. /boot

    C. Sector 8192

    D. Front

28. Which of the following best describes the contents of the / filesystem within Linux?

    A. The / filesystem is the root filesystem and contains temporary files.

    B. The / filesystem is the root's home directory.

    C. The / filesystem is used for storage of the device and to swap information.

    D. The / filesystem is the root filesystem and is the logical root of the hierarchy within Linux.

29. Which of the following commands will send the output of the `grub2-mkconfig` command to the correct location for booting?

    A. `grub2-mkconfig --output=/boot/grub2/grub.cfg`

    B. `grub2-mkconfig --file=/boot/grub2.menu`

    C. `grub2-mkconfig --file=/boot/grub.lst`

    D. `grub2-mkconfig --output=/boot/menu.lst`

30. Which command will change into the current user's home directory?

    A. `cd !`

    B. `cd home`

    C. `cd ~`

    D. `cd /home`

31. Which of the following commands writes an image called from the current directory named `raspbian.img` to the SD card mounted at /dev/sdc?

    A. `dd if=raspbian.img of=/dev/sdc bs=1M`

    B. `imgwrite raspbian.img > /dev/sdc`

C. `imgw raspbian.img | cat /dev/sdc`

D. `dd raspbian.img > /dev/sdc`

32. When troubleshooting a problem, you look through `.bash_history` to determine commands that you've recently executed. However, the file does not contain information from your current session. Which command can you use to view the commands that have been executed during the current session?

A. `cmdhist`

B. `cmds`

C. `pwd`

D. `history`

33. Which option should be sent to `grub-install` if you want to install the boot images within a directory other than `/boot`?

A. `--boot`

B. `--image`

C. `--boot-directory`

D. `--b`

34. Which command should be run in order to make changes take effect for a GRUB2 configuration change?

A. `update-grub`

B. `grub-update`

C. `grub-config`

D. `grub-ins`

35. Which of the following commands will set the environment variable JAVA_PATH equal to /home/user/java2 when using the Bash shell?

A. `invoke JAVA_PATH=/home/user/java2`

B. `export JAVA_PATH=/home/user/java2`

C. `envvar JAVA_PATH=/home/user/java2`

D. `echo JAVA_PATH=/home/user/java2`

36. Which option in the `.bashrc` sets the number of commands to keep in the `.bash_history` file?

A. `HISTLIMIT`

B. `HISTORYFILE`

C. `HISTFILESIZE`

D. `HISTNUM`

37. Which of the following commands will cause `nl` to number all lines, including blank lines, for a file called `code.php`?

A. `nl code.php`

B. `nl -a code.php`

C. `nl -n code.php`

D. `nl -b a code.php`

38. Which command can be used to create an octal representation of a given plaintext file?

   A. oct

   B. cat

   C. list

   D. od

39. Which command and option can be used to format text with pagination in a double-space format, including page numbers?

   A. pr -d

   B. pag -db

   C. cat -pd

   D. print -d

40. Of the following options for the tail command, which option outputs the last lines beginning at the 30th line from the start of the file rather than the end of the file?

   A. -n +30

   B. -n 30

   C. -30

   D. +30

41. Which option to the uniq command causes the matching to be done in a case-insensitive manner?

   A. -c

   B. -f

   C. -i

   D. -n

42. Which of the following commands prints the username and real name of all users in /etc/passwd in a tab-separated format?

   A. cut -d: -f 1,6 /etc/passwd

   B. sed 's/://' /etc/passwd

   C. awk -F: '{print $1,$5}' OFS="\t" /etc/passwd

   D. cat -o "\t" /etc/passwd

43. Which option to cp will preserve symlinks in a recursive copy?

   A. -f

   B. -d

   C. -a

   D. -b

44. Which of the following key combinations is a technique for moving to the 23rd line of a file in Vi?

    A. 23G

    B. /23

    C. i23

    D. ZZ

45. Which option to the top command changes the update interval?

    A. -d

    B. -t

    C. -n

    D. -f

46. Which of the following commands will display the process id, the real user id, the filesystem access user id, and command for processes on the system?

    A. listproc -uf

    B. ps -eo pid,euser,fuser,comm

    C. ps -e pid,user,comm

    D. ps -fa

47. Which command can be used to search the contents of all files below your current location for files that contain the characters DB?

    A. grep -r "DB" *

    B. grep -ri "DB" *

    C. cat * | less

    D. cat *.txt | grep DB

48. Which of the following commands will locate all files that begin with the name DB, starting from the current directory?

    A. locate "DB*"

    B. find ./ -name "DB*"

    C. whereis "DB*"

    D. find "DB*"

49. Which of the following files is the location used to gather information about load average for use in the uptime command?

    A. /proc/uptime

    B. /proc/loadavg

    C. /proc/load

    D. /proc/utime

50. The system contains an NFS mounted filesystem that has become unreachable. Which option should be passed to umount in order to force the unmounting of the filesystem?

   A. -nfs

   B. --fake

   C. -f

   D. -n

51. Which option to fsck causes the operation to prompt when attempting a repair action?

   A. -y

   B. -f

   C. -r

   D. -a

52. Which of the following files is updated dynamically with information about currently mounted filesystems?

   A. /etc/fstab

   B. /etc/files

   C. /boot/fstab

   D. /etc/mtab

53. Which option to repquota causes the output to be printed in a human-readable format?

   A. -h

   B. -s

   C. -p

   D. -f

54. When running the df command, you need to change the scale such that the report shows terabytes instead of bytes. Which option will accomplish this task?

   A. -ST

   B. -BT

   C. -j

   D. -T

55. What command can be used to create an image of important metadata for an ext3 filesystem?

   A. e2image

   B. e3image

   C. dumpe2fs

   D. dumpe3fs

56. Which option to `mke2fs` is used to check for bad blocks during filesystem creation?

   A. -a

   B. -b

   C. -c

   D. -d

57. Which of the following commands changes the ownership of the file `Class.java` to the user `steve` and the group `developers`?

   A. chgrp steve:developers Class.java

   B. chown steve.developers Class.java

   C. chown developers.steve Class.java

   D. chown Class.java steve.developers

58. Which of the following best describes the difference between HISTSIZE and HISTFILESIZE in Bash?

   A. HISTSIZE is the number of overall history entries to keep in the `.bash_history`, while HISTFILESIZE sets the number of commands to keep for the current session.

   B. HISTFILESIZE is the number of overall history entries to keep in the `.bash_history`, while HISTSIZE sets the number of commands to keep for the current session.

   C. HISTSIZE is the size of root's history, while HISTFILESIZE sets the overall system history.

   D. HISTSIZE and HISTFILESIZE are the same.

59. Which configuration option can be set within `/etc/default/grub` to affect the behavior of the system after a failed boot?

   A. GRUB_RECOVER

   B. GRUB_NOFAIL

   C. GRUB_RECORDFAIL_TIMEOUT

   D. GRUB_RECOVER_TIMEOUT

60. Which options to du will print a summary of information in a human-readable format?

   A. -sh

   B. -h

   C. -s

   D. -su

61. Which option to the `find` command causes it to follow symbolic links?

   A. -S

   B. -H

   C. -P

   D. -L

Chapter

25

Practice Test 2

THE FOLLOWING IS A PRACTICE TEST FOR
THE COMPTIA LINUX+ EXAM 104

1. To which file should you add an entry in order for a host to be blocked using TCP Wrappers?

   A. `/etc/hosts.deny`

   B. `/etc/tcp.wrappers`

   C. `/etc/wrap.config`

   D. `/etc/tcpwrap.conf`

2. Which of the following best describes the SQL `WHERE` keyword?

   A. `WHERE` can be used with `SELECT`, `INSERT`, `UPDATE`, and `DELETE` operations.

   B. `WHERE` can be used with `SELECT`, `UPDATE`, and `DELETE` operations.

   C. `WHERE` is a standalone statement that enables selection of specific criteria.

   D. `WHERE` is used within `GROUP BY` clauses.

3. Which of the following commands creates an alias for the ps command such that the option auwx is included when the user types psa?

   A. `alias "ps auwx" = "psa"`

   B. `alias psa=ps uawx`

   C. `alias psa="ps auwx"`

   D. `psa="ps auwx"`

4. Which of the following conditionals in a Bash script will test if the variable DAY is equal to SUNDAY?

   A. `if ($DAY == "SUNDAY")`

   B. `if ($DAY -eq "SUNDAY")`

   C. `if [[ $DAY == "SUNDAY" ]]`

   D. `if [ DAY = "SUNDAY" ]`

5. Which of the following commands is necessary for making a variable defined in your current shell available to child processes?

   A. `export`

   B. `source`

   C. `let`

   D. `def`

6. You are watching another administrator perform some work on a server. As part of that work, the admin uses the following command: `. variables.sh`. Which of the following is the equivalent of `. variables.sh`?

   A. `let variables.sh`

   B. `set variables.sh`

   C. `source variables.sh`

   D. `var variables.sh`

7. Which of the following commands adds `~/code/bin` to the path?

A. `PATH=~/code/bin:$PATH`

B. `PATH=/code/bin:$PATH`

C. `PATH=/home/code/bin:$PATH`

D. `PATH=PATH:~/code/bin`

8. Which of the following shows a valid Bash function called `sayHello`?

A. `function sayHello () { echo "hello"; }`

B. `function sayHello{}`

C. `function sayHello() { echo Hello }`

D. `function sayHello() { echo Hello };`

9. Which of the following commands sends an e-mail to root with the subject of `Update` and the content of the file `/etc/hostname`?

A. `mail root > /etc/hostname`

B. `mail -s Update root > /etc/hostname`

C. `mail -s Update root < /etc/hostname`

D. `mail root -s Update /etc/hostname`

10. Files that should be copied to a user's home directory when their account is created should be placed in which of the following directories?

A. `/etc/usertemplate`

B. `/etc/template`

C. `/etc/skel`

D. `/etc/userskel`

11. Which of the following is a valid UPDATE statement in SQL?

A. `UPDATE tablename WHERE columnname is 1;`

B. `UPDATE tablename SET columnname = 1;`

C. `UPDATE tablename USING columnname AS SOURCE;`

D. `UPDATE tablename HAVING columnname = 1;`

12. Which of the following commands launches Orca with speech capabilities?

A. `orca --no-setup --disable main-window`

B. `orca --screen`

C. `orca --screen-reader`

D. `orca --no-setup -s`

13. Which of the following areas within an Ubuntu system contains information and settings for accessibility?

    A. Accessibility

    B. Access and Help

    C. Universal Use

    D. Universal Access

14. Which command can be used to set the delay and repeat rate for a keyboard?

    A. keyboard

    B. kbdrate

    C. kbd

    D. keyrate

15. Which of the following locations stores the configuration for LightDM?

    A. /etc/lightdm/

    B. /etc/lightdm.conf

    C. /etc/lightdm-conf

    D. /etc/lightdm.d

16. Which variable is used to indicate the screen on which GUI applications will be shown?

    A. DISPLAY

    B. SCREEN

    C. LIST

    D. XWIN

17. Which of the following commands displays statistics and information about windows in X windows?

    A. xinfo

    B. xstats

    C. xwin

    D. xwininfo

18. Users can be added or removed for access to the X server. Which command facilitates this?

    A. xauthorization

    B. xhost

    C. xwin

    D. xconnect

19. Which option to useradd sets the number of days between password expiration and when the account is disabled?

    A. -n

    B. -f

   C. -e

   D. -g

20. Which of the following commands displays the current mail aliases known on the server?

   A. getent aliases

   B. getalias

   C. listalias

   D. mail aliases

21. Which of the following configuration lines in /etc/hosts.deny creates a deny-by-default policy where clients will need to be specifically allowed in /etc/hosts.allow?

   A. *.*

   B. All: *

   C. ALL: ALL

   D. LOC: ALL

22. Which of the following describes the result of running the atq command as root?

   A. The current cron and at jobs for root will be listed.

   B. The current at jobs for all users will be listed.

   C. The current cron and at jobs for all users will be listed.

   D. The last 10 entries in the at log will be shown.

23. Which of the following commands can be used to set the time zone on a Debian system?

   A. tzconfig

   B. /etc/timeconfig

   C. timeconfig

   D. timecfg

24. Which command option can be used to remove all cron jobs for a given user using the crontab command?

   A. -d

   B. -e

   C. -r

   D. -l

25. Which option to the crontab command enables you to work with a different user's cron jobs?

   A. -u

   B. -m

   C. -d

   D. -e

26. Which of the following commands displays the available character maps?

  A. charmap

  B. charmap -l

  C. locale -m

  D. mapinfo

27. Within which directory hierarchy will you find information regarding the available time zones on the server?

  A. /usr/zoneinfo

  B. /usr/share/zoneinfo

  C. /etc/zoneinfo

  D. /etc/tz.conf.d

28. When deleting a user from the server, you need to maintain their home directory rather than deleting it. Which option of the following commands deletes the user <username> but preserves their home directory?

  A. userdel <username>

  B. userdel -r <username>

  C. userdel -h <username>

  D. userdel -p <username>

29. After deleting a group, you need to search the filesystem for files owned by the group using its group ID. Which option to the find command will search using the group ID?

  A. -user

  B. -group

  C. -groupid

  D. -gid

30. Which of the following commands changes the group name from admins to serveradmins?

  A. groupmod -g admins serveradmins

  B. groupmod -n serveradmins admins

  C. groupchg -n serveradmins admins

  D. groupchg admins -n serveradmins

31. Which command is used to parse log file entries on a systemd-based system?

  A. logger

  B. journalentry

  C. jrnctl

  D. journalctl

32. The drift file, as specified in `/etc/ntp.conf` on a Red Hat system, is stored in which location by default?

- **A.** `/var/lib/ntp/drift`
- **B.** `/var/ntp/drift`
- **C.** `/usr/share/ntpdrift`
- **D.** `/usr/share/lib/ntpdrift`

33. Which option to the `ntpdate` command configures the version to use, such that an older NTP server could be queried?

- **A.** `-o`
- **B.** `-v`
- **C.** `-e`
- **D.** `-r`

34. Within which directory are `systemd` journals stored by default?

- **A.** `/var/log/systemd`
- **B.** `/var/systemd/journal`
- **C.** `/var/log/journald`
- **D.** `/var/log/journal`

35. Which option to the `logrotate` command specifies the mailer to use?

- **A.** `-o`
- **B.** `-s`
- **C.** `-m`
- **D.** `-v`

36. Which option to date changes the output to UTC regardless of the current time zone?

- **A.** `-u`
- **B.** `-t`
- **C.** `-s`
- **D.** `-v`

37. Which of the following commands can be used to delete a print job on a system that uses the lp print system?

- **A.** `lpdel`
- **B.** `rmprint`
- **C.** `rm -print`
- **D.** `lprm`

38. Which character combination sets the body of the message to STDIN when using the `mail` command?

   A. <

   B. >

   C. <<<

   D. |

39. Which of the following commands deletes a group from a Linux system?

   A. groupdm

   B. grouprm

   C. groupdel

   D. delgroup

40. Which of the following syslog facilities captures messages from the lp printing facility?

   A. auth

   B. messages

   C. lpr

   D. root

41. Which of the following subnet masks represents a /23?

   A. 255.255.255.0

   B. 255.255.0.0

   C. 255.255.255.255

   D. 255.255.254.0

42. An entry in `/etc/nsswitch.conf` indicates `hosts: files dns`. In which order will `/etc/hosts` be queried for a host name lookup?

   A. The `/etc/hosts` file will be examined first.

   B. The `/etc/hosts` file is not related to host name lookup.

   C. The `/etc/hosts` file will be queried second.

   D. The `/etc/hosts` file will be queried last.

43. Which port needs to be allowed through the firewall for standard LDAP traffic to be received by the server?

   A. TCP port 25

   B. TCP port 443

   C. TCP port 143

   D. TCP port 389

44. Which option to ssh changes the username to use for logging into the server?

   A. -v

   B. -i

   C. -l

   D. -u

45. Which option to ping disables name resolution?

   A. -d

   B. -D

   C. -f

   D. -n

46. Which of the following commands shows various statistics for a network interface such as packets and bytes received and transmitted along with errors and other such conditions?

   A. ifconfig

   B. ifstat

   C. if -s

   D. ifcond

47. Which option to dig causes it to use IPv6 only for communication?

   A. -ipv6

   B. -6

   C. -v6

   D. -IPv6

48. What is the limit for domains and characters when using the search option in /etc/ resolv.conf?

   A. Three domains and 128 characters

   B. Six domains and 256 characters

   C. Twelve domains and 1024 characters

   D. Fourteen domains and 1024 characters

49. When using the host command, which option displays the SOA record from each of the authoritative DNS name servers for the given domain?

   A. -N

   B. -n

   C. -C

   D. -a

50. You need to specify an additional localhost address and host name for a server in order to support a specialized network configuration. Which line in /etc/hosts sets the host name with a unique IP address in the correct range for localhost?

   A. `127.0.1.1 host.example.com host`

   B. `192.168.0.1 host.example.com host`

   C. `host.example.com 127.0.0.1`

   D. `host.example.com 172.16.31.32`

51. Which of the following options to `ifup` tells the command to ignore errors and continue?

   A. `--continue`

   B. `--C`

   C. `--ignore-errors`

   D. `-h`

52. Which option to `passwd` can be used to unlock an account that was locked with the `passwd` command?

   A. `-S`

   B. `-l`

   C. `-u`

   D. `-w`

53. Which of the following is the correct syntax to connect using `ssh` to host.example.com on port 2200?

   A. `ssh -l 2200 host.example.com`

   B. `ssh host;example.com`

   C. `ssh host.example.com:2200`

   D. `ssh host:2200 -d example.com`

54. Which of the following scenarios prevents all users from using cron except those specifically allowed?

   A. Create an /etc/cron.allow with the specified users.

   B. Add an entry of * to /etc/cron.deny.

   C. Create /etc/cron.deny, and add specified users.

   D. Add deny=users to cron.allow.

55. Which option in /etc/sudoers sets the destination address for administrative and security e-mails related to sudo?

   A. `mail`

   B. `mailto`

   C. `secmail`

   D. `adminmail`

56. Which of the following commands displays a listing of who is logged into the server along with the date and time that they logged in?

    A. whois

    B. who

    C. loggedin

    D. curusers

57. Which port should be allowed through a firewall for NTP communication?

    A. Port 139

    B. Port 161

    C. Port 123

    D. Port 194

58. Which option to nmap causes it to scan using UDP?

    A. -sT

    B. -sS

    C. -sP

    D. -sU

59. Which of the following commands retrieves the ssh host key fingerprint from a server?

    A. ssh-keygen

    B. ssh-hostkey

    C. ssh-keyscan

    D. ssh-key

60. Which of the following options to lsof searches an entire directory tree for open instances of files or directories?

    A. -d

    B. +D

    C. -f

    D. -i

Chapter

26

Practice Test 3

THE FOLLOWING IS A PRACTICE TEST FOR
THE COMPTIA LINUX+ EXAM 201

1. When using mdadm in monitor mode, which option sets the polling interval?

    A. --delay

    B. --internal

    C. --interval

    D. --poll

2. Which options to mdadm will start an array, assuming that there is one RAID device on the server?

    A. --assemble

    B. --start

    C. --get

    D. --begin

3. Which of the following commands can be used to set the first partition of the first SATA device to a RAID type?

    A. sfdisk /dev/sda1 fd

    B. sfdisk --id /dev/sda 1 fd

    C. sfdisk /dev/sda 1 fd

    D. sfdisk /dev/list fd 1

4. Which of the following is a persistent name that can be used across systems to identify a SCSI device?

    A. iSCSIID

    B. /dev/sd

    C. iLUN

    D. WWID

5. Which of the following represents a valid mode for iscsiadm for discovering iSCSI targets?

    A. discovery

    B. discover

    C. find

    D. list

6. Which command is used to build the LVM cache file?

    A. lvmcache

    B. lvcache

    C. vgscan

    D. vgcache

7. Which of the following commands displays the current hostname as known to the kernel?

    A. cat /etc/passwd

    B. sysctl -n kernel.hostname

    C. `sysctl -n net.host`

    D. `less /etc/hosts`

8. Which option within `/etc/ssh/sshd_config` is used to provide the name of a file that will be displayed prior to logging in via ssh?

    A. Banner

    B. LoginBanner

    C. MOTD

    D. Message

9. Which option to a configure script is used to set the location to which the resulting compiled code will be installed?

    A. `--location`

    B. `--dest`

    C. `--last`

    D. `--prefix`

10. Which options are encompassed when the `-a` option to `rsync` is invoked?

    A. `-rlpt`

    B. `-rlptgo`

    C. `-rpfsxl`

    D. `-rlptgoD`

11. When troubleshooting an issue from the console, kernel messages continually print, making it difficult to perform the troubleshooting. Which option to `dmesg` will stop messages from being sent to the console?

    A. `-D`

    B. `-off`

    C. `-E`

    D. `-O`

12. Which option to `netstat` displays information regarding multicast group membership?

    A. `-m`

    B. `-g`

    C. `-r`

    D. `-a`

13. Which option to the `ip` command displays DNS names rather than merely IP addresses?

    A. `-n`

    B. `-f`

    C. `-r`

    D. `-a`

14. Which of the following commands and options enables you to examine timing related to listening sockets?

A. ss -o

B. netstat -rn

C. ping -f

D. ls -l

15. Which of the following dd commands writes the contents of linux.img to /dev/sdb1?

A. dd if=linux.img > /dev/sdb1

B. dd of=/dev/sdb1 > linux.img

C. dd if=/dev/sdb1 of=linux.img

D. dd if=linux.img of=/dev/sdb1

16. Which of the following IP address and subnet mask pairs represents a private network in a /24 size?

A. 192.168.3.0/255.255.255.128

B. 172.16.19.128/255.255.0.0

C. 192.168.2.0/255.255.255.0

D. 10.168.1.0/0.0.0.255

17. Which option to rsync creates a backup for each destination file transferred?

A. -a

B. -b

C. -c

D. -d

18. Which option to the tar command preserves permissions?

A. -x

B. -v

C. -z

D. -p

19. When viewing the results of a traceroute, you see !H. To what does !H refer?

A. Network unreachable

B. Host available

C. Host unreachable

D. High length

20. Assuming that policy routing has been enabled in the kernel, which option to the ping command can be used to mark the outgoing request appropriately in order to indicate that the packet should be processed according to a particular policy?

A. -m

B. -a

    C. -p

    D. -k

21. Which environment variable can be used to specify the default device on which the mt command will operate?

    A. TAPEDEVICE

    B. MTDEVICE

    C. MTTAPE

    D. TAPE

22. When creating a backup for a system, which directory should be included so that most configuration files will be backed up?

    A. /var

    B. /opt

    C. /etc

    D. /bin

23. When working with a patch file, which option can be used to have the patching process ignore whitespace?

    A. -w

    B. -i

    C. -e

    D. -p

24. When working in ping mode, which option to iscsiadm sets the delay between two ping requests?

    A. -a

    B. -e

    C. -i

    D. -o

25. Which option to hdparm checks the current power mode for a drive?

    A. -a

    B. -C

    C. -d

    D. -f

26. Which file contains information on swap spaces and devices?

    A. /proc/swapspace

    B. /proc/swap

    C. /etc/swap

    D. /proc/swaps

27. Which systemd target will boot into rescue mode?

   A. init

   B. rescue

   C. recovery

   D. recover

28. Which option to fsck will report statistics such as CPU time used on completion of the fsck operation?

   A. -s

   B. -r

   C. -l

   D. -f

29. Which make target for the kernel is used to answer no to every question when creating a config file?

   A. allconfig

   B. config

   C. allnoconfig

   D. menunoconfig

30. Which of the following files provides information on memory utilization including free memory, buffers, cache usage, and several additional items?

   A. /proc/cpuinfo

   B. /proc/memtime

   C. /proc/memuse

   D. /proc/meminfo

31. Which option to the modinfo command can be used to determine the options that a given module accepts?

   A. -o

   B. -p

   C. -e

   D. -f

32. Which option to lspci displays the kernel driver (module) being used for a given device along with modules capable of being used for the device?

   A. -d

   B. -j

   C. -k

   D. -f

33. After updating source files related to udev, which command should be used in order to update the hardware database index?

 A. udevadm update

 B. udev update

 C. udevhw update

 D. udevadm hwdb -u

34. You need to look for files that are overriding each other when loading with systemd. Which of the following commands can help to show the files that are overridden with systemd?

 A. systemd-delta

 B. systemd-override

 C. systemd --override

 D. systemctl --override

35. Which of the following commands installs the GRUB bootloader on the second SCSI disk?

 A. grub-load /dev/sda

 B. grub-install /dev/sdb

 C. grub-load /dev/sdb

 D. grub-install /dev/sdb2

36. Which of the following commands can be used to list the UUID for each appropriate device in the computer?

 A. uuid

 B. ubid

 C. diskid

 D. blkid

37. When using the dm-crypt command, which type of encryption is used by default?

 A. Plain

 B. SHA-256

 C. LUKS

 D. Loop

38. You are creating an El Torito bootable CD with mkisofs. Which option is necessary to specify the boot image file?

 A. -el

 B. -b

 C. --torito-boot

 D. --tor

39. You are running `fstrim` on all filesystems. The exit code is 64. To what does an exit code of 64 refer with the `fstrim` command?

    A. Success

    B. All disks failed

    C. Some disks failed

    D. General failure

40. Which of the following is the correct option and format for adding an Ethernet and IP ARP entry, where `<address>` is the IP address and `<hardware address>` is the MAC address?

    A. `arp -d <address>`

    B. `arp -c <address> <hardware address>`

    C. `arp -a <hardware address> <address>`

    D. `arp -s <address> <hardware address>`

41. Which of the following options to the `iwlist` command displays information on the available transmit power for a given interface?

    A. `power`

    B. `txpower`

    C. `rcpower`

    D. `transmitpower`

42. Which scan mode for `nmap` provides an Xmas scan?

    A. `-sT`

    B. `-sS`

    C. `-sP`

    D. `-sX`

43. Which option to `tcpdump` sets the snapshot length of packets to capture?

    A. `-s`

    B. `-l`

    C. `-d`

    D. `-c`

44. Which option to `journalctl` displays the output in reverse, with newest entries first?

    A. `-n`

    B. `-r`

    C. `-f`

    D. `-b`

45. Which of the following is the default location of the LVM cache?

    A. `/etc/lvm/cache`

    B. `/etc/lvm/.cache`

    C. `/etc/lvmcache`

    D. `/home/lvm/.cache`

46. On which port does the `ping` command operate for ICMP echo requests?

    A. 53

    B. 1337

    C. 33433

    D. No port is used for ICMP.

47. Which `systemd` target can be used as an alternative to rescue mode when recovery is not possible in rescue mode?

    A. `emerg`

    B. `recover`

    C. `control-recover`

    D. `emergency`

48. When performing an `rsync` across devices, you receive errors that file ownership cannot be preserved, likely due to missing users or groups on the destination system. Which option should be removed from the `rsync` options in order not to preserve user and group ownership?

    A. `-go`

    B. `-o`

    C. `-no-ownership`

    D. `-remove-owners`

49. Which option to `ping` enables the bypass of the routing tables?

    A. `-q`

    B. `-r`

    C. `-b`

    D. `-A`

50. On which port and protocol is the first probe sent with `traceroute`?

    A. UDP/33434

    B. UDP/1337

    C. ICMP

    D. IGMP

51. When working with tape devices, which of the following device names typically indicates the first non-rewinding SCSI tape device on the system?

    A. /dev/st0

    B. /dev/tape0

    C. /dev/nst0

    D. /dev/tape/st0

52. When choosing directories to back up, which directory hierarchy should be included in order to ensure that mail files, such as user spool files containing mail, are backed up?

    A. /var

    B. /mail

    C. /etc

    D. /usr

53. Which option to the patch command makes a backup of files?

    A. -d

    B. -b

    C. -s

    D. -c

54. Which option to hdparm displays information such as the size in sectors and the starting offset for the drive?

    A. -e

    B. -w

    C. -h

    D. -g

55. When booting into rescue mode with systemd, a message is sent to all logged-in users informing them of the impending reboot. Which option to systemctl can be used to prevent this message from displaying?

    A. --suppress

    B. --no-wall

    C. --quiet-mesg

    D. --no-mesg

56. When checking an ext4 filesystem with fsck, which option can be used to display progress indicators?

    A. -p

    B. -f

    C. -C

    D. -d

57. Which target for the kernel is used to provide a minimal kernel config?

  A. `minconfig`

  B. `min`

  C. `tinyconfig`

  D. `configsmall`

58. Which of the following files contains the udev hardware database?

  A. `/etc/udev/hwdb.cfg`

  B. `/etc/udev.d/hwdb.txt`

  C. `/etc/udev/hwdb.db`

  D. `/etc/udev/hwdb.bin`

59. Which option to `systemd-delta` can be used to display differences among files in the instance where files are overridden?

  A. `--show-diff`

  B. `--diff`

  C. `-s`

  D. `-d`

60. Which option to the `mount` command mounts a partition using its UUID?

  A. `-u`

  B. `-U`

  C. `-t`

  D. `-i`

Chapter

27

Practice Test 4

THE FOLLOWING IS A PRACTICE TEST FOR
THE COMPTIA LINUX+ EXAM 202

1. Which option within a BIND zone configuration stanza for a master zone is used to specify whether or not slave servers should be notified when there is a change to the zone?

    A. `slave-notify`

    B. `notify-slave`

    C. `notify`

    D. `a-notify`

2. Which option to `dnssec-keygen` enables specification of the key size to use?

    A. `-b`

    B. `-f`

    C. `-e`

    D. `-a`

3. Which option to `named-checkzone` suppresses output except for the exit code?

    A. `-s`

    B. `-q`

    C. `-p`

    D. `-f`

4. When creating a zone file, a record contains the following: www IN A 192.168.1.1. To what does the IN refer in the record?

    A. Internal

    B. Internet

    C. Inner

    D. IN Priority

5. On which port does `rndc` listen by default?

    A. 53

    B. 1053

    C. 953

    D. 530

6. Which type of DNS record indicates the Start of Authority?

    A. A

    B. IN

    C. SOA

    D. NS

7. Which option to the `dig` command sets the server to which the query will be sent to 192.168.3.2?

    A. `@192.168.3.2`

    B. `server=192.168.3.2`

    C. `server=non-default`

    D. `--query-dest=192.168.3.2`

8. Which configuration directive for BIND sets the forwarders to which queries will be sent?

    A. `forward-dest`

    B. `forward-ip`

    C. `forwarding`

    D. `forwarders`

9. Which BIND configuration directive sets the IP address from which queries will be sent?

    A. `query-source`

    B. `query-ip`

    C. `query-origination`

    D. `source-ip`

10. Which option to `named-checkzone` enables a dump of the zone in canonical format?

    A. `-D`

    B. `-d`

    C. `-c`

    D. `-o`

11. When using `named-checkconf`, which option should be used if BIND is operating in a chroot environment?

    A. `-c`

    B. `-t`

    C. `-f`

    D. `-r`

12. Which option to `htpasswd` specifies password encryption using bcrypt?

    A. `-B`

    B. `-b`

    C. `-m`

    D. `-C`

13. Which configuration option for Apache changes how the version information is returned by the server for server-generated documents?

    A. `Version`

    B. `ServerVersion`

    C. `ServerTokens`

    D. `VersionToken`

14. Which of the following is the primary configuration file for an Apache2 server?

    A. `apache2.conf`

    B. `apache.conf`

    C. `http.cfg`

    D. `httpd.conf`

15. Which directive in a Squid configuration enables the setting of the port on which Squid will listen for connections?

    A. `tcp_port`

    B. `http_port`

    C. `listen_host`

    D. `ip_listener`

16. Which Apache directive sets the location of the public key for an SSL-based virtual host?

    A. `SSLCertificateKeyFile`

    B. `SSLCertificateFile`

    C. `SSLCertificatePublicKey`

    D. `SSLCertFile`

17. Which SSL-related directive sets the available list of cryptographic ciphers available on an Apache server?

    A. `SSLCipherList`

    B. `SSLCiphers`

    C. `SSLCipherSuite`

    D. `SSLCryptoList`

18. When using an `AuthGroupFile` with Apache, which of the following is the correct format for a group called `AdminGroup` with members `steve` and `tim`?

    A. `Group: steve, tim`

    B. `Group: steve tim`

    C. `AdminGroup: steve tim`

    D. `AdminGroup: steve, tim`

19. Which Apache web server log file format sequence is used to log the number of bytes in the response, including HTTP headers?

    A. `%b`

    B. `%B`

    C. `-b`

    D. `-B`

20. Which argument to the ca.pl helper script can be used to create a new certificate authority hierarchy?

    A. -ca

    B. -genca

    C. -newca

    D. -canew

21. You are looking for files related to the SSL configuration on the server. After looking in /etc/ssl, within which other directory might the files reside?

    A. /etc/sslconfig

    B. /usr/share/ssl

    C. /etc/pki

    D. /etc/private

22. On which port does the nmbd Samba daemon listen on?

    A. 139

    B. 445

    C. 143

    D. 137

23. Which message type can be used by smbcontrol to facilitate a new browse master election by nmbd?

    A. force-election

    B. new-election

    C. send-election

    D. notify-election

24. Which mode of the Samba net command is used to work with Active Directory?

    A. rpc

    B. ads

    C. ad

    D. actived

25. Which of the following configuration options for NFS facilitates the use of an NIS netgroup called admins within a host definition for an export?

    A. -admins

    B. group=admins

    C. @admins

    D. admin=rw

26. Which of the following formats is correct for specifying a username of Steve and a password of Boo for a Samba mount command?

  A. -o username=Steve,password=Boo

  B. -username Steve -password Boo

  C. -credentials=Steve,Boo

  D. --credentials=Steve,Boo

27. To which level should security be set within a Samba configuration in order for Active Directory security to be used?

  A. ads

  B. ad

  C. domain

  D. controlDomain

28. Which of the following options to the showmount command displays both host and directory information for mounted directories?

  A. -a

  B. -b

  C. -c

  D. -d

29. Which of the following commands lists the current Samba shares?

  A. smbstats

  B. smbstatus -S

  C. smbshares

  D. smbd -shares

30. You need to create a new user for Samba. However, you executed the command smbpasswd -a and subsequently found out that the specified user already exists. What will be the result of running smbpasswd -a on an existing user?

  A. The user information will be overwritten with new information.

  B. The password will be changed.

  C. An error will occur.

  D. A duplicate entry will be created.

31. The Samba configuration for your Linux server does not use the standard port for SMB shares. Which option to the smbclient command enables setting the port?

  A. -a

  B. -p

  C. -b

  D. -d

32. Which option within a host stanza in dhcpd.conf is used to specify the reserved IP address for a DHCP reservation?

   A. ip-address

   B. address

   C. ethernet address

   D. fixed-address

33. Which of the following describes a primary difference between slapadd and ldapadd?

   A. The ldapadd command is used when the server is running, whereas slapadd works with the database while the server is offline.

   B. The ldapadd command is used to add entries to the local database, whereas slapadd is used to add entries to a remote database.

   C. The ldapadd command has been deprecated in favor of slapadd.

   D. The ldapadd command is used for OpenLDAP, whereas slapadd is used for Active Directory.

34. When radvd starts, it will exit if a given interface does not exist. Which interface option changes this behavior?

   A. StartAlways

   B. StartIfMissing

   C. IgnoreIfMissing

   D. MissingOK

35. Which option in dhcpd.conf sets the default time for the DHCP lease for a given pool?

   A. lease-duration

   B. default-lease-time

   C. default-time

   D. lease-time

36. Which of the following configuration lines in /etc/nsswitch.conf provides group membership information from local files and then LDAP?

   A. groupmembers: files ldap

   B. groups: files ldap

   C. group: files ldap

   D. group [files ldap]

37. The sssd.conf file is divided into sections. Which section of sssd.conf specifies overall or general parameters for the daemon?

   A. [general]

   B. [service]

   C. [sssd]

   D. [main]

38. Within which file is the configuration related to the pam_limits.so module stored?

    A. limits.conf

    B. pam_limits.conf

    C. pamlimit.conf

    D. limitproc.cfg

39. Which option to slapcat specifies the file to which the output will be written?

    A. -f

    B. -l

    C. -o

    D. -d

40. Which changetype in an LDIF file is used to indicate that an entry should be changed?

    A. change

    B. modify

    C. mod

    D. update

41. Within which objectClass does the LDAP attribute mail reside?

    A. inetOrgPerson

    B. mailOrg

    C. orgMail

    D. organization

42. Which of the following operators is used to test whether a value is greater than another value with Sieve?

    A. >

    B. greater-than

    C. ge

    D. gt

43. Within which directory are configuration files for Dovecot stored?

    A. /usr/dovecot

    B. /etc/dovecot

    C. /etc/dovecot.conf.d

    D. /etc/dove.cfg.d

44. Which of the following is the sendmail command to print the mail queue?

    A. sendmail -q

    B. sendmail -bp

    C. `sendmail -bq`

    D. `sendmail -mailq`

45. Which of the following commands deletes all of the messages in the Postfix deferred queue?

    A. `postsuper -d DEFERRED`

    B. `postqueue -d DEF`

    C. `postsuper -d ALL deferred`

    D. `postqueue -d ALL`

46. Which of the following options can be used with `postcat` to display only the body of the message?

    A. `-m`

    B. `-e`

    C. `-h`

    D. `-b`

47. Which of the following Sieve tests will match on a message that is greater than 500 KB?

    A. `if message > 500`

    B. `if size :over 500K`

    C. `if messagesize > 500K`

    D. `if size :morethan 500`

48. Which of the following commands produces a password appropriate for use with Dovecot?

    A. `dovepass`

    B. `doveadm pw`

    C. `dovepasswd`

    D. `doveadm pass`

49. Which configuration parameter in a Postfix configuration sets the limit on an individual message?

    A. `message_size_limit`

    B. `message_max`

    C. `message_size`

    D. `max_message_size`

50. Which of the following `address-part` structures is used to indicate the entire e-mail address with Sieve?

    A. `:email`

    B. `:address`

    C. `:all`

    D. `:full`

51. When testing the SMTP protocol using a tool like Telnet, which of the following lines specifies the destination address as part of the SMTP conversation?

    A. `RCPT TO`

    B. `MAILTO`

    C. `DEST`

    D. `TO`

52. Which of the following `iptables` targets is used to create a port redirection?

    A. `PORTDIR`

    B. `PORTREDIR`

    C. `REDIR`

    D. `REDIRECT`

53. Which Pure-FTPd directive is used to limit bandwidth for authenticated users?

    A. `-T`

    B. `-B`

    C. `-b`

    D. `-t`

54. Which of the following commands connects to `www.example.com` on the standard HTTP port?

    A. `nc www.example.com`

    B. `nc www.example.com 80`

    C. `nc www.example.com:80`

    D. `nc www.example.com:http`

55. Which of the following commands clears `iptables` rules for a given chain?

    A. `iptables -P`

    B. `iptables -C`

    C. `iptables -F`

    D. `iptables -N`

56. Which OpenSSH configuration directive is used to specify the users who will be allowed to log in using SSH?

    A. `AllowUsers`

    B. `PermitUsers`

    C. `UsersAllowed`

    D. `AllowedUsers`

57. Which of the following commands prevents packets from going out on an interface different from the interface on which the packet was received?

   A. `iptables --no-redirect`

   B. `echo "1" > /proc/sys/net/ipv4/conf/all/rp_filter`

   C. `echo "1" > /proc/sys/net/ipv4/conf/all/redirect_filter`

   D. `echo "1" > /proc/sys/net/ipv4/conf/all/pf`

58. Which of the following commands creates a local port-forwarding scenario where connections to port 8080 will be sent to www.example.com on port 80 through the server at ssh.example.com?

   A. `ssh -forward 80:www.example.com:8080 ssh.example.com`

   B. `ssh -p 8080:www.example.com:80 ssh.example.com`

   C. `ssh ssh.example.com -F 8080`

   D. `ssh -L 8080:www.example.com:80 ssh.example.com`

59. When using `netstat -a`, which file is consulted for port-number-to-name translation?

   A. `/etc/portnum`

   B. `/etc/services`

   C. `/etc/portnames`

   D. `/proc/sys/net/ipv4/ports`

60. Which option within a LOG target for `iptables` sets a string that will be prepended to log entries?

   A. `--log-prefix`

   B. `--prepend`

   C. `--log-prepend`

   D. `--log-str`

Appendix

Answers to Review Questions

Chapter 1: System Architecture (Domain 101)

1. C. SATA disks are addressed as /dev/sdX, just like a SCSI disk. /dev/hdX is a traditional ATA disk. The other options do not exist.

2. B. Current interrupt (IRQ) assignments are contained in the file /proc/interrupts. Therefore, viewing the contents of the file with a command such as cat will work. There is no view command, thus making answer A incorrect. Likewise, there is no /dev/irq file, thereby making answers C and D incorrect.

3. C. The /dev/fd0 interface is typically the first floppy disk in a Linux system. There is no /dev/hd0 or /dev/flop0, thereby making answers A and B incorrect. While there is a /dev/sda interface, that will be the first SCSI or SATA disk within the system.

4. D. Configuration files for udev are found in /etc/udev, which makes answer D correct. The other options do not exist.

5. A. The modprobe command loads the module and its dependencies, if applicable. The lsmod command is used to list currently loaded modules, making answer B incorrect. The insmod command will load a given module but not its dependencies. Answer D, rmmod, is used to remove a module from memory.

6. B. The lsusb command is used to obtain a basic list of USB devices on a system. The other commands are not valid. In the case of answer D, the ls command is valid, but there is no --usb option.

7. D. The /etc/hotplug/usb directory contains scripts that run when a given device is plugged in. The other directories don't exist, so those options are not correct for this question.

8. C. The keyword single given on the Linux kernel command line will boot the system into single-user mode. The other options are not valid.

9. A. The Shift key, if pressed when control has first been handed to GRUB, will cause the GRUB menu to be displayed.

10. D. The dmesg command displays the contents of the kernel ring buffer. On many Linux distributions, this log is also saved to /var/log/dmesg. The other options shown for this question are not valid commands.

11. C. Runlevel 1, sometimes displayed as runlevel s or S, is single-user mode in which many services are not started. Runlevel 5 and Runlevel 6 are used for other purposes and runlevel SU is not a valid option.

12. D. Scripts are stored in /etc/init.d on a system using SysVinit. You may sometimes find these linked from /etc/rc.d/init.d as well. The other options are not valid for this question.

13. A. The `init` command can be used to access different runlevels. Runlevel 6 is used for rebooting the system. Answer B will shut down the system entirely, not reboot it. Answer C will place the system into single-user mode. Answer D is not a valid option.

14. C. The `telinit` command can be used to refresh the system after changes have been made to `/etc/inittab`. Notably, answer B will reboot the system, but that was not an option given the question asked. Answers A and D are not valid commands.

15. D. The `runlevel` command displays the current runlevel for a system. Answer B is not a valid option for the `init` command, and adding `sudo` in front of the `init` command makes no difference. Answer A is not a valid command.

16. C. Unit configuration files are stored in `/lib/systemd/system`. The other directory options for this question are not relevant or do not exist by default. Operating system files are typically stored in `/usr/lib/system` and those related to `systemd` can be found in the `/usr/lib` hieararchy.

17. A. The listing shows a symbolic linked file located in the current directory, linked to `.configs/fetchmail/.fetchmailrc`. The file is owned by the `root` user and `root` group, and it was created on July 8, 2014.

18. B. The `systemctl` command is used to work with services and targets. The `list-units` command is used to list targets. The other commands are not used for this purpose or do not exist with the required option.

19. C. The `-nn` option displays both numbers and device names, thus making answer C correct. The `-n` option (answer B) displays only numbers. The other two options do not exist.

20. D. The `lsmod` command is used to list currently loaded kernel modules, thereby making answer D correct for this question. The `insmod` command (answer A) is used to load modules. Answer C is a valid command but not a valid option for that command, while answer B does not exist.

21. C. The `--show-depends` option shows the modules that depend on the specified module. The options shown in the other answers do not exist.

22. B. The `wall` command is used to send a message to all users, thereby making answer B correct. The `cat` command is used as a means to concatenate or view files, while `tee` is used to send output to standard output and a file. Finally, `ssh` is the secure shell client command, and it is not used for the purpose specified.

23. B. Checking to ensure that the disk is detected in the BIOS is a good first step in troubleshooting. Answer A, unplugging the disk, won't help it to be detected. Restarting the web server won't help detect the disk, and the `disk-detect` command does not exist.

24. D. The `/proc/bus/usb` directory contains information about USB devices. The other directories are not valid for this purpose.

25. B. The `root=/dev/sda2` option will cause the given kernel to load `/dev/sda2` for its root partition. The `rootpartition` option is not valid, and the format of the `root={hd0,3}` is not valid in this context.

26. C. You begin an editing session with an E when the boot option is highlighted. You can then make changes, and when finished, press B to boot the system.

27. A. The ls command from within the grub > prompt will show the available partitions in a format such as (hd0,1).

28. D. The file /var/log/dmesg will typically contain historical messages from the current booting of the system. On some distributions of Linux, this information is also in /var/log/boot.log.

29. C. Out of the options given, the systemctl status command is the most appropriate. The telinit and sysctl commands are not used for this purpose. Likewise, the --ls option is not valid for systemctl.

30. B. The isolate option is used to move the system into the target specified, thereby making option B the correct one. The other options do not exist.

31. A. The initctl reload command causes Upstart to reread its configuration files.

32. B. The --list option will show all services on a system along with their status for each runlevel.

33. C. USB devices are generally considered to be hotplug devices. Hotplug devices describe those devices that can be inserted and removed while the system is "hot," or powered on, whereas coldplug devices are those that must be inserted and removed when the system is powered off.

34. D. The root partition is mounted after device initialization. System services, including multi-user mode, start after the root partition is mounted. The other two options, A and C, take place prior to the kernel initializing device drivers.

35. A. With cable select, ATA drives will be detected in the order in which they are plugged in on the cable from the motherboard. It's likely that the drives need to be swapped physically on the cable.

36. B. The umount command is used to unmount drives within a running system. The other commands do not exist.

37. D. The ESP is typically mounted at /boot/efi.

38. A. The mount command is used to mount drives in Linux. The source and destination mount points are expected as arguments. Drive partitions begin at the number 1, making the first partition number 1.

39. D. Of the options presented, running dmesg is a common way to find out the location to which the kernel has assigned the drive. Rebooting the system is not a good option, though it would work. There is no such thing as /var/log/usb.log, and the location of the drive may change regardless of port, depending on how the drive may be detected in the system.

40. B. From these options, only B will shut down the system immediately. Answer A will cancel a shutdown.

41. C. The `ExecStart` option indicates the command to be executed on startup of a `systemd` service.

42. D. The `systemctl get-default` command will show the default target. The other commands and options are not valid.

43. A. The `enable` option configures the service to start on boot. The `start` option, answer D, is used to start a service immediately. The other options are not valid for this command.

44. C. The `/proc` filesystem contains information about currently running processes and additional information about the kernel and current boot of the system.

45. C. The `-t` option to `lsusb` will print output in a tree-like format so that you can see which devices are connected to which bus. The other arguments to `lsusb` are not valid, and the `usblist` command is not real.

46. A. SCSI supports 7 to 15 devices per bus, depending on the type of SCSI.

47. D. If a working device does not appear in `lsmod`, it typically means that the kernel has a driver already loaded by virtue of being compiled into the kernel itself rather than loaded through a module. The use of `systemd` (answer A) or `initramfs` (answer B) has no effect.

48. C. The `-w` option causes the module to wait until it's no longer needed prior to unloading. The `-f` option forces immediate removal and should be used with caution. The other options are not valid for `rmmod`.

Chapter 2: Linux Installation and Package Management(Domain 102)

1. D. The partition containing `/var` should be the largest for a mail server because mail spools are stored within this hierarchy. The `/etc/` hierarchy is usually small, as is `/usr/bin`. The `/mail` directory does not exist by default.

2. C. The `rootnoverify` option is used to specify a non-Linux kernel, one that GRUB should not attempt to load. The `initrd` option is used for specifying the initial RAM disk, thereby making option A incorrect. The remaining options, B and D, are not valid options for GRUB.

3. C. The `noexec` option will prevent programs that reside on the partition from being executed. The `noexec` option is used frequently for mounting the `/tmp` partition.

4. A. The `update-grub` command sends its output to STDOUT. Therefore, you must redirect using > and send that output to the correct file. The other options are not valid for this purpose. Answers C and D are not valid commands while answer B contains invalid options and an invalid location for the destination file.

5. B. MBR-based disks can be partitioned with up to four primary partitions, one of which can be further partitioned or extended into logical partitions.

6. D. The `ldconfig` command updates the current shared library cache and list. `ldconfig` reads `/etc/ld.so.conf` and incorporates any changes found within it. The other commands listed as options for this question do not exist.

7. B. The `upgrade` option for `apt-get` will upgrade the system to the latest version of software for packages already installed. The `apt-update` command does not exist nor does the `-U` option to dpkg. The `apt-cache` command is used to work with the package cache.

8. C. The `yum install` command will install a given package. The `update` option will update a package. The other options listed do not exist.

9. C. Root's home directory is `/root` on a Linux system. While the `/home` directory does exist, there is no `root` or `su` user within that hierarchy by default. The `/` directory is the root of the filesystem but not root's home directory.

10. A. rpm2cpio sends its output to STDOUT by default, and therefore that output needs to be redirected to a file in most cases.

11. B. 0x82 is Linux swap while 0x83 is Linux. NTFS is 0x07 and FAT32 is 0.0c.

12. B. The `/usr` hierarchy contains many of the programs that run on a Linux system. Other notable directories for programs are `/bin` and `/sbin`.

13. B. GRUB begins its count at 0, and in this scenario there are two operating systems. Therefore, because Linux is first in the configuration file, its number would be 0, which is then sent to the `default=` option.

14. A. The `/etc/default/grub` file can be used for this purpose. You may also edit `/boot/grub/grub.cfg`, but this was not an option given for this question.

15. B. The `deplist` option displays the dependencies for the given package. The `list` option displays information about a specific package, while the other two options are not valid.

16. A. The `-ivh` options will install a file using `rpm`, displaying both verbose output and hash marks for progress. The other options presented do not exist or do not accomplish the specified task.

17. B. The `export` command is used to set environment variables in Bash. The other commands are not valid for this purpose.

18. D. The `yumdownloader` utility will download an RPM package but not install it. The `yumdownloader` utility is part of the `yum-utils` package. The other options listed for this question do not exist.

19. A. The `apt-cache` command is used to work with the package cache, and the `search` option is used to search the cache for the supplied argument, in this case `zsh`. The `apt-get` command is used to work with packages themselves, while the `apt-search` command does not exist.

20. C. The `GRUB_DEFAULT` option, when in the `/etc/default/grub` file, is used to configure the operating system that will boot by default. The other options do not exist in this context.

21. A. The ro option, which is the default for GRUB, will initially mount the root partition as read-only and then remount as read-write.

22. D. Configuration files related to the repositories for YUM are located in /etc/yum.repos.d. Of the other options, /etc/yum.conf is a file and not a directory, and the other directories do not exist.

23. A. The -V or --verify option will check the files in a given package against versions (or checksums) in the package database. If no files have been altered, then no output is produced. Note that output may be produced for files that are changed during installation or for other reasons. Note also the use of an uppercase V for this option as opposed to the lowercase v for verbose.

24. C. The -o option can be used to specify a destination file to which output will be sent instead of STDOUT. The other options listed in this question do not exist.

25. A. The menu.lst and grub.conf files are used in GRUB Legacy, that is, prior to GRUB 2. This therefore makes answer B incorrect.

26. D. The ldd command will list the libraries on which the command's argument depends.

27. B. Swap space is used when there is insufficient RAM on a system.

28. B. The /etc/lib directory is not typically associated with library files and does not typically exist on a Linux system unless manually created. The other options either contain system libraries or can be used for that purpose.

29. C. The apt-get update command will cause the package cache to be updated by retrieving the latest package list from the package sources. There is no cache-update option or update option to apt-cache. The upgrade option is used to update the system's packages and not the cache.

30. C. The file sources.list located in /etc/apt contains the list of repositories for Debian packages. The other file locations do not exist by default.

31. A. The /boot partition will typically be much less than 500 MB but should not be undersized. The used space within /boot will increase as more kernels are added such as during an upgrade process.

32. B. The pvcreate command initializes a physical partition for future use as a logical volume with LVM.

33. D. The grub-install command is used to install GRUB onto a disk and the second SATA disk would be /dev/sdb, therefore making answer D the correct option. You can use grub-install on different disks in order to provide an alternate or backup boot option.

34. A. The dpkg-reconfigure program will cause an already-installed package to be reconfigured or changed. The -r option for dpkg is for removal of a package, thus making answer B incorrect. There is no reconf option for dpkg or reinstall option for apt-get.

35. C. The lvcreate command is used to create logical volumes with LVM. The pvcreate command initializes physical volumes prior to creating logical volumes. The command in the other two options for this question do not exist.

36. A. Physical volumes are initialized first, followed by volume group creation, and then logical volume creation.

37. D. aptitude provides the terminal-based interface rather than the standard command-line interface of the other tools listed in this question.

38. D. The -search option performs a search of various fields such as the package name and description.

39. B. The rpm -q kernel command will show the kernel version. You can also use uname -r for the same purpose.

40. C. The GRUB_DEFAULT option in /etc/default/grub will set the operating system to boot by default.

41. A. The exclude option can be used to exclude certain packages. The argument accepts wildcards, and therefore excluding all kernel* updates will create the desired behavior.

42. B. The partition type 0x83 should be created for a normal Linux partition. Type 82 is used for swap, while 84 is an OS/2 partition. There is no L type.

43. B. The grub-mkconfig command should be run after making a change to the /etc/default/grub file so that a new configuration file can be created with the changed option(s).

44. B. The -s option to dpkg searches for the given package and provides information about its current status on the system. The apt-cache command is not used for this purpose, and the -i option for dpkg installs a package. The apt-info command does not exist.

45. C. The lvmdiskscan command looks for physical volumes that have been initialized for use with LVM.

46. B. The --resolve option will download the dependencies of the package being downloaded. The other options shown within this question are not valid for the yumdownloader command.

47. A. The -i option to dpkg will install a previously downloaded package. The other commands don't exist, and the -U option for dpkg does not exist.

48. D. GRUB Legacy begins counting at 0 and separates the disk letter and partition with a comma, therefore making 0,0 the first partition on the first disk. Answer A is not the first disk on the system and answers B and C contain nonexistent partitions or devices.

Chapter 3: GNU and Unix Commands (Domain 103)

1. B. The env command will print the current environment variables from Bash. The printenv command will also perform the same operation. The other commands listed in this question do not exist.

2. D. The set command can be used for a variety of purposes to change how the shell environment works. One such option is -C, which prevents output redirection such as that done with > from overwriting a file if the file already exists.

3. C. The man command displays documentation for the command given as the argument. The other options listed for this answer do not exist.

4. D. The uname command is used to print system information, and the -a option prints all information available to uname.

5. A. The g option, also known as global or greedy, will apply the matched operation to the entire line rather than just the first instance of the match. The other options apply as they would for a Perl Compatible Regular Expression.

6. C. The -l option provides the number of lines given as input. For example, wc -l /etc/passwd would print the number of lines in the /etc/passwd file. The other options given in this question are not valid for the wc command.

7. C. Both head and tail print 10 lines of output by default.

8. B. The -rf options to rm will recursively remove contents of a directory, including other directories. The -f option alone will not work in this case because of the additional directories. The other options given for rmdir do not exist.

9. D. The -type option causes find to limit its search to directories only, whereas the -name option limits the names of returned elements. Note the use of the wildcard due to the phrasing of the question. Also note the use of ./ to denote beginning the search in the current directory.

10. A. The cat command will display the contents of the file /etc/passwd and then pipe that output to the awk command. The awk command then parses its input, splitting along the specified separator for /etc/passwd, which is a colon (:). The output is then printed and piped to the sort command. The sort command in option B will not work because the cut command requires an argument. Likewise, the echo command in option C will only echo /etc/passwd to stdout. The split command can also be used to split input but does so on a fixed width manner which is generally not feasible when working with the passwd file as input. Also, the tr command is a typical companion to the awk command and helps to substitute the characters from awk output.

11. C. The -l option for ls produces long or listed output, and -t sorts by timestamp. The -r option reverses the order, and -a is needed to include hidden (dot) files, thus making answer C correct.

12. A. The timestamp of the file will change when touch is run on a file that already exists.

13. D. The -i option will cause both cp and mv to be interactive, that is, prompt before overwriting. The -f option will force the command to run while -r is recursive.

14. C. The tee command will send output both to stdout and to the specified file, thus making answer C correct. Option A will redirect output to the correct file but not to stdout simultaneously. The other answers will not work for this question. It should be noted that there is no specific formatting included with cat or tee. If formatting is needed for text processing, the fmt command can be used.

15. A. The -p option will cause mkdir to create additional levels of directories without error. Running mkdir without options will not work in this case. The -r and -f options to mkdir do not exist.

16. B. The -R option will copy directories recursively. Note that if the -i option is not enabled, the recursive copy will overwrite files in the destination. The -v option adds verbosity but does not cause any recursion, and the -Z option does not exist.

17. C. The file command can be used to determine which type of file is being used. This can be particularly helpful for files without extensions where you are unsure if you should view the contents of the file. Option A, grep, is used to look within files but would not be helpful in this case. The telnet and export commands are not used for this purpose.

18. C. The dd command is used to create disk images, among other things. In this case, the input file is /dev/sda1 and the output file is output.img. It's also common to add the blocksize option by using the bs argument, such as bs=1M.

19. B. The cut command uses a tab as its default delimiter. This can be changed with the -d option. You might use the cut command in order to apply text filters to one or more files so that they can be further processed later. For example, you might cut certain fields and create new files that can be connected together using the join or paste commands. You can use the unexpand command if you need to convert spaces to tabs and the expand command to convert tabs to spaces. However, you can also change the delimiter that is used by cut.

20. A. The -z option will unzip the file while -x will extract from the tar archive, and -f is used to indicate the file on which to perform the aforementioned operations. It's typical to add -v for verbose output as well.

21. D. The fg command will bring a command to the foreground if it has been backgrounded with either & or with the bg command. You might background a command or process so that it continues running after logout.

22. B. While the ps auwx command combined with grep will provide information on the running Apache instances, it will provide much more information than is required or useful for this problem. The pgrep command provides only the process IDs and therefore meets the criteria presented in the question.

23. D. The top command is used to monitor continuously things like CPU and memory usage, and the -p option monitors a single process. By using the run quotes with the pidof command, the process ID is provided as input to the -p option.

24. D. The free command displays overall memory usage for both RAM and swap and can be used to determine when additional memory might be needed.

25. A. You need to write the changes to the file; therefore, you'll need :w. The addition of q will also quit. Note that you could use ZZ to write and quit as well. The dd command deletes a line whereas x deletes a single character.

26. D. The -n option changes the number of lines of output for both head and tail to the number specified. The other options listed in this question are not valid for head, and the -f option follows a file with tail as the file grows.

27. A. The `uptime` command shows basic information such as that described in the question along with the number of users logged into the system and the current time. The `bash` command is a shell environment, and the `ls` command will not display the required information.

28. D. The `screen` command starts a new terminal that can be disconnected and reconnected as needed. Processes running from within the screen session do not know that they are running in a screen session, and therefore this meets the criteria needed to satisfy this question. The `fg` or `bg` commands will not meet the criteria, and the `kill` command will stop a process.

29. C. The `-9` option invokes SIGKILL, which will force the process to end. The -15 signal is the default, and the `-f` and `-stop` options do not exist. Certain commands may have been started with nohup, meaning that they are immune to hangups that might be issued with other signals. Note that you can kill a group of commands with the pkill command rather than individually with kill.

30. C. Within Bash, the number 1 represents stdout and 2 represents stderr. Redirecting both means combining them in the manner shown in option C.

31. B. The `nice` command, when run without arguments, will output the priority for the currently logged-in user, which is normally 0. The `renice` command can be used to change the priority of running processes. The other two commands shown as options for this question do not exist.

32. D. Within a regular expression, * represents zero or more characters, and in this case the problem doesn't care whether a person is using /bin/bash or /usr/bin/zsh. Likewise, a . matches a single character, but in the case of bash and zsh we need to look at the first and optionally a second character, thus the ? making the second . optional. Finally, the $ anchors the pattern at the end of the string and is also key for this regular expression. The egrep command is equivalent to grep -e and fgrep is equivalent to grep -F, both of which are deprecated. For more information on regular expressions see regex(7).

33. A. The different levels of the manual are accessed by preceding the argument with the desired level. The other options, such as `--list`, do not exist in this context.

34. C. The o command opens a new line below the current cursor location. The a command begins an insert mode session at the character after the cursor, not the line. The i command begins an insert mode session at the current cursor location.

35. A. Sending -HUP as part of the `kill` command will restart a process. Of the other answers, -9 will kill the process completely. The other two answers do not exist as valid means to kill a process.

36. B. The `history` command will display your command history, including commands from the current session. You can specify how many lines of history to display, as shown in the answer for this question. Note that .bash_history will not show the current session's history.

37. C. The `jobs` built-in command shows the list of jobs running in the background. Its output includes a job number and the status of the job.

38. B. The `find` command beginning with the path and then the -name argument will locate all of the files called .bash_history. The output from the `find` command should be piped to xargs, which can then build further commands from standard input. Note that this question and solution assume that all users use the Bash shell and are keeping history.

39. C. The `tail` command provides the end portion of the file given as an argument. Adding the `-f` option will cause the output to update as new lines are added to the file being tailed.

40. D. The `nl` command will prepend line numbers onto the file given as its argument. The output is then sent to stdout. Of the other answers, `wc -l` will print the number of lines in the file but not prepend those numbers onto each line, as was asked for in this question.

41. A. The `xz` command can compress and decompress files in a variety of formats, one of which is `lzma`.

42. A. The `find` command is used for this purpose. Adding `-type f` will limit the search to only files, and the `-mtime` option will limit to modification time in day format.

43. C. The `mv` command is used to move files, and `*.txt` will look for all files with a `.txt` extension. Note the fully qualified destination with a `/` preceding the name `tmp`.

44. D. The `pwd` command prints the current working directory. The `cd` command changes directory.

45. A. The file first needs to be sorted to group common zip codes together. After that, piping the output to `uniq` will display the unique zip codes, and the `-c` option provides a count.

46. A. Preceding the command with `!` will search history and execute the specified command. For example, `!vi` will start your last vi session.

47. C. The `killall` command is used to terminate processes using their name.

48. C. The `?` will search backward in a file within vi. The `/` is used for searching forward. The h key will move the cursor to the left one character, and the x key will delete a character.

Chapter 4: Devices, Linux Filesystems, and the Filesystem Hierarchy Standard (Domain 104)

1. A. The `which` command returns the full path to the given command, and it is useful for determining both whether a given command is available and the location from which the command will run.

2. A. The `chgrp` command can be used to change group ownership of a file. The order is `chgrp <groupname> <target>`.

3. C. The file is almost certainly a hard link to the original script. While `ls` won't show this information, the `stat` command will show that it is a link and also show the inode to which the file is linked.

4. A. The `-i` option to `df` produces information on inodes across all filesystems. The `ls -i` option will produce inode listings but only for the current directory. The `-i` option is invalid for `du`, and `dm` does not exist as a command.

5. C. The `-y` option will attempt to repair automatically, essentially answering y, or yes, instead of prompting. Of the other options, only `-V` is valid and will produce verbose output.

6. D. The first step is to use `fdisk` to create one or more partitions, then format the partitions, and then mount the partitions for use. The `fdisk` command is used with various types of disks including MBR-based partitions.

7. B. The `tune2fs` command can be used for this purpose but should be used with care because it can result in data corruption.

8. B. The addition of journaling in ext3 increased filesystem reliability and performance.

9. C. The `-S` option displays output in a format such as u=rwx,g=rx,o=rx. The other options listed in this problem do not exist.

10. B. The `-s` option to `ln` creates a symbolic link or symlink.

11. C. The `whereis` command displays pertinent information about the command given as its argument. For example, entering `whereis apache2` on a Debian system will show the binary location, configuration file location, and other relevant details.

12. A. The `PRUNEPATHS` option accepts a space-separated list of paths to remove from the results. The other options listed in this question do not exist.

13. D. The `/srv` hierarchy is used for data for server programs. The `/etc` hierarchy is configuration information, while `/var` is also used for data files but variable ones such as mail files. The `/tmp` directory is for temporary files.

14. C. The chmod command is used for this purpose, and the u+s option sets the sticky bit for the user on the specified target.

15. C. The `-a` option mounts all filesystems in `/etc/fstab` that are currently available. Of the other options listed, only the `-f` option is available and it is a shortcut to the "fake" option that does nothing except perform a dry run of the mount.

16. B. The `mkswap` command formats a swap partition. The `fdisk` command is used to create the partition itself but not format it. The other two options do not exist.

17. A. The `tune2fs` command displays a lot of information about filesystems including the number of times that the filesystem has been mounted.

18. A. The `-g` option displays progress of the dump. The other options listed do not exist.

19. D. The `quotacheck` command is used to update the quota file for the given filesystem. The `quota -u` command will display the current quota for a given user. The other commands do not exist.

20. A. The du command will report on disk usage in a recursive manner, unlike the other commands shown here.

21. C. The `/etc/fstab` file is used to store information about the filesystems to mount within the system.

22. D. The `/media` mount point is used for removable media. See `https://wiki.linuxfoundation.org/en/FHS` for more information on the FHS.

23. A. The `/etc/mtab` file contains currently mounted filesystems. Note that `/etc/fstab` contains filesystem information but not about which filesystems are currently mounted.

24. B. The -r option causes umount to attempt to remount in read-only mode. The -v option is verbose mode, and the -f option forces the operation. The -o option does not exist.

25. C. The 022 umask value will translate into 644 permissions on a new non-executable file.

26. B. The l within the listing indicates a symlink. There is no way to tell if a file or directory is temporary. A directory will display a d instead of an l. Symbolic links are not copies of files but rather are akin to shortcuts. Changes to the contents of the symlink change the source file as well.

27. B. The repquota command is used for this purpose, and the -a option will display information for all filesystems.

28. C. The updatedb command will update the database used by the locate command.

29. A. The type built-in command returns the location that the shell will use in order to run the given command. The find command cannot be used for this purpose, and the other commands do not exist.

30. B. The -R option will perform the change ownership in a recursive manner.

31. D. The proper order is the device (UUID or partition), followed by the directory to mount that device, followed by its type and options, and then the dump and fsck settings.

32. A. The blkid command will show partition UUIDs. You can also get this information with the lsblk -no UUID <partition> command. The other commands shown in this question do not accomplish the required task.

33. D. The xfs_info command is equivalent to xfs_growfs -n.

34. B. The mkfs.btrfs command is used to create btrfs filesystems and does not require the drive to be partitioned.

35. C. The usrquota option will enable user-level quotas on the given mount point. This is typically set within /etc/fstab.

36. A. The best option among these choices is to change the group to www-data and change the permissions such that the group can write into the directory. Option B should never be used because it enables world writing to the directory. The other options will not allow the web server group to write into the directory.

37. A. The tune2fs command is used for this purpose, and the -c option sets the mount count for the specified partition.

38. B. The parted command can be used to resize partitions in such a way. The mkfs command is not used for this purpose, and the other two options do not exist.

39. C. The VFAT filesystem is known as vfat to the mount command, and the other elements of the mount command are standard.

40. D. The c option in gdisk is used to change the partition name. The n option creates a new partition, the v option verifies the disk, and the b option creates a backup of GPT data to a file.

41. C. The -b option prints known bad blocks. The -f option is used to force the display of information, and the other options don't exist.

42. B. The -A option checks all filesystems in /etc/fstab, while the -M option excludes the root filesystem. The fsck that will run will be dependent on the type of filesystem. For example, e2fsck will be executed for ext2 partitions.

43. B. The quotaon command signifies that quotas should be enabled for the given filesystem. This would imply that a quota file has already been created. Quotas can be edited with the edquota command.

44. C. The fsck option, which is represented as a number in the /etc/fstab file, sets the order in which the device is checked at boot time.

45. D. The -c option creates the files for the first time. The -f option is used to force checking, -u is used for user quotas, and -m is used to not attempt remounting as read-only.

46. C. The debugfs command can be used for this purpose. When opening with -c, the filesystem will be opened in catastrophic mode, meaning that it will be opened read-only and will not read inodes when opening.

47. D. The -inum option searches for files by their inode number. This can be useful when searching for the files involved in hard links.

48. C. The -R option sets the recursive option, which means that chgrp will traverse the given directory and perform the group ownership change operation throughout the specified hierarchy.

Chapter 5: Working with Shells, Scripting, and Data Management (Domain 105)

1. C. The source command is used to execute commands from a file. A typical use case is to create functions or variables that are then available for use within the current session. The other commands listed do not exist.

2. B. While it's true that every user has a .bash_logout, the file exists in their home directory and therefore can be edited by the user. Thus, to ensure that the required command is executed at logout, the file /etc/bash.bash_logout must be used.

3. B. The env -u command will unset an environment variable for the current session. The unset command can also be used for this purpose.

4. A. The env command, when used as #!/usr/bin/env bash, will determine the location of the Bash interpreter automatically. This makes the resulting script more portable for systems where Bash may not be located in /bin/. You can use this command as a way to customize shell scripts for cross-platform use. Small scripts can be created for most of the commands in the book and those scripts can help automate many system administration tasks.

5. D. The SELECT command is used for this purpose, and the * selection retrieves all data. SELECT statements include the query part followed by the FROM keyword and then the data source, which in this case is a table called users.

6. B. The PS1 variable usually has its default set in /etc/profile and is used as the shell prompt. Users can customize the prompt to include hostname, working directory, and other elements.

7. A. The alias command is used for this purpose, and its format is name=value, thus making option A correct. The ln command cannot be used for this purpose because it will not accept command-line arguments for the target in such a format as shown in the options.

8. B. User-based configuration files are located in the order .bash_profile, .bash_login, and .profile. Only the first file found is executed and the others are ignored.

9. C. The $1 variable is automatically available within Bash scripts and represents the first command-line argument. The $0 variable is the script itself. The other variables listed in this question do not exist by default.

10. D. The fi construct is used to indicate the end of an if conditional within a Bash script. In many languages, if conditionals are scoped by braces such as { }, but in shell scripting, fi is used to denote the end of the condition.

11. B. The DELETE FROM statement deletes all of the data from the given table. Note that MySQL is typically case sensitive, thus creating the need to follow the same case for the virtualusers table object.

12. A. The DESC or DESCRIBE command is used to provide a description of the columns and column types for a table. Of the other commands shown as options, only SELECT is a valid SQL command, and it is used to retrieve data and not a description of the table itself.

13. B. The seq command is used to print a sequence of numbers in a variety of formats. The answer for this question provides a starting point (0), an increment (1), and the final number (5), thus resulting in six numbers being displayed as output.

14. B. The echo command is used to display its argument, regardless of whether the command is used inside a shell script or from the command line itself. The env command is used to display environment variables and therefore does not meet the need specified in the question. The var_dump command is used within PHP, and ls is used to display contents of directories.

15. A. The SUID bit enables the program to run as the user who owns the file regardless of who executes the program. Using SUID is typically not recommended for security reasons.

16. D. The exec command executes the script given as its argument and will then exit the shell. The source command does not exit the shell.

17. C. The double-ampersand sequence executes commands only if the previous command within the command line exited cleanly.

18. C. The read command awaits user input and places that input into the specified variable. The exec command is used to execute commands, and the other options are not valid for the purpose described.

19. A. Parentheses are used to denote a function, such as `myFunction()`. The parentheses are optional but are then followed by curly braces containing the commands to be executed when the function is called.

20. A. The `ORDER BY` clause is used for this purpose, and the `ASC` keyword needs to be added in order to make the display in ascending order.

21. C. The `||` sequence indicates an alternate command to run if the initial preceding command does not exit cleanly. The `&&` sequence executes only when the preceding command exits cleanly, so it's the opposite of what the question was asking.

22. C. The `elif` keyword is used to create an alternative execution path within a shell script. The other constructs such as `else if` and `elsif` are used in other languages.

23. C. The `unalias` command is used to remove a previously defined alias. The `rm` command will remove regular files but not aliases. The other commands do not exist.

24. D. You minimally need to be able to read the file being sourced; therefore, `chmod 400` will correctly set the permissions. Any `chmod` that gives additional permissions is not necessary.

25. C. The `for` loop construct in this case will require the variable name `LIST` to be preceded with a dollar sign (`$`), thus making option C correct. The other options will not work for the purpose described.

26. A. An inner join is the default type of join performed by SQL when columns are joined in the manner specified. An outer join, whether left, right, or both, is used to return rows that are not in a particular table as well.

27. C. The `-lt` operator is used to test for "less than" conditions within a script. The other operators are not valid for use in a shell script.

28. B. The `-e` option checks to ensure that a file exists, and it is typically used in the context of a conditional within a shell script. The other options may work within shell scripts but are not tests for file existence.

29. C. The `/etc/skel` directory contains files to be copied to the user's home directory. The other directories listed for this question do not exist by default.

30. A. The `UPDATE` statement uses the `SET` keyword to indicate the column or columns to change. The `WHERE` clause is optional.

31. D. The syntax begins with `INSERT INTO<table>`. This syntax is then followed optionally by the names of the columns to which values will be inserted, followed then by the `VALUES` keyword and finally the values to be inserted.

32. C. The `--norc` option causes Bash to execute without reading the `/etc/bash.bashrc` file or the local `~/.bashrc` file. The other options listed do not exist as options for Bash.

33. A. Array creation in a shell script involves parentheses when used in this manner. You can also use square brackets to define individual elements, as in `ARRAY[0] = "val1"`.

34. C. The `-p` option displays declare statements in a way that the commands are fully qualified and could then be used as input for another command, either through piping or redirection to a script.

35. A. The `.bash_profile` file, if it exists in your home directory, will be executed on login. Note that placing the function in `/etc/profile` would technically work, but then the function would be available to all users, which is not what the question is asking.

36. B. The `readonly` command displays the list of read-only variables that have been declared in the current session. The other commands listed for this question do not exist.

37. A. The only SQL statement that can utilize a `GROUP BY` clause is the `SELECT` statement. The other commands listed are valid but not for use with `GROUP BY`.

38. C. Square brackets are used to denote the beginning and end of the test portion of a `while` loop in a shell script. Other languages generally use parentheses for this purpose.

39. B. The `test` built-in will return `true` and can be used to test for the value existence of a variable not being null. Note that the behavior of the `test` built-in differs depending on the number of arguments.

40. C. The `HOME` environment variable, set automatically to the user's home directory, is consulted when the command `cd ~` is entered. The other paths beginning with `HOME` do not exist by default, and the `MAILPATH` environment variable shown contains a list of locations where mail is checked when using the shell interactively.

41. B. The `TMOUT` variable can be set in a given user's shell, and they will be logged out after the value given (in seconds) of inactivity. The other environment variables listed here do not exist.

42. B. Just as with an `if` statement where the statement is ended with `fi`, so too is a `case` statement ended with the word *case* spelled backward. The curly brace shown as option D is used to close `case` statements in many languages but not for shell scripts.

43. A. The provided answer performs command substitution and places the value from the resulting command into a variable. Note the use of +%s formatting on the date, which then formats the output as seconds since the epoch, as specified in the question. Option C will provide the date within the `DATE` variable but will not format it as specified.

44. B. Wrapping a variable in curly braces, `${FILEPATH}`, will ensure that the variable is interpolated or expanded correctly, even when used in a place where it might not normally be expanded, such as within a quoted string.

45. B. In shell scripts, the commands to execute begin at the do keyword and end at the done keyword. Other languages generally use either curly braces or tabs.

46. D. The `-r` test determines whether a given file exists and can be read by the current user. The `-e` test only checks to see if the file exists, while `-s` determines if the file exists and has a size greater than zero. There is no -a file test.

47. A. The `-r` option to declare will create or mark the variable as read-only. The `-p` option prints output in a format that can be reused. The `-x` option declares the variable for export.

48. D. The `*)` sequence is used to denote a default set of statements that will be executed if no other case matches within the set.

Chapter 6: Understanding User Interfaces and Desktops (Domain 106)

1. A. The greeter is configured through /etc/lightdm/lightdm.conf using the greeter-session option. The other answers provided here are not valid.

2. B. The Screen section of xorg.conf is used to logically bind a given graphics card and monitor, each of which would be defined in its own respective section in the configuration file. The other options shown for this question do not exist.

3. A. Frequency options are one of Hz, k, kHz, M, or MHz, thereby making uHz an unavailable option.

4. C. The systemctl set-default command is used for this purpose, and the target of multi-user is used to boot to the command line. You also need to remove the word splash from /etc/default/grub and run update-grub as well.

5. A. The DISPLAY variable can be used to send the windows of an X session remotely to another computer when using protocols like ssh. There is no XTERMINAL or XDISP environment variable, and XTERM is typically a terminal window and not an environment variable.

6. D. The Welcome option sets the message to be displayed to users within the display manager when they login. For users who are remote, the RemoteWelcome message can be used for the same purpose.

7. C. The Shift key can be used to enable and disable sticky keys within GNOME and other operating systems for accessibility purposes.

8. A. The Disable keyword is used to ensure that a given module is not loaded. Note that a Load statement for the same module takes precedence over the Disable statement, but Disable can be used to unload modules that are loaded by default.

9. A. The Orca project provides assistive screen-reading capabilities within GNOME. Of the other options given, the screen command is valid but it is not used for this purpose.

10. C. The xrandr command can be used to change resolution, and changing the resolution to something like 800×600 would make icons and other items appear larger.

11. D. The allow-guest option changes the behavior of guest login for LightDM, and disallowing guest login would generally make the computer somewhat more secure, though if someone has physical access to the device they might be able to get access in other ways.

12. C. The XFree86 -configure command tells the XFree86 server to query for hardware and create a configuration for the recognized hardware. Note that you may still need to edit the resulting configuration file because of unrecognized hardware or to account for specific configuration items.

13. B. The XkbModel configuration option is used to set the type of keyboard being used, such as pc105 for a 105-key keyboard. The XkbLayout option defines the layout of the keyboard, such as US for United States–style keyboards.

14. B. The VertRefresh option is used for this purpose, and it accepts a range of values in the manner shown. The other options given for this question are not valid for the purpose described.

15. D. The xdpyinfo command displays various elements about the current display(s) along with information about X itself.

16. C. The linear acceleration profile is enabled by setting the AccelerationProfile to 6 within xorg.conf. The 0 setting is known as classic, while -1 provides constant acceleration (no profile), and 7 is known as limited, which performs the same as linear but with a maximum amount of speed and acceleration.

17. A. The /usr/share/fonts hierarchy is used for storage of fonts. Another path that might contain font information is /usr/share/X11/fonts, but that was not among the choices given for this question.

18. C. Kernel versions beginning with 2.6.26 include native support for Braille displays in Linux.

19. A. The DontZoom option prevents the specified key combinations from changing the video mode. Of the other options, the DontZap option changes the behavior of the Ctrl+Alt+Backspace key combination. The other options don't have any effect and are not valid in xorg.conf.

20. A. The gok command, short for GNOME On-screen Keyboard, is the program to start the on-screen keyboard. The Caribou program will be the successor to gok.

21. C. The gdmsetup program is used to configure various options for the login window and environment, including those for local and remote users. The other options shown for this question are not used for this purpose or do not exist.

22. D. The kmag program magnifies items on a desktop and is used as an assistive technology. In general, kmag can be used with other window managers as well.

23. C. The greeter-show-manual-login option, when set to true, will require the user to enter a username for login rather than selecting the username from a list.

24. B. The Appearance section of the GNOME Control Center is used to set many aspects of how the desktop appears and behaves, including the choice of a high-contrast theme.

25. B. Mouse gestures are commonly associated with assistive technologies and help to facilitate uses of programs by moving the mouse in a certain way. Mouse gestures could be used for login and to capture screenshots, but those are not adequately or generally descriptive of their use.

26. D. The Alt+Super+S keyboard shortcut activates the screen reader in GNOME 3.9 or later. The Super+S shortcut enters Overview. The other shortcuts provided do not have a special meaning by default.

27. D. The startx command kicks off the display manager after login to a local terminal. The other commands shown do not exist or will not work for the purpose described.

28. B. The BlankTime option, which is set to 10 minutes by default, causes the monitor to go blank but not actually go into standby or other power-saving modes.

29. C. The xwininfo command displays information about a given window within an X session. The other commands listed for this answer are not valid.

30. A. The Mouse button displays keys to move the mouse. The Compose button shows a compose keyboard, and the other options are not valid.

31. C. The xhost command is used to control access to the X server. A host is added with the + sign and removed by preceding the command with the - sign.

32. B. The ForwardX11 option must be enabled in order for X connections or windows generated from the X server to be sent over an ssh connection.

33. D. The FontPath directive provides another location in which the server can find fonts. The other options do not exist within the context of an xorg.conf configuration file.

34. D. With an on-screen keyboard, users can utilize a pointer such as a mouse to select keys on the keyboard.

35. C. Bounce keys cause the interface not to react when keys are accidentally pressed in succession or held down.

36. B. The Alt+Ctr+F1 key combination is used to get to a terminal prompt, and it is helpful in situations where the X server won't start properly.

37. B. The autologin-user option is used to define a user who will be automatically logged in to the system. The other options given in this question do not exist.

38. C. The AccessX utility is used on legacy or older systems to set many of the accessibility options. The functionality provided by AccessX can typically be found in one of the utilities provided by the native X window manager, dependent on the window manager in use.

39. A. The export shell command sets an environment variable. In this case, the DISPLAY environment variable needs to be set. The env command shown will not set the variable.

40. A. The Menus option displays the menu options for a given application so that those options can be manipulated with the keyboard. The Activate option helps to work with the desktop and other applications. The other options shown for this question are not valid.

41. B. The /etc/lightdm/lightdm.conf.d directory contains individual *.conf configuration files for various settings, and it is typically parsed along with the /etc/lightdm/lightdm.conf file.

42. C. In runlevel 3, accessed through the telinit command, the X server is not typically executed. Runlevel 6 will shut down the system. Runlevel 1 switches to single-user mode, while runlevel 5 is a multi-user mode in which X is usually running.

43. C. The VideoRam option, which can be expressed in bytes, configures the amount of RAM available to the video card.

44. A. The ColorDepth option sets the color depth for a given monitor display. A typical value might be 24 for this option.

45. B. The Identifier option provides a unique description of each of the server layouts in an X configuration. The other options shown for this question do not exist.

46. A. The mkfontscale command will create a fonts.scale file that describes outline fonts on the system, and it is used for configuration of fonts that are manually added to the system.

47. A. Display Power Management Signaling (DPMS) enables additional power-saving modes, such as a full sleep mode, which enables further energy efficiency for the display.

48. B. The Emacspeak program provides another visual assistive technology as an alternative to Orca. The other technologies listed here are not related to visualization or assistive technologies.

Chapter 7: Administrative Tasks (Domain 107)

1. C. The /etc/passwd file contains various pieces of information about users on a system, such as username and real name, along with user id (UID) and login shell. The file is world-readable.

2. B. The format for cron is [minute hour day-of-month month-of-year day-of-week] thereby making option B correct for this question.

3. C. The file /etc/localtime, which can be an actual file or a symbolic link, is used to indicate the local time zone. The other files listed as options do not exist.

4. B. The /etc/cron.allow file is a list of users who have permission to create and remove their own cron jobs. The /etc/crontab file is used to store cron jobs, and the other files do not exist.

5. B. The chage command is used for this purpose, specifically with the -E option. When provided with a date, chage will expire the account on that date. When provided with -1, the expiration will be removed.

6. D. Within the /usr/share/zoneinfo hierarchy you will find information on the various regions and time zones available. The files within this hierarchy can be symlinked to /etc/localtime.

7. B. The at command is used to run a series of commands that you enter. Unlike with cron, you can schedule commands from the command line to be executed in the same order as entered, rather than having to create a specific script for the commands. The syntax shown in option B sets the time to be one hour from now.

8. B. The `userdel` command is used for this purpose and the `-r` option (lowercase) deletes both the home directory and mail spool files. The `-R` (uppercase) option informs the `userdel` command to use a `chroot` directory.

9. A. The `/etc/skel` directory contains files that are automatically copied to a user's home directory when that user is created. The other directories listed for this question do not exist by default.

10. C. Use `anacron` when you need to schedule a job on a computer that might be off when the job is scheduled. `anacron` will take care of running the job at its next available time.

11. B. The `+%s` option will format the date as seconds since January 1, 1970. This option is used frequently in scripting and elsewhere for obtaining a unique timestamp that can be parsed easily as an integer. The other options will not work.

12. C. The `--list` option shows the available character sets on the system. The other options given for this question do not exist.

13. C. The `LC_TIME` environment variable is used to control the display and behavior of the date and time, and it can be changed to a different locale in order to achieve the desired display and behavior of date and time formatting. The other options shown for this question do not exist.

14. B. The `atq` command shows a list of jobs that have been scheduled with the `at` command. The other commands don't exist with the exception of option D, which shows the `at` command but with an invalid option, `--jobs`.

15. D. Setting a user's shell to `/bin/false` will prevent them from logging in interactively to the system, such as with ssh. The other options shown for this question are all valid shells and would allow an interactive login.

16. B. UTF-8 provides multibyte character encoding, and it is generally accepted as the standard for encoding moving forward. ISO-8859 is single-byte encoded. The other answers are not valid. UTF-8 is capable of encoding all of the characters defined by Unicode. Another popular, though legacy, encoding is ASCII.

17. A. The `groupmod` command is used for this purpose, and the `-n` option is used to change the group name. The other commands listed do not exist.

18. A. The `/var/spool/cron/crontabs` directory contains a file for each user who currently has one or more cron jobs or entries. Note that the other files listed here are not valid for this purpose.

19. C. The `atrm` command removes jobs given their ID. The ID can be obtained with the `atq` command. The `atq` and `at -l` commands shown will list jobs but not delete them. The `rmat` command is not valid.

20. D. The `tzselect` command will, by default, display a step-by-step menu to select a time zone. The eventual output will include a region/time zone line, such as America/Chicago, as output.

21. B. The `getent` command is used to display entries based on the `/etc/nsswitch.conf` file. One use case for `getent` is when integrating with Microsoft Active Directory or another

LDAP service to check if the connection can be made to the LDAP server. The usermod command is valid, but it is not used for this purpose, and the other commands shown for this question are not valid.

22. B. The /etc/login.defs file contains various configuration items such as the minimum and maximum user and group IDs to be used on the system.

23. C. The /etc/crontab file is a plaintext file that is treated as a system-wide cron file. As such, the file is generally not associated with any single user and it's not necessary to run a special command after editing this file.

24. D. The TZ environment variable is used for this purpose and the general format is as shown, thus making option D the correct answer.

25. A. The /etc/cron.daily directory contains files such as scripts that are executed daily. There are corresponding cron.hourly, cron.weekly, and cron.monthly directories that run on their respective schedules, as indicated by the name of the directory.

26. C. Setting LANG=C is an alias for POSIX compatibility and will cause programs to bypass locale translations. The other options shown for LANG are not valid.

27. B. The -m option causes the user's home directory to be created. By default, if this option isn't specified and CREATE_HOME has not been set, the home directory won't be created. The -h option displays help text and the other options shown are not valid.

28. A. The usermod -L command locks an account by placing an ! at the beginning of the encrypted password. If the user has another means to log in, such as with an ssh key, using usermod -L will not prevent their login. This option is frequently used when creating special purpose accounts.

29. C. The LC_ALL variable can be used to set environment variables such as the locale, and the variable will then override others. This can be used when there is a need for a temporary change. The other variables listed here are not used for this purpose and are not created by default.

30. A. The format when adding a username places the username between the schedule and the command to run, thereby making option A correct. The other options shown for this question are invalid. In the case of option B, there is no schedule. In the case of options C and D, the schedule is incorrectly formatted.

31. C. The passwd command is used for this purpose. The -a option displays all users but requires the use of -S to indicate status. The -S option alone will not produce a report for all users, and the --all option is an alias for -a.

32. D. The chage command is used for this purpose. The -d option sets the days since the last password change, and it is measured in days since January 1, 1970. The -W option is the number of days of warning for changing a password, and the -l option displays a list of the various settings related to the account.

33. B. The file /etc/anacrontab contains information about the jobs, such as the job name and delay, among other information. The other files listed do not contain anacron-related information about jobs.

34. A. The ln command is used for this purpose, and the -s option creates a symbolic link while -f forces or overwrites the destination. The other options or order of commands are not valid.

35. B. The /etc/cron.deny file contains a list of users who cannot create cron scheduled tasks. The file /etc/cron.allow is used to provide a list of users who are allowed to create cron jobs. The other two files do not exist by default.

36. B. The /etc/shadow file contains usernames, UIDs, and encrypted passwords and is not readable by any non-root user on the system due to the sensitive nature of the encrypted passwords. The /etc/passwd file contains usernames and UIDs but not encrypted passwords. The other two files listed for this question do not exist.

37. D. There is no direct relationship between the UIDs and GIDs on a system. UIDs represent users, whereas GIDs represent group IDs. On some systems, the UID and GID number will match for regular users, but this is not a requirement and is more of a coincidence.

38. B. The dpkg-reconfigure command is used to cause the configuration questions to be asked again. The tzdata package is the name of the package on Debian-based systems. The two apt- commands shown are not valid.

39. A. The usermod command is used for this purpose. The -d option changes the home directory, whereas -m moves the contents. The other commands shown for this question are not valid.

40. D. The -G option is a list of supplemental groups to which the user will be added. A lowercase -g option provides the primary GID. The -l option causes the user not to be added to the lastlog and faillog databases. There is no -x option.

41. A. The crontab command can be used for this purpose and the -l option is used to list the crontab entries. The -u option is needed to specify a user other than the current user.

42. A. The -r option creates a system user, which will typically entail no expiration, no home directory, and a UID below 1000. The -s option defines the shell and is not typically used for this purpose. The -a and -S options do not exist.

43. B. The /etc/gshadow file contains secure information such as an encrypted password for groups, where applicable. The /etc/group file contains general information on groups. The other two files listed as options do not exist.

44. C. The LC_MONETARY variable is used by certain programs to determine the localization for currency.

45. B. groupdel cannot delete groups unless there are no users who have the given group as their primary GID. There is no -f or -r option. The groupadd command can be used to add a new group to the system.

46. A. The id command shows the username, UID, primary group and GID, along with supplemental groups. The passwd and chage commands are not used for this purpose. There is no getid command.

47. D. The -c option changes the comment field in /etc/passwd. The comment field is typically associated with the real name of the account. The -R option indicates a chroot directory, while -d indicates a change of home directory. There is no -n option.

48. D. The find command should be used for this purpose. The correct syntax is shown in option D. The grep command will merely look in the specified files for the number 1501, and the -u option to grep includes byte offsets, which is not applicable for this question.

Chapter 8: Essential System Services (Domain 108)

1.   C. The journalctl command is used to work with the systemd journal. On systemd-based systems, journalctl is a central command for debugging and troubleshooting.

2.   C. The kern facility receives messages from the kernel for logging purposes. Of the other options, syslog is used for logging messages about syslog itself. The other two options shown are not valid syslog facilities.

3.   D. ntp.org provides a free service for time synchronization. When you use pool.ntp.org as the target, you will typically receive an NTP server that is geographically close to your location, or at least as close as possible. Setting your address to 127.0.0.1 or 192.168.1.100 will use a local server, but only if that server has an NTP service.

4.   A. The service used for logging on a computer managed by systemd is called systemd-journald. You use journalctl to view logged entries rather than the standard Linux toolset.

5.   B. The newaliases command re-creates the aliases database on servers running Postfix, sendmail, and qmail. There is no need to restart the mail server after running newaliases. The alias command shown in option C will create an alias for the command shell but is not related to Postfix.

6.   D. Configuration files for CUPS are found in /etc/cups. However, it is also common to manage CUPS through its web interface. The other directories listed are not valid.

7.   A. The Allow directive is used for this purpose and the addresses 192.168.1.1 through 192.168.1.127 signify a /25 in CIDR notation, thereby making answer A correct. Note that option B, with a /24 netmask would allow the addresses too but would also allow 192.168.1.128 through 192.168.1.255, which is larger than should be allowed.

8.   B. The ntpdate command provides a command-line interface that immediately changes or sets the time according to the NTP server given as its argument. The ntpd answer provided in option A will run the NTP daemon and would not be appropriate for a script. The other two commands are not valid.

9. B. Typically, the `Connection refused` message from an NTP-related command means that the daemon is not running. There is no indication that the `ntpq` command is querying a different server; therefore, whether the network is up or down is irrelevant. The permission-based options for this answer are not valid based on the error message indicated.

10. D. The `hwclock` command is used both to query and set the hardware clock, such as the one maintained by the system firmware or BIOS. The `ntpdate` command is used to set the local system time, but it is not related to the hardware clock. The other commands are not valid.

11. B. Qmail directories are contained within `/var/qmail` by default. The queue directory is `/var/qmail/queue`. The other directories are not valid on a default configuration of qmail.

12. D. The info severity level provides information messages for a given facility. Of the options given, emerg is used for emergency messages and not normally used by applications, whereas debug is the highest or most verbose level of logging available through syslog. Configuration for syslog is typically found in `syslog.conf` or `syslogd.conf` within the `/etc/` hierarchy.

13. B. The `driftfile` configuration option sets the location of the `driftfile` for `ntpd`. The drift file helps to maintain time accuracy. The location shown is the default for Red Hat Enterprise Linux.

14. A. The `mail` option is used to send the log to the specified e-mail address on completion of the `logrotate` process. The other options shown do not exist as options in `/etc/logrotate.conf`.

15. C. The `journalctl` command is used for this purpose and the `--disk-usage` option displays the disk space used by journal log files, which are typically stored in `/var/log/journal`. Journal-related configuration is found in `/etc/systemd/journald.conf`.

16. D. The `mailq` command is used on Postfix servers in order to view a summary of the current mail queue. Details of the queue include the ID of the mail being sent along with one or more of the e-mail addresses involved in the transaction. The `mailq` command may also work with newer versions of sendmail.

17. C. The `ntpq` command provides an interactive, menu-like interface into the NTP server. You can use `ntpq` to check statistics on peers, for example. The `ntpdate` command shown as option B is used as a command-line means to set the time. The `ntpd` command shown as option A would execute the NTP daemon itself.

18. D. The format is user: destination for the aliases file, thereby making option D correct. The other options are not valid syntax for the aliases file.

19. B. The `-f` option indicates the file to which messages will be logged. The `-d` option is used for debugging, while `-v` prints the version of `klogd`. There is no `-l` option for `klogd`.

20. C. Individual configuration files for various log file rotation policies are found in `/etc/logrotate.d`. This directory is included from the primary configuration file `/etc/logrotate.conf`.

21. A. The `lpr` command places a file (or standard input) into the print queue for `lpd` to work with. The `lpq` command prints the current queue. There is no `lpx` command.

22. C. The -bp option to the sendmail command prints information about the current queue. There are no -queue or -f options that are relevant for this question. The -bi option is used to work with the aliases database.

23. A. The -w option sets the hardware clock to the current system time. The -s option does the opposite, setting the system time to the hardware clock. There is no -a or -m function for hwclock.

24. D. TCP port 631 is used as the administrative interface into CUPS. Visiting an active CUPS server on that port will show the administration website for working with print queues and other configuration items related to CUPS.

25. A. The -q option causes sendmail to attempt to deliver messages from the queue. Add the -v option to display verbose output.

26. B. The requirements of multiple e-mail addresses prevent the use of .forward; therefore, it will need to be accomplished in /etc/aliases. The format for multiple e-mail addresses is to separate them with a comma, thereby making option B correct.

27. A. The --systohc will set the hardware clock according to the current system time. The use of --utc is required in order to ensure that the time is set to UTC. If --utc is omitted, the time will default to whatever was used the last time the command was run, which could be UTC but might also be localtime instead. Therefore, the best option is A.

28. D. The postsuper -d command deletes messages from the queue. The ALL keyword causes all messages to be deleted from the queue. You should take care when performing this action because it is irreversible. There is no -remove option to postqueue and the -f option for postfix is not relevant. The rm -rf command shown is not specific enough, and it is generally not recommended to remove files from a mail queue manually.

29. A. The URL shown will display the jobs area of the local CUPS server with a query string name of which_jobs and a value of completed. The other URLs shown are not valid.

30. C. Just as the tail -f command will continuously update the display as new content is added, so too does the -f option display new entries for journalctl. The -t option shows messages for the given syslog identifier. There is no -tail or -l option.

31. B. The $UDPServerRun option is used for the purpose described. The port on which the server should listen is then provided as the value for this option. The other options shown are not valid configuration items for rsyslogd.

32. A. The postqueue -f command is used to flush the queue. The command will process all of the e-mails that are awaiting delivery. The other commands are not valid for this purpose.

33. C. The -g option specifies the maximum offset or skew that can be adjusted for when synchronizing time. When set to 0, there is no offset check.

34. A. The SystemMaxFileSize option controls the size of the journal log file to ensure that a log does not cause problems related to disk usage. The SystemMaxUse option controls overall size of journal files and the default for SystemMaxFileSize is 1/8 of the SystemMaxUse setting to allow for rotation of files.

35. C. The lpstat command is used for this purpose. The lpstat command displays information about printers, print jobs, and related information. The -W option specifies which jobs to display, completed or not completed. The lpq command shown as an option is used to view the queue, and the other options are not valid.

36. D. The postrotate option within a configuration for log rotation can be used for this purpose. After postrotate, a line typically follows with the script or commands to execute. The other options shown for this question are not valid.

37. B. SMTP operates on TCP port 25, and if other servers are contacting your SMTP server, then you'll need to listen on this port and allow traffic to it as well. Port 23 is used for Telnet, port 110 is POP3, and port 143 is IMAP, none of which are necessary for SMTP traffic.

38. A. The makemap command is used to create the hashed database in the correct format for sendmail to use. The other commands are not valid for sendmail.

39. A. The configuration file for syslog-ng is stored in /etc/syslog-ng and is named syslog-ng.conf. There is typically not an /etc/syslog directory, even on systems without syslog-ng.

40. C. The application could theoretically use any of the logging facilities, depending on the type of application being developed. However, the requirement to log to a custom log file means that the logs will have a different name and possibly location than the standard logs. Therefore, logging to any of the standard or system-level facilities is not appropriate for this scenario, thereby making one of the local (local0 through local7) facilities appropriate.

41. B. The usermod command with the -aG option is used to append a group onto the user's list of groups. In this case, the user needs to be a member of the lpadmin group.

42. D. The nocompress option is used to prevent the log file from being compressed or zipped as part of the rotation process. This might be needed on systems where compression negatively affects performance or where additional processing is necessary.

43. D. The -s option sets the date and time as specified within the command. If there is another means to set the date automatically, it may override the change. For example, if ntpd is running, that process may alter the date even after it has been set with date -s.

44. B. The mailstats command is used for the purpose described. Of the other options, the mailq command will display the current mail queue but not statistics on mail that has been processed. The other two options are not valid commands.

45. D. The logger command is used to send messages to syslog and can be executed in a shell script context in order to take advantage of the robustness of syslog without having to write separate log management into the script.

46. A. The systemctl command is used for controlling services. In this case, restart should be sent to the CUPS service as denoted by the name cups.service.

47. C. The use of - indicates that syslog does not need to sync to disk for every log entry. This can greatly improve performance for busy systems but may cause log entries to be lost if the sync process has not been run prior to a system crash or other issue.

48. A. The Port configuration option is used for this purpose and is used as an alternative to the Listen directive. With the Listen directive you will specify address:port. However, option C, while valid syntactically, will only listen on the localhost IP address of 127.0.0.1 and not all interfaces.

Chapter 9: Networking Fundamentals (Domain 109)

1. A. The netstat command can be used for this purpose, and the -r option displays the current routes. The addition of -n prevents DNS lookups, which can help with performance.

2. A. The ifconfig command can be used for this purpose, and it requires the addition of the -a option because the adapter is currently down. The ifup command can be used to bring up an interface, but it does not display information by default. The netstat command displays information about the network but not with the -n option.

3. D. Private IP addresses are found within the 10.0.0.0/8, 172.16.0.0/12, and 192.168.0.0/16 ranges, thus making an address in the 143 range a public IP address.

4. C. The route command is used for this purpose, and adding a route is done with the add option. The default gateway is added using the default gw keywords followed by the IP address of the gateway and the adapter.

5. A. The host command enables changing of the query type with the -t option. Using ns as the type will query for the nameservers for a given domain. There is no all type, and the other options are also invalid.

6. B. Traditionally, UDP/53 is used for DNS queries, but with a primary and secondary server it is assumed that zone transfers may occur. DNS zone transfers typically take place over TCP/53.

7. B. The -I option enables the choice of interface. A lowercase -i option sets the interval, while -a indicates an audible ping. Finally, -t enables a TTL-based ping only.

8. D. A /27 with a netmask of 255.255.255.224 splits a subnet into four segments of 32 addresses, thus enabling 30 usable addresses.

9. A. The host or dig commands can be used for this purpose by setting the type to mx. The mx type will query for the mail exchanger for the given domain. There is no smtp type.

10. B. The localhost address for IPv6 can be written as ::1. Addresses shown like 127 represent the IPv4 localhost range, but they are not written properly for IPv4 or IPv6.

11. A. The -T option causes traceroute to use TCP packets. This option, which requires root privileges, can be helpful in situations where a firewall may be blocking traceroute traffic. The -i option chooses the interface, while the -s option chooses the source address. A lowercase -t option sets the Type of Service (ToS) flag.

12. C. The ifup command is used to bring up network interfaces, and the -a option brings up those interfaces marked as auto. The ifconfig -a command displays information on all interfaces, and there is no ifstat command. The ifdown command can be used to bring interfaces down or offline.

13. D. The hostname command is used to return the hostname and domain. When given the -d option, just the domain name is returned to STDOUT, thereby making it appropriate for use in a script.

14. A. The ip command with the monitor option/subcommand will display netlink messages as they arrive. There is no netlink subcommand for ip and the route command will not work for this purpose.

15. D. The -6 option, as in traceroute -6, executes an IPv6 traceroute. The other options shown for this question are not valid. It would be rare for the traceroute6 command not to be available and still have the traceroute -6 command available.

16. A. The syntax is database: databasename with additional databasenames separated by spaces, as shown in the correct option for this question.

17. A. The @ symbol is used to indicate a server to which the query will be sent directly. This can be quite useful for troubleshooting resolution problems by sending the query directly to an authoritative name server for the domain. Of the other options, -t sets the type and the other choices are not valid.

18. D. SNMP traffic takes place on ports 161 and 162. Though the traffic is usually on UDP, the TCP ports are also reserved for SNMP. Ports 110 and 143 are used for POP3 and IMAP, respectively, while 23 and 25 are for Telnet and SMTP. Finally, ports 80 and 443 are for HTTP and HTTPS.

19. A. The getent command is used for working with NSS databases, and getent hosts will display the available hosts using the databases configured in /etc/nsswitch.conf.

20. D. A /25 in CIDR notation represents half of a /24 in address space, therefore making 255.255.255.128 the masked bits. The 255.255.255.0 answer is /24 while 255.255.255.192 is /26. Finally, 255.255.0.0 is /16.

21. C. The configuration option is called nameserver, and the value for the option is the IP address of the desired nameserver. There are several options that affect how name resolution is performed, such as the number of attempts and timeout. See resolv.conf(5) for more information.

22. D. The /etc/services file contains standard port-to-protocol information based on the well-known and assigned ports from IANA. If you'd like to provide a custom name for the service, you can do so by editing this file. There is no /etc/ports or /etc/p2p file by default, and /etc/ppp is usually a directory for the point-to-point protocol daemon and related services.

23. A. The route command can be used for this purpose, and the syntax includes the network range, denoted with the -net option, followed by the word netmask and the masked bits, followed by the word gw and the IP address of the gateway. The other options shown are invalid for a variety of reasons, including missing keywords and options and order.

24. A. The netstat command is used for this purpose and the -a option displays all sockets, listening and non-listening. Note that it's frequently helpful to add the -n option, or combine them as in netstat -an, in order to prevent name lookup. Doing so can significantly improve performance of the command.

25. A. The correct format is IP address followed by canonical hostname followed by any aliases for the host. You can use entries in /etc/hosts to override DNS lookups, which can be useful in preventing those names from resolving or to provide a different resolution.

26. C. The ifconfig command for configuring interfaces begins with the device followed by the IP address, which is then followed by the netmask keyword and the netmask to add. Because this is a /24, the netmask is 255.255.255.0.

27. C. IPv4 addresses are 32 bits in length and IPv6 addresses are 128 bits. Both IPv4 and IPv6 can be used on internal and external networks alike, and there is indeed subnetting necessary with IPv6.

28. D. ICMP is a layer 3 protocol, meaning that it does not use ports for communication. TCP/43 is used for whois, while port 111 is used for sunrpc. UDP/69 is used for TFTP.

29. B. The ip route command can be used for this purpose, and its syntax uses a change command and the via keyword. The same operation could be completed with the route command, but that would require first deleting the existing gateway and then re-adding a new default gateway.

30. C. Secure Shell, or ssh, operates on TCP port 22 by default. TCP/23 is used for Telnet; TCP/25 is SMTP, and TCP/2200 is not associated with a well-known service.

31. B. The nc command is used to start netcat, and the -l option causes it to listen. The -p option is used to specify the port on which netcat will listen. The -s option specifies the local source address, and it is not used for this scenario.

32. A. The soa type is used to query for Start of Authority records for a domain. Note that in many cases, dig will attempt to look up the domain within a given command and may not appear to have had an error. For example, when running option D (dig -t auth example.com), you will receive information about example.com and there will be a line in the output that dig has ignored the invalid type of auth.

33. A. The search option is used for this purpose, and it can be provided with multiple domain names, each separated by a space or tab. The domain option is valid within /etc/resolv.conf, but it does not allow for multiple domain names.

34. C. The ping6 command is used to ping IPv6 addresses. Unique local addresses are the IPv6 equivalent of RFC 1918 private addresses in IPv4. In IPv6, fc00::/7 is the unique local address space. Note that there is no -6 option to the normal ping command.

35. A. The route command can be used for this purpose and in the scenario described, a reject destination is used for the route. The other options shown are invalid because they use invalid options to the route command.

36. B. The `tracepath` command provides the maximum transmission unit (MTU) of the hops, where possible. Both `traceroute` and `tracepath` can be used internally or externally, and both provide IPv6 capabilities. Certain options with the `traceroute` command can require root privileges, but not enough information was given in the question for that to have been the correct option. The `tracepath6` command provides native IPv6 capabilities.

37. D. The `-c` option provides the count of the number of pings to send. The `-n` option specifies numeric output only, while `-p` specifies the pattern to use for the packet content. Finally, the `-t` option sets the TTL.

38. B. NXDOMAIN is the status for a non-existent domain or host, basically meaning that the host for which the query was sent does not exist. A normal status when there has not been an error is `"NOERROR"`.

39. A. In order to facilitate the scenario described, the syntax for `ifconfig` uses the device followed by the protocol, `inet6` in this case. Next, the keyword `add` is used to indicate that an additional IP address is being added. Finally, it is followed by the address itself.

40. C. LDAP over SSL, or LDAPS, operates on port 636. Port 53 is used for DNS, port 389 is used for normal, non-SSL LDAP, and port 443 is used for HTTP over SSL.

41. D. The best option for this question is to add an entry for the host in `/etc/hosts`. Doing so will always cause DNS queries to resolve to `127.0.0.1`. The other options are not as robust because they rely on `www.example.com` always having the same IP address, or the solutions require additional maintenance to constantly add new IP addresses if `www.example.com`'s IP address changes.

42. A. The `ip route flush cache` command should be executed after changing the routes. The other commands shown for this question are not valid.

43. A. SPF records are stored in the `txt` record type in DNS, thereby making `-t txt` the correct option for this question. Of the other answers, only `-t mx` is valid and returns the mail exchangers for the given domain.

44. B. TCP is a connection-oriented protocol that uses a three-way handshake to establish a connection. ICMP does not use ports for communication, while UDP is connectionless. IP is the core Internet Protocol, and it does not use a handshake.

45. D. There are 1,048,576 IP addresses in the `172.16.0.0` private range. There are 16,777,216 in the `10.0.0.0` range and 65,536 in the `192.168.0.0` range.

46. C. The only viable possibility of those listed is that ICMP traffic is blocked. TCP traffic is obviously passing because of the ability to get there using HTTP, and DNS must also be working.

47. C. The `G` signifies a gateway within the route table.

48. A. The `axfr` type is a zone transfer, and the `@` symbol signifies the server to which the query will be sent. There is no `xfer` type, and option B is just a normal query for the domain sent to the specified server.

Chapter 10: Security (Domain 110)

1.   A. If /etc/nologin exists, users will be prevented from logging into the system. The root user can still log in, assuming that root logins are enabled within the ssh configuration.

2.   B. The find command is used for this purpose, and the permission can be described as 4000 to indicate the presence of the setuid bit. The -type option can be used for changing the type of object to be returned, but it is not relevant for the scenario described.

3.   B. The lsof command can be used for this purpose, and with the -i option it will display the network ports along with their process. The netstat command will display network ports but not the process with the -a option. The ps command is used for processes but not network ports. Finally, there is no netlist command.

4.   A. The fuser command can be used to determine which process is using a given file. The ls command will show files, and find can be used to find files but not specifically for this purpose. The ps command does show processes but it is not necessarily tied to a particular file.

5.   D. The chage command is used for working with account aging information such as expiration date, password change, days between password changes, and so on. The -l option lists information for the given account. The usermod command is used to make changes to an account, and the other two commands are not valid.

6.   A. The nmap command is used to scan for open ports. The nmap command will scan for open TCP ports to the address or addresses specified. The other commands shown do not scan for open ports to external (off-host) IP addresses.

7.   B. The ssh-keygen command is used to create a key pair for use with ssh instead of a password. Of the other options, the ssh command does exist but the -k option is used to disable GSSAPI credential forwarding and not for the purpose described.

8.   B. The format is username (or other specifier) followed by hard or soft, depending on the limit type, then the keyword followed by the value for that given keyword.

9.   A. The file authorized_keys, stored in the .ssh directory in your home directory, contains public keys that are authorized to log in to the server using their corresponding private key.

10. C. The -p option shows the process ID to which a given port is connected, and it is useful for displaying information about which process is listening on a given port. The -a option shows listening and non-listening sockets, while -n disables name lookups. The -l option shows listening sockets only.

11. D. Loading of alternate files is accomplished using the -f option. Doing so facilitates exactly the scenario described, being able to examine logins from old log files. The -a option controls the location of the display for the host, while -t controls the display of the logins as of the specified date and time. There is no -e option.

12. D. The w command shows currently logged-in users along with information such as uptime and load average. The fuser command is used to show open files, and the -u option to ls controls the display for file listings. There is no listuser command.

13. A. The -u option is correct for this purpose. An uppercase -U option sets the user context for listing privileges. The -s option sets the shell, and the -H option sets the home directory.

14. B. The NOPASSWD option causes sudo to not prompt for a password for a given sudo command. This is useful for scripted scenarios where a password prompt would cause problems.

15. C. The ulimit command shows such limits, and the -a option shows all limits for the currently logged-in user. The other commands are not valid.

16. C. The syntax to block access to every service uses the ALL keyword followed by the address or network to which the policy will apply.

17. A. The correct format is YYYY-MM-DD for the usermod command.

18. C. The disable option is used for the purpose described and can be set to yes or no. The other options are not valid for this scenario. Configuration for xinetd is controlled by /etc/xinetd.conf.

19. A. The file is named id_rsa by default, and the public key is named id_rsa.pub. For DSA keys, the names are id_dsa and id_dsa.pub.

20. C. The -c option executes a single command but does so without an interactive session. The -s option specifies the shell to be used. There is no -u or -e option for the su command.

21. C. The send-key option followed by the name of the key sends the key to the key server specified by the keyserver option. This is a typical scenario for sending a locally generated public key to a public server for others to use. The other options shown as potential answers do not exist.

22. B. There is no special option necessary in order to execute a single command on a remote host with ssh. The -s option requests a subsystem and is not related to this scenario. The -e option specifies an escape character.

23. D. The ssh-add command is used to list currently loaded keys, and it is used in conjunction with ssh-agent. There is no -l option to ssh-agent and the -l option to ssh specifies the login name to use. There is no ssh-list-keys command.

24. C. While any text editor can be used, it is highly recommended to use the visudo command to edit /etc/sudoers. Using visudo enables syntax checking, which will help to prevent issues with an invalid configuration causing problems for those who rely on sudo.

25. A. The systemctl command will be used for this purpose, and the subcommand is disable. There is a stop subcommand, but it will only stop the given service rather than prevent it from starting on boot. The other options are invalid for various reasons including that they use systemd as the command name rather than systemctl.

26. B. The chage command can be used for this purpose, and the -E option accepts days since 1/1/1970. There is no -e option to passwd, and -l for usermod will not perform the action described. There is no chguser command.

27. A. Setting -P0 will cause no ping requests to precede the scan, and it is useful for the scenario described. There is a -s option, but it is not used for this purpose. The other options are not valid.

28. C. The maxlogins parameter is used to control the number of simultaneous logins for a given account.

29. B. The file ssh_known_hosts, typically kept in /etc/, is used for the purpose described. Note that on some systems this file and other ssh-related configurations may be found in /etc/ssh/. The answers that indicate ~ or within /root are incorrect because the question specifies a server-wide list.

30. C. The date of the last password change, as measured in days since January 1, 1970, is contained in the third field of a shadow entry. The expiration date would be the eighth field, as separated by colons.

31. A. The format for local forwarding uses the -L option followed by the local port and then the remote host:port combination. This is typically followed by the user@host credential and destination information for the ssh connection itself.

32. C. The option is called X11Forwarding, and it must be set to yes in order for the destination server to forward X-based windows to the local client computer. The other options shown are not valid.

33. A. The --gen-key subcommand is used for the purpose described. The other options shown do not exist.

34. D. The % is used to denote a group within /etc/sudoers, and it provides an excellent way to facilitate an administrative privileged group.

35. A. The -p option sets the port for login, and it is useful for scenarios where you cannot use the host:port syntax. There is no -P or @ option with ssh, and the -l option specifies the login name.

36. A. The -s option sets the type of scan, and when followed by an uppercase S, it sets the option to SYN. The T option is a Connect() scan. There is no Y option or -type option for nmap.

37. C. The wtmp file, stored in /var/log is used to store recent login information and must be read with the last command due to its format. The other logs listed for this question are not default logs found on a Linux system.

38. A. The -i option for ssh is followed by the private key to use for authentication. Doing so implies that the public key is in the authorized_keys file on the remote host. The -k option disables sending of GSSAPI credentials, while -f is used to request backgrounding of ssh. There is no --key option.

39. A. The -n option facilitates the scenario described, and it will exit non-zero rather than prompting. The -i option sets the login name, and it is not valid for this scenario. The -q and the --noprompt options do not exist.

40. C. The ssh-keygen command is used for this purpose, and the -t option specifies the type of key to generate. There are no key-related generation options for the ssh command. Overall host keys are stored in /etc/ssh/ssh_host_rsa_key and /etc/ssh/ssh_host_rsa_key.pub for RSA keys, and /etc/ssh/ssh_host_dsa_key and /etc/ssh/ssh_host_dsa_key.pub for DSA keys.

41. B. Lines can be commented out of /etc/inetd.conf with a pound sign or hash mark (#). After making changes to /etc/inetd.conf, you should restart the service. Many systems also utilize /etc/inetd.d/ to store configuration files related to specific services.

42. A. The -L option to usermod can be used to lock an account. The lowercase version, -l, is used to change a username. The other commands do not exist.

43. B. The file pubring.gpg, found in ~/.gnupg, contains the public keyring.

44. C. The file .gpg-v21-migrated, when present, indicates that gpg version 2.1 or later is in use and the files have been migrated for that version or a later version.

45. D. The find command is used for this purpose, and the -perm option is needed, specifically as the 2000 permission to indicate setgid. Note the use of / to indicate that the entire server will be searched. The grep command shown cannot be used for this purpose because it looks for the presence of the string setgid within files located in the current directory only.

46. C. The update-rc.d command creates symbolic links from a service file in /etc/init.d/ to the appropriate locations in /etc/rc.d/* for each runlevel. The other commands shown are not valid.

47. A. Single-user mode is typically runlevel 1. In runlevel 1, no network services are started. Runlevel 2 has networking but typically not services. Runlevel 5 is full multiuser with networking, and runlevel 6 is reboot.

48. C. The single dash - is the typical option passed to su for login. There is no -u or -U option, and the -login option does not exist. There is a --login option (with two dashes), but that is not what's shown.

Chapter 11: Capacity Planning (Topic 200)

1. D. The -p option to iostat displays information on devices and partitions. The -c option shows CPU utilization, and -d shows device utilization. There is no -a option.

2. B. Filters are used within iptraf to define traffic that should be included or excluded when monitoring. For this scenario, you could define the source IP address as your own and the destination as that of the interface being monitored and then look specifically for destination port 22 for ssh.

3. D. The `vmstat` command is used to display extended information about performance including blocks in and out. The `iptraf` command is used to provide network-level monitoring, and the other two commands listed are not valid.

4. C. The `iotop` command is used to monitor disk usage, such as reads and writes on a per-process basis in real time. The `top` command does not provide disk usages, and `iostat` does not provide information in a per-process manner. Finally, `free` provides aggregate information on memory.

5. D. Nagios provides advanced monitoring capabilities appropriate for the scenario described. Nagios works using various plugins that monitor numerous aspects of devices and systems. ntop and mrtg both provide graphical statistics but do not have the alerting capabilities specified.

6. B. The `w` command shows a variety of useful information including load average, logged-in users, and other uptime information. The `uptime` command does not show who is currently logged in. There is no `swap` or `sysinfo` command.

7. B. The `free` command shows current memory usage for both RAM and swap space, including total available, current amount used, and current amount free. The other commands shown as options do not exist.

8. B. Pressing Shift+F within `top` enables you to choose which columns display as well as the sort order for these columns. In the scenario described, you can view the processes using the highest amount of memory.

9. A. The `df` command displays information on disk usage, and it can help with planning disk utilization over time. For example, if you note that disk utilization is increasing significantly, you can prepare to bring more disk online or even to change the log rotation schedule such that logs are rotated faster, thereby freeing up space.

10. C. `Cacti` is a graphing tool that uses both scripts for gathering performance data as well as SNMP. The graphs can help you visualize the performance of networks and systems alike. The `pstree` command is used to show a tree-like structure of processes.

11. A. The `ps` command provides information on processor and memory usage for individual processes. You can use this information to predict capacity.

12. A. The -p option enables monitoring of one or more process IDs. If you're monitoring more than one process ID, separate each with a comma. The -s option sets the sort order. The -a and the -e options do not exist.

13. C. The -a option displays statistics for each socket, both listening and non-listening. Included in this information are the send and receive queues. This information can be used to gauge performance and potential bottlenecks.

14. B. The `iptraf` tool is used for monitoring network traffic in real time to provide statistics on usage and throughput. The tool is graphical in nature, but it is appropriate for use over an ssh connection without an X server installed. The other commands listed as options are not valid Linux commands.

15. C. The pstree command displays current processes in a tree-like structure, with parent processes connected to child processes. The pstree command makes it easy to see processes in a grouped format to check for potential high resource usage.

16. A. The sar command can be used for this purpose, and when provided with numbers in the format displayed, it will update every X seconds for Y executions, as in the answer with sar -u 2 10, which will update every two seconds for 10 executions.

17. A. The htop command enables advanced scenarios for working with processes through a graphical interface created with ncurses. This means that the interface is appropriate for use through ssh, for example.

18. C. The wa statistic shows time spent waiting for I/O, and it can be used to measure or find a bottleneck related to disk. The us statistic is time spent on user space processes, while sy is time spent on kernel processes. There is no statistic called io within vmstat.

19. C. The -p option to pstree shows process IDs along with the standard pstree output. The -a option displays command-line arguments for commands. There is no -i or -b option.

20. C. The RSS column is Resident Set Size, and it indicates the amount of physical RAM that is allocated to the given process.

21. B. The lsof command is used for this purpose, and it can help if there are large files that may be affecting performance. The ls command does not show whether a file is open.

22. B. The l key will list open files for a given process, assuming that lsof is installed. The L key performs a library trace if ltrace is available.

23. D. The steal column shows the percentage of time that was spent waiting due to the hypervisor stealing cycles for another virtual processor.

24. B. While all of the commands and programs listed are typically available on modern Linux distributions, all of them need to be installed separately except the top command, which is usually available for performance troubleshooting and monitoring.

25. A. Load average with the uptime command is displayed in 1-, 5-, and 15-minute increments.

26. B. The /proc/swaps file can be used to gather information quickly, especially within a script, on swap space.

27. C. The ntop program monitors network interfaces and provides web-based reporting on bandwidth utilization by protocol and host. Both mrtg and Nagios can provide similar information but typically not on a per-protocol or per-host basis.

28. B. Providing information from ps in a wide format can be helpful for viewing the command line of a given command. The a option displays all processes while the o option enables the choice of columns for output.

29. A. When no interval or count are provided, the gathered statistics are displayed for each interval in which statistics were gathered. For example, if sar gathered statistics every five minutes since the last restart, then each of those data points is displayed.

30. C. The -i option is needed for this case, and the format for the port is preceded by a colon.

31. C. The -m option causes the disk-related statistics to use megabytes as the scale rather than the default kilobytes.

32. B. If the Stat column within the output of a ps command shows D, then there is a process in uninterruptible sleep, meaning that it cannot be killed and is typically waiting on I/O. A process in Sl is in normal sleep for a multithreaded process. Rebooting the server is the only way to clear processes that are in uninterruptible sleep, assuming that they don't wake up of their own accord. Finally, the -n option to vmstat selects how the header is displayed.

33. B. The -d option is used to set the delay, and the interval is tenths of a second, thereby needing 100 such intervals to equal 10 seconds.

34. A. The vmstat command displays both memory and CPU usage information. The iostat command does not display memory information. Once you know the command, then it's a matter of the correct syntax for per-second updates for 10 seconds.

35. D. The netstat -s command displays aggregate statistical information for networking, including the total packets received and the number of packets forwarded. The ifconfig command does not show packets forwarded. The ls command is not used for networking, and the ipstat command does not exist.

36. A. On a system with one processor, a load average of 1.00 would indicate high utilization. However, with two processors that load average equals approximately 50% capacity. Even at 50% capacity, it might be a good idea to examine what is causing that utilization with the top or ps command.

37. B. When a 0 interval with no value for count is sent as an argument to sar, the overall averages since last restart will be displayed, and the program will exit.

Chapter 12: Linux Kernel (Topic 201)

1. B. The make oldconfig command will integrate the existing configuration file into the new configuration for the kernel. You still need to take care for items that have moved or changed within the new kernel to ensure that the configuration is correct.

2. A. Kernel source code is usually kept in /usr/src/linux.

3. D. The xz command is used to both compress and decompress files. When used with the -d option, the file provided as an argument is then decompressed.

4. A. The legacy zImage format is limited to 512 KB in size, while bzImage does not have such a limitation.

5. B. The menuconfig target provides a graphical-styled interface for choosing kernel options, and it is appropriate to use over an ssh connection. Be careful compiling a kernel over ssh, though. If you choose the wrong options, the server may not boot successfully. Thus, make sure that you have another means to access the console.

6. A. The `mkinitrd` command is used on older systems to create the initial RAM disk. The initial RAM disk is used to load—some might say preload—essential modules for things like disks and other vital components needed for booting.

7. C. When available, bzip2 is used to compress a bzImage. bzImage describes a different format for compressed kernel images that can go above the 512 KB limit that normally applies to a zImage.

8. B. The kernel config is placed in `/usr/src/linux/.config`. It's a good idea to make a backup of this file in case you need to re-create the kernel from source in the future or for reference.

9. B. The `lsmod` command is used to display currently loaded modules. This is useful for scenarios where you are migrating from the stock or distribution-provided kernel to a custom kernel and need to know which modules to compile into the new kernel.

10. B. The clean target removes most compiled files, though some may be left such as those related to kernel compilation. The mrproper `make` target removes compiled files from previous compiles of the kernel but also cleans the `.config` file as well. The config target is used to configure options for the kernel but should not be used until after mrproper.

11. B. The LOCALVERSION option, found within the General Setup area, can be used to append custom versioning based on your local needs.

12. C. Dynamic Kernel Module Support (`dkms`) is used for building kernel modules outside the kernel source tree.

13. B. The depmod command is used to create a list of modules. The list is kept in a file called `modules.dep`, the location of which is dependent on the distribution of Linux in use.

14. D. The udevadm command is used to work with the udev interface to the kernel, and the `monitor` subcommand displays kernel uevents and other udev events in real time.

15. A. The `lsusb` command displays information about the USB kernel interface. The `-t` option causes that display to be formatted in a tree-like structure that can be helpful for visualizing how the devices are connected to the computer.

16. A. The `-a` option displays all values and their current settings for `sysctl`. The `-b` option is binary and displays values without any newlines. The `-d` option is an alias for `-h`, which is help display. There is no `-c` option.

17. B. The `modprobe` command examines dependencies for a given module and loads both the dependencies and the requested module.

18. B. The `deb-pkg` target creates `.deb` files that are then suitable for management through the Debian package management system. Similar targets are available on other systems, such as `rpm-pkg` for Red Hat and CentOS systems.

19. B. The `uname` command is used for this purpose, and the `-r` option displays the kernel version number.

20. C. Information for sysctl is found within /proc/sys. Within that directory is a hierarchy of directories eventually leading to a normal file, the contents of which are the value for the variable.

21. C. Rules related to udev are stored in /etc/udev/rules.d. The /etc/udev hierarchy contains the udev.conf configuration file along with other components related to the configuration of udev.

22. A. The modinfo command provides information on a given kernel module. You can use modinfo to find out the parameters needed for a given module and the modules on which it depends, among other information. The modprobe command is used to load a module. There is no tracemod or modlist command.

23. C. Within /usr/src/linux/Documentation you will find extensive documentation on the kernel source code, including instructions on how to compile the kernel as well as the various elements found within the kernel itself.

24. B. The -k option shows the kernel driver associated with a given PCI device, and it can also be helpful when planning a new kernel compile. The -t option displays information in a tree-like structure, and -n uses numbers instead of device names. There is no -a option.

25. C. The insmod command inserts a module into the running kernel. It does not, however, attempt to resolve dependencies but rather outputs an error if there are dependent modules or kernel symbols that are not available.

26. B. The -r option removes the named kernel modules and attempts to remove any modules on which the named module depends, where possible. The -d option sets the root directory for modules, while -v is verbose and -f forces the module to load.

27. B. The modules_install make target is used to install modules that have been previously compiled using the modules target. The instmod and modinst targets are not valid.

28. B. The /etc/modprobe.d directory is used for storing configuration information related to modules such as that used for blacklisting purposes but also for other configuration information such as udev and module options.

29. C. The lsmod command displays a list of currently loaded modules. Included in the list is the size of the module in memory and what, if anything, is currently using the module.

30. B. The dracut command is used to create the initial RAM disk for newer systems and has replaced the legacy mkinitrd command used for the same purpose.

31. B. The rmmod command removes modules from a running system. In order to use rmmod, the module cannot be in use or depended on by other currently loaded modules. The other commands shown are not valid.

32. B. Variables and values placed in /etc/sysctl.conf will take effect on boot. The other files listed are not valid.

33. D. The file /proc/kallsyms provides a way to view the currently loaded kernel symbols. This can be helpful for resolving module dependencies. Note that on legacy systems, this file might be called /proc/ksyms.

34. B. The `--show-depends` option displays the dependencies for a given module. The other options are not valid for the `modprobe` command.

35. A. The `systool` utility can be used to show currently loaded options for a given module. The `modinfo -r` command is not valid, and while `modinfo` shows information about a module, it does not include core size and other settings. The `lsmod` command cannot be used for this purpose, and there is no `infmod` command.

36. B. The `/proc/sys/kernel` hierarchy contains vital configuration information for a kernel. These settings can be changed on a running system.

37. C. The kernel ring buffer, or log messages related to the kernel, can be viewed using the `dmesg` command. The messages normally rotate displaying the latest messages only, but this can be changed through configuration options.

Chapter 13: System Startup (Topic 202)

1. B. The `/etc/systemd/system` directory is the recommended location to store unit files for `systemd`. The other locations are not valid.

2. C. The `systemctl` command is used for this purpose and then with the `daemon-reload` subcommand. The `reboot` option would work to reload the `systemd` configuration but is not correct because it requires the entire server to reboot, which is not what this question asked.

3. B. The `/etc/inittab` file contains the various runlevels and what to run at the given runlevel. For example, runlevel 1 is single user, runlevel 6 is reboot, and so on. The other files listed do not exist.

4. B. The SYSLINUX bootloader is used for FAT filesystems to create rescue disks and to assist with the installation of Linux in general. Syslinux also describes an overall project containing other specialty bootloaders. The other options listed for this question are not valid bootloaders, though.

5. A. ESP uses the legacy FAT filesystem type for its underlying format. There is a specification for how the ESP partition must be created on top of the FAT format for bootloaders and kernel images. Note that the partition is typically FAT32, but it can be FAT16 if only Linux systems will reside on the drive.

6. C. `initrd` is used for an initial root filesystem for early drivers. `initrd` is configured to load within the grub configuration file for a given operating system.

7. B. The `fsck` command is used to diagnose and repair hard drive problems in Linux. The `defrag` command is not available in Linux.

8. D. The `telinit` command can be used for this purpose, and passing 1 as the argument will switch the system into single-user mode. The other commands shown are not valid.

9. A. The --install option is used followed by the partition to which extlinux will be installed for boot.

10. C. The format for the mount command is [partition] [target], thereby making option C correct. The other options are not valid because the arguments are in the wrong order.

11. B. The command to install GRUB is grub-install, and the first SATA drive is /dev/sda. A device listed as hda is typically a PATA drive, thereby making those options incorrect.

12. D. The -n option changes the boot order for the next boot only and boots from the specified partition. The -b along with -B modifies and then deletes the option. The -o option sets the boot order. The -c option creates a boot number.

13. A. ISOLINUX provides a means by which CD-ROMs formatted as ISO 9660 can be booted. It's very common to have live CDs or rescue/recovery CDs that use ISOLINUX for boot. The other bootloaders are not valid for this purpose or don't exist.

14. A. The /usr/lib/systemd hierarchy contains files related to systemd configuration. The user directory within the hierarchy is used for user unit files, and the system files are stored in /usr/lib/systemd/system.

15. B. Due to the decidedly insecure decisions made with the design of Microsoft's UEFI, a shim is often needed to enable Linux to boot on a system with UEFI. The file shim.efi can be used as an initial bootloader for this purpose.

16. A. Priority order for systemd configuration files are those within the /etc hierarchy, followed by files in the /run hierarchy, and then followed by files in the /lib hierarchy.

17. D. Scripts for starting and stopping services are located in /etc/init.d on a SysV init-based system. The other directories listed within this option are not valid.

18. C. The systemd-delta command is used to determine overridden configuration files. Of the other commands, diff is valid, but not for this purpose. The systemctl command is also valid, but again not for the purpose described.

19. B. The chkconfig --list command displays all services that will be executed on boot along with the setting for each service for each runlevel. Of the other commands, the init command is valid, but it does not have a --bootlist option. The other commands are invalid.

20. B. The bcfg command within the UEFI shell is used to configure bootloaders on a UEFI-based system. The command can accept various parameters to configure how the bootloader and kernel will load on boot. Of the other commands shown, grub-install is valid but not within the UEFI shell.

21. B. The Master Boot Record, or MBR, is the first sector on a disk, and it contains information about the structure of the disk. If the MBR becomes corrupt, all data on the disk may be lost. The other options shown for this question are not valid.

22. A. The bootloader is mounted into /boot/efi. The other directories do not exist.

23. D. The rescue.target is used to assist in recovery by loading a minimal base system and then going to a shell akin to single-user mode or runlevel 1.

24. A. The configuration file is called isolinux.cfg, and it is typically located in /boot/isolinux or /isolinux. The other options shown are not valid filenames for this question.

25. D. The file pxelinux.0 must exist within /tftpboot on the TFTP server in order for a system to use PXELINUX for booting. The other files are not valid or necessary for PXELINUX.

26. D. The update-rc.d utility can be used to manage SysV init scripts on Debian or Ubuntu and other distributions. When using update-rc.d, you supply the script name and the utility will take care of creating symlinks to the appropriate runlevels.

27. B. The e key, when pressed at the right time during boot, will send you into the GRUB shell, where you can change parameters related to boot such as the kernel options and other related parameters.

28. B. The systemctl command is used for this purpose, and the get-default subcommand will display the default target for boot. On many distributions, the default target is graphical.target. The other subcommands shown for this question are not valid.

29. A. The -r option repairs the filesystem, while the -y option causes fsck to assume "yes" instead of prompting. The -v option is verbosity. There is no -m or -x option for fsck.

30. D. The --boot-directory option enables you to specify an alternate location for GRUB images rather than the default /boot. The other options shown for this question are not valid.

31. D. The isolate subcommand followed by the desired target is used to switch between runlevels with a systemd-based system. The other subcommands shown are not valid for systemctl.

32. C. The runlevel defined as initdefault is the default runlevel for the system. The other options shown do not exist.

33. B. The initramfs system is used instead of initrd to create the filesystem-based loading process for key drivers that are needed for boot.

34. A. The systemctl command is used for this purpose, and the set-default subcommand is necessary to affect the desired behavior. The target file is simply called multi-user.target.

35. C. The shim.efi bootloader loads another bootloader, which is grubx64.efi by default. The other options are not valid filenames for the purpose described.

36. D. The /etc/rc.d hierarchy contains symbolic links to files found within /etc/init.d. These symlinks are then used for executing the scripts at the appropriate runlevel. For example, on boot the system will execute the scripts found in the runlevel directory for each runlevel executed at boot time.

37. A. default.target is the default target unit that is activated by systemd on boot. The default target then starts other services based on the dependencies.

Chapter 14: Filesystems and Devices (Topic 203)

1. D. The file `/etc/mtab` lists the currently mounted filesystems. The `/etc/fstab` file lists overall filesystems for the computer, but it does not distinguish between mounted or unmounted filesystems. The other options listed for this question do not exist.

2. C. The `-t` option sets the filesystem type as ext2, ext3, or ext4. The `mke2fs` command is typically symlinked from `/sbin/mkfs.ext2`, `/sbin/mkfs.ext3`, and `/sbin/mkfs.ext4`. The `-f` option forces `mke2fs` to create a filesystem. The `-a` and `-e` options do not exist.

3. B. The file `/etc/auto.master` contains the configuration for `autofs`. The other files listed as options are not valid for this scenario.

4. C. The `mkisofs` command creates an ISO filesystem, which can then be written to a CD or DVD. The other commands listed are not valid.

5. A. The `cryptsetup` command is used to set up and help configure dm-crypt volumes. The other commands shown for this question are not valid.

6. B. The `mkswap` command is used to format a swap partition. The other commands are not valid.

7. B. The `-c` option sets the maximum mount count. The `-C` option sets the current number of mounts. The `-b` and `-a` options do not exist.

8. D. The `-f` option, also known as fake, is helpful for situations where you need to debug the mount process or when you need to add an entry into `/etc/mtab` for a previously mounted filesystem. The `-l` option shows labels, and `-v` is verbose. There is no `-q` option.

9. C. The letters `ro` indicate that the filesystem has been mounted read-only, meaning that it is not possible to perform a write to the filesystem. The other possible option is `rw`, indicating that the filesystem has been mounted as read-write.

10. C. Bad blocks are shown with the -b option. The -f option forces `dumpe2fs` to perform the requested operation, and the other command options do not exist.

11. D. btrfs is based on the copy-on-write principle, and it is generally considered more advanced than ext4 and its predecessors. FAT is a legacy filesystem primarily used for DOS and its follow-ons, like Windows.

12. B. The `xfs_info` command, which is functionally equivalent to `xfs_grow -n`, displays information about an XFS-formatted filesystem.

13. A. The `blkid` command shows information about partitions including their type, their UUID, and other basic information. The other commands shown for options do not exist.

14. C. The `-t` option, which can accept a comma-separated list of types, specifies that only filesystems of the listed type are to be unmounted. This is useful in conjunction with the

-a option, which unmounts all filesystems except /proc. The -v option is verbose and -f forces the operation to continue.

15. D. The sync command writes unwritten data to the disk immediately, and it is useful to run just prior to attempting an unmount operation.

16. B. The swapon command enables swap space, making it available for use as virtual memory. The mkswap command formats the space. The other two commands are not valid.

17. C. The -f option specifies that xfs_check should check the contents of the named file for consistency. The -v option sets verbosity, and there is no -d or -a option.

18. B. The -w option causes debugfs to open the filesystem in read-write mode. There is also a -c option to open in catastrophic mode for filesystems with significant damage. The -rw, -r, and -n options are not valid.

19. D. The smartd daemon monitors SMART-compatible disks for notable events, and it can be configured to send alerts when events occur. The other commands listed are not valid for this scenario.

20. A. The -f option forces fsck to run on an otherwise clean filesystem. This can be helpful for times when you suspect that there is an error on the filesystem, and you need to verify this as part of the troubleshooting process. This can also be helpful to prepare the filesystem for conversion, such as might be the case with a tool like btrfs-convert.

21. A. The block size for import or restore must match the block size used on export or dump. Block size is specified with the -b option, thus making option A correct. The other options are not valid for xfsrestore.

22. B. A filesystem with the word defaults for its mount options will be mounted read-write (rw), suid, with the ability to have executables (exec). The filesystem will be auto-mounted (auto), but users will not be able to mount it (nouser). Character and block special devices will be interpreted (dev), and operations on the disk will be performed in an asynchronous manner (async).

23. D. The smartctl command controls how SMART monitoring is done for a given device, assuming that the smartmon utilities have been installed. The smartd option represents the overall daemon for monitoring SMART events.

24. A. Within /etc/fstab, the filesystem to be mounted (such as /dev/sda1) is found first, followed by the destination location to which the filesystem will be mounted. The type of filesystem follows next, along with any options needed for the filesystem. The dump utility indicator follows the options, and finally the pass or fsck order is last. The last field determines the order in which filesystems are checked by fsck on boot.

25. A. Password-based Key Derivation Function 2 (PBKDF2) is used for key derivation for the password-based cryptography used with LUKS. SSL is Secure Sockets Layer, and it is typically used for encryption of HTTP traffic. Both RSA and DSA are encryption algorithms, but they are not related to this question.

26. B. The btrfs subvolume create command creates a btrfs subvolume. The other commands are not valid.

27. C. The -z option sets the maximum size for files to be included in the dump. The -b option sets the block size, but it is not related to what is being asked for in this scenario. The -s option sets the path for inclusion in the dump, and -p sets the interval for progress indicators.

28. C. The -e option sets the behavior, such as continue, remount read-only, or panic when an error occurs at the filesystem level. The -f option forces whatever operation you're requesting to continue, even if there are errors. The -d and -k options are not valid.

29. D. The -n option causes mount not to write to /etc/mtab, and it is particularly useful for the scenario described. The -a option mounts all filesystems in /etc/fstab. There is no -b or -m option.

30. A. The swapoff command deactivates swap space, thereby making it unavailable as virtual memory on the system. The other commands shown as options are not valid.

31. A. The Where= directive specifies the location for the final mounted filesystem.

32. C. The --show option displays information about the swap spaces on the computer, including how much swap space is currently being used. The -a option activates all swap spaces. There is no --list option and -h displays help.

33. A. The mkfs.fat or mkfs.vfat commands are valid for creation of FAT filesystems. There is no -f option to mkfs and there is no mkfat command.

34. D. The tune2fs command is used for working with ext2, ext3, and ext4 filesystems. The -j option adds a journal. The other commands are not valid.

35. A. The snapshot subcommand of btrfs subvolume creates a snapshot. The other commands shown are not valid.

36. A. The -L option forces the log to be cleared or zeroed out, which may cause a loss of data. The -v option sets verbose output, while -V prints the version. The -d option performs a dangerous repair, which can be used on a read-only filesystem.

37. C. The -o option enables the setting of one or more options for the mount command and ro is read-only. Note that the -r option will also mount as read-only. The other options shown are not valid.

Chapter 15: Advanced Storage Device Administration (Topic 204)

1. B. The file /etc/mdadm.conf is the configuration file used for RAID setups that use md. The other files listed are not valid.

2. D. A partition type 0xFD is used for software RAID arrays. This can be set or viewed using a tool such as fdisk. The other options shown are not valid partition types.

3. C. The /dev/disk/by-id directory contains symbolic links to /dev/sd, such as /dev/sda. Because WWIDs can be used to identify a device across systems, they are often used within the context of SANs. The other directories listed as options do not exist.

4. A. The iscsiadm command is used for administration of iSCSI devices on a Linux system. The other options shown for this question are not valid.

5. C. The pvdisplay command shows information about a given physical volume. You can use pvdisplay to view the device on which the PV is built along with the extent size of the PV. The other commands shown are not valid.

6. D. The DEVICE configuration line contains a list of devices that can be used for an array. The keyword DEVICE is then followed by a space-separated list of devices.

7. B. Logical unit numbers (LUNs) that contain the characters fc are those found through Fibre Channel. Therein lies the difference between options B and C, where option C contains the letters scsi, which would usually represent a local disk. The other options are not valid.

8. C. The multipath command is used for administration of devices such as LUNs and can be used for finding the path to LUNs for a server, such as in a SAN configuration. The other commands are not valid, with the exception of ls, which is valid; however, the option shown is not related to LUNs but rather to a combination of various flags to the ls command.

9. C. The fstrim command is used to remove blocks that are not in use. The fstrim command is frequently used in a SAN configuration to give back unused storage to the SAN. The fstrim command can also be used with solid-state drives for the same purpose. The other commands shown are not valid.

10. B. NVMe-capable drives are named /dev/nvme*. No special drivers are needed other than those found in the native kernel on a modern system. The other answers do not exist as paths by default.

11. A. The scsi_id command generates a SCSI identifier based on page 0x80 or 0x83 of the vital product data on a device. The other commands are not valid.

12. D. AOE, or ATA over Ethernet, sends ATA commands directly over Ethernet. AOE commands are sent at a lower layer of the OSI model than TCP/IP or even IP, but they are not routable. The other acronyms shown are valid but not for the purpose described. PXE is a boot protocol, POE is used for power over Ethernet, and iSCSI is a storage protocol, though not related to ATA.

13. B. The hdparm command can be used to get or set values related to the low-level configuration of drive settings for both IDE and SATA devices. The other commands shown for this question are not valid.

14. A. The next step is typically to create a volume group (or more than one) with vgcreate based on the newly created physical volumes.

15. B. The -E option signals that an extended option follows, such as stripe_width. The -f option forces an operation but should not be necessary for this solution, and the -e option sets the behavior on error. There is no -extend option.

16. D. The file /proc/mdstat contains information on RAID arrays including RAID personalities found on the system, the devices that compose the array, and other pertinent information. The other files shown are not valid.

17. A. The iscsid daemon creates and maintains connections to iSCSI targets, making them available in Linux. The iscsiadm command is used for administrative purposes, and the other commands shown are not valid.

18. C. The nvme module, available on modern systems, is used as a driver for NVMe devices on Linux. You can examine the nvme module with the modinfo command.

19. B. The directory /sys/class/fc_host contains other directories based on the Fibre Channel connections available. Within those host directories will be found the WWN (World Wide Name) in a file called port_name. The other directory hierarchies are not valid.

20. A. The --create option enables creation of a RAID array that will use md. The typical argument is the /dev/mdN device. The other options listed are not valid for mdadm.

21. B. The file iscsid.conf, typically found in either /etc/ or /etc/iscsid/, is used for configuration related to the iscsi daemon. The other configuration files are not valid for iscsid.

22. C. The /dev/mapper directory contains information about multipath devices such as logical volumes. The other directories are not valid.

23. C. The --monitor option is used to actively watch an array for issues such as disk failure. The monitoring can be done as a daemon and run in the background, thereby alerting when there is an issue.

24. A. The -o ro option mounts the drive in read-only mode. The rw mode is read-write. Mounting in read-only is useful if you need to diagnose the drive without potentially destroying any information on the drive. The other options are not valid.

25. B. The lvcreate command is used to create a logical volume from previously created physical devices and volume groups. Using lvcreate is the final of three steps in the process for using LVM prior to actually using the logical volume.

26. B. The MAILADDR option sets the destination address for mail about RAID events that are noted by mdadm when in monitor mode.

27. A. The vgscan command looks for both physical volumes and volume groups related to an LVM configuration. The vgscan command is run at system startup, but it can also be run manually. The other commands are not valid.

28. D. A partition type of 0xFD is used for software RAID arrays. This can be set or viewed using a tool such as fdisk. The other options shown are not valid partition types.

29. C. The pvscan command displays a list of physical volumes on a given server. The PVs displayed are those that have been initialized with pvcreate for use with LVM.

30. B. The interactive console is accessed by calling multipathd with the -k option. Once in the console, you can obtain help by typing help. The other options shown are not valid for multipathd.

31. A. The -a or --available (sometimes known as --activate) option sets whether the logical volume can be used. There is no -b -or -c option, and the -d option is used for debugging.

32. A. The file lvm.conf is a primary configuration file for LVM. Within lvm.conf, typically found in /etc/ or /etc/lvm/, you can set things like filters for devices to include or exclude from the vgscan process. The other commands shown are not valid.

33. B. The snapshot option creates a snapshot of a logical volume. The other options shown are not valid.

34. C. The -w option writes a new value to the given kernel parameter. The -a and -A options both list all values. There is no -k option.

35. D. The sdparm command is similar to the hdparm command. Whereas hdparm is used for IDE and SATA, sdparm is used for SCSI devices. The other commands shown are not valid.

36. A. The directory /etc/fcoe contains information related to the FCoE configuration on a given system. The other directories are not valid for FCoE.

37. D. The lspci command is used for this purpose. NVME devices are listed with the name nVME or NVMe; therefore, adding -i to grep will make the search case insensitive. You'd use this in order to ensure that the devices are detected. The other commands are not valid, with the exception of the lspci command, but you cannot grep for scsi for this scenario.

Chapter 16: Networking Configuration (Topic 205)

1. C. The ip command defaults to the INET family if not otherwise specified with the -f option. The command attempts to guess the correct family and falls back to INET. The other families listed as options for this command are not valid for use with the ip command.

2. B. The ifconfig command is used for this purpose, followed by the interface. The hw keyword is used for the hardware address, which is then followed by the hardware class, in this case ether. That is followed by the new MAC address (not depicted in the options). The other commands are not valid.

3. D. The -n option causes route to use numeric values only, performing no name resolution. This option is useful for the scenario described. The -e option causes the output to be in netstat format. There is no -d or -f option for the route command.

4. A. Because you're working with MAC addresses, the arp command will be used. The -d option removes or deletes an ARP entry, which would be appropriate here so that the MAC address resolution occurs again. The netstat command is not used for this purpose. The hostname and dig commands work with name resolution but not for MAC addresses or the ARP table.

5.   A. The iw command is used for this purpose. When you're using iw with a specific device, the dev keyword appears next followed by the device name. Finally, the command to execute on that device, in this case the link command, is used.

6.   B. The iwconfig command, which is similar to the ifconfig command, works with an individual wireless interface to set and display parameters. Of the other commands, the ifconfig command is valid but not used for wireless. The other commands are not valid.

7.   C. The iwlist command can be used for this purpose, and the scan subcommand is used to look for local access points and wireless networks. The iwconfig command does not have a scan subcommand. Likewise, there is no subcommand called get for the iwlist command, and there is no iw-scan command.

8.   B. The -o option removes newlines from the output, thereby making the output more suitable for the grep command. The -l option specifies the number of loops for the ip addr flush command; The -f option specifies the protocol family. There is no -n option.

9.   B. The mtu option can be used to set the value for the maximum transmission unit (MTU) for a given interface. The metric option sets the interface metric. The other options are not valid.

10. B. A route will need to be added in order to utilize the reject destination, thereby making option B correct. Option C deletes the route but does not create a reject route. Option D deletes the default route, and option A is not valid.

11. A. The -s option creates an ARP table entry. The -d option removes an entry. The -c and --add options do not exist.

12. A. The ss command provides many of the same functions as netstat, but it can show some extended information, such as memory allocation for a given socket. The free command shows memory usage but not by socket. The other two commands do not exist.

13. D. The -t option shows TCP connections, while -a shows active sockets. The -n option disables name resolution.

14. C. This solution requires a way to filter out the bind user; therefore, answers that grep for bind or specify bind as the user are incorrect. However, the lsof command allows for negation with the caret ^ character. Therefore, listing all files except bind requires the syntax shown.

15. D. The -f option is a flood ping. This will effectively cause the interface to send and receive large amounts of traffic, usually making it easier to find on a switch. The -a option is an audible ping, emitting a sound on ping. The -c option sends a certain count of pings. There is no -e option.

16. B. The netcat command provides a method for opening and communicating on both sides, server and client, for a TCP connection. The netcat command avoids some of the issues with Telnet capturing characters specific to the Telnet protocol. The netstat command does not test connectivity, and ping does not do so at the TCP level. There is no nettest command.

17. C. The -D option lists the interfaces on a given computer. The -d option dumps compiled matching code, and -i selects an interface. There is no -a option.

18. B. The -R option requires that an attempt at name resolution be performed. The -n option does the opposite; that is, it disables name resolution. There is no -b or -a option.

19. A. The ping6 command performs the same as the IPv4 ping command, but it does so for IPv6. The other commands are not valid on Linux.

20. B. The ip command can be used for this purpose. When used with the addr object and the -6 option, only information about IPv6 addresses will be shown. The first option, simply ip addr, will show all addresses including IPv4. The other commands are not valid.

21. A. The ifconfig command is used for this purpose, and ARP can be disabled by preceding the word arp with a minus sign, as shown. If no minus sign is present, then ARP will be enabled. The other commands will not work for this scenario.

22. C. The dev option specifies the device to use for the route being specified. This is a typical use case for many routes to reduce the chances of the kernel guessing incorrectly. The other options shown for this question are not valid.

23. C. The -p option shows the process IDs associated with a given socket within the ss output. The -a option is for all sockets, while -l is for listening sockets. The -f option is used to specify the protocol family.

24. A. The -i option shows interface information in a table-like format. Information such as transmit and receive bytes as well as the MTU for the interface and other information is shown. The -r option shows routes, while -l shows listening sockets. There is no -t option.

25. D. The /etc/network directory contains information on network interfaces and contains directories that further contain scripts to be executed when interfaces are brought up or down. The other directories listed do not exist.

26. C. The -I option tells traceroute to use ICMP for requests. The -T option is TCP SYN. The -A option performs AS path lookups, and the -i option configures traceroute to use the specified interface.

27. B. The mtr command provides a unique way to view real-time information about each hop in a route between hosts. Both the traceroute and route commands are valid, but the options shown for each are not. There is no liveroute command.

28. C. Internally, the hostname command uses gethostname. This can be useful to know when troubleshooting address resolution issues such as conflicting results for host naming. The other functions are not valid.

29. A. The grep command and the -i option should be used in order to make the grep case-insensitive. When used with -v, grep will exclude the argument, thus doing the opposite of what's needed here. The kernel ring buffer will probably not contain information about DHCP, therefore making dmesg not the correct option.

30. B. Only alphanumerics, minus/dash, and dot are valid for hosts in /etc/hosts.

31. B. Options within /etc/resolv.conf are preceded with the options keyword followed by one or more options such as debug.

32. B. The -c option clears the kernel ring buffer after the first read. The -C option clears it immediately. The -e option displays relative time and local time. There is no -a option.

33. D. The systemctl command is used for this purpose. Adding the -u option specifies the unit for which journal entries are desired.

34. A. The /etc/hostname file typically contains only the hostname of the local computer rather than the hostname and domain name. This is then read at boot time to set the hostname for the computer. The /etc/hosts file contains information on various hosts for name resolution purposes. The other files do not exist.

35. C. The /etc/sysconfig/network-scripts directory contains configuration information for a Red Hat system. The other directories shown do not exist.

36. B. The traceroute6 command is used for tracing IPv6 routes. The other commands do not exist.

37. C. The PARANOID wildcard specifies that the hostname and IP must match. The ALL keyword is also a valid wildcard in TCP Wrappers for use in both /etc/hosts.allow and /etc/hosts.deny.

Chapter 17: System Maintenance (Topic 206)

1. C. The kernel sources now use xz compression. Previously, these sources had used bzip2, and prior to that they used gzip. There is no xy compression algorithm.

2. C. The -a option provides archive mode, which is a substitute for several other options. The -r option is recursive, the -o option indicates that ownership should be preserved, and the -f option enables a filter.

3. A. The -c option indicates the creation of a tar file. The -d option is used for diffing or differencing between two tar files, the -b option provides block size, and -f specifies the file for use with tar.

4. C. The --remove-files option removes files from the filesystem after adding them to the archive. The -r option appends files to the end of an archive, the -d option provides a diff between the filesystem and an archive, and the -f option specifies the file.

5. D. The -p option specifies the number of slashes to be stripped from the beginning of the path for patching. Both the -p1 and -p0 options are quite common. The -s option specifies silent operation. There is no -strip option.

6. A. According to the man(1) page for the make command, the name Makefile, with an uppercase M, is the recommended name for the file. The name makefile is valid as a default, but it is not the recommended option. The other files are not valid as default names.

7. D. The clean target is typically included in most Makefiles for projects in order to remove files leftover from a previous compilation. The other targets are not valid.

8. D. The configure script, which is usually included in source code packages, customizes the software based on the local environment. The other script names shown are generally not used.

9. B. The /usr/src directory is the recommended location for source code according to the Filesystem Hierarchy Standard. Many administrators use /usr/local/src instead, but this is not specified in the FHS.

10. B. The gunzip command is used to uncompress files that have been compressed using gzip compression.

11. C. The bs option is used to specify block size. Various suffixes are possible such as M, which is equivalent to megabytes, and K, which is equivalent to kilobytes.

12. C. The tapetype directive defines a friendly name for a destination. The destination is then further configured within a corresponding define directive. The other directives are not valid for Amanda.

13. D. Tape devices are found within /dev/st*, thereby making st0 the first device.

14. C. The /etc/issue file is used to provide a message to users, such as a login banner, prior to local login. The other files shown are not valid for the purpose described.

15. A. The --delete option removes files that no longer exist on the host system when syncing with archive mode in rsync. The other options shown are not valid for rsync.

16. D. The wall command displays a message to all logged-in users. The command is sometimes used to communicate an impending reboot or shutdown of the server. The other commands shown are not valid.

17. B. The --exclude option excludes files matching a pattern from the archive. This option can greatly reduce the size of an archive by excluding unnecessary files from the archive. The -x option is the only other valid option that extracts files from an archive.

18. C. The contents of the file motd, an abbreviation for Message of the Day, are displayed when a user logs in successfully. Among the other options, the contents of /etc/issue are displayed prior to local login. The other filenames are not valid for this purpose.

19. B. The -f option specifies the filename and -v is verbose, making both of those options required based on the scenario. The -x option extracts from the archive.

20. C. Executing the configure script from the current directory typically means prefacing the script name with ./, as shown in the correct option.

21. A. The -z option will uncompress a tar file that has been compressed with gzip. The -x option extracts, while -c creates a tar file. Finally, -f specifies the tar file to work with.

22. B. The file /etc/issue.net is used to provide a message for remote logins such as Telnet. The other files listed are not valid for the purpose described.

23. D. The poweroff target of systemd, accessed using the systemctl command, is used for halting the system and then attempting to remove power on compatible systems. The halt target stops the system but does not attempt to remove power, while reboot simply restarts the system. There is no stop target.

24. A. The uname command displays information about the kernel, processor type, and other relevant components that might be helpful when compiling software.

25. D. The --modify-window option modifies how file synchronization is determined. The default behavior is to match to the nearest second. This option is useful for synchronizing between filesystem types, such as Microsoft FAT, which don't have the precision of Linux-based filesystems.

26. B. The -b option specifies that a backup should be made during the patching process. The -l option tells patch to ignore whitespace. The -r option specifies a reject file. There is no -a option.

27. D. The install target installs the final compiled files in their appropriate location and makes them executable, if applicable. Of the other options, distclean is sometimes included as a target to return source files to their pristine state. The other targets listed are not valid.

28. C. Compression using the xz program is indicated with the -J option. The -j option indicates bzip2 compression. The -x and -c options are extract and create, respectively.

29. B. The --size-only option examines whether the files being synchronized are the same size. This can be helpful for situations where there may be significant time skew or other issues preventing the normal differencing mechanisms from working properly. The other options shown are not valid for rsync.

30. A. The --decompress option uncompresses an xz file, while the --stdout option sends the output to standard out. The other options shown are not valid.

31. B. The -c option sends output to STDOUT. The -d option decompresses, while -f forces an operation. Finally, -s reduces the memory footprint for bzip2.

32. D. The Bacula Director configuration file is called /etc/bacula/bacula-dir.conf by default. The other files are not normally used as part of a Bacula configuration.

33. B. The rewind subcommand for the mt command rewinds the tape to the beginning. This subcommand can be shortened to rew instead of rewind. The other subcommands shown do not work with mt.

34. A. The -r option is needed to specify reboot and the format for counting time from now. It is prefaced with a plus sign (+), thereby making option A correct. Of the other commands, specifying +15 without the -r option simply shuts down the computer in 15 minutes, and specifying the time as 00:15, as in option D, will reboot the computer at 12:15 a.m.

35. B. The -q option suppresses all warnings. The -v option is verbose, while -L displays the license. The -r option is recursive.

36. C. The -e option, also available as --rsh=ssh, uses ssh as the means for transport, thereby ensuring an encrypted tunnel over which the synchronization process will occur. The other options shown are not valid.

37. B. The --help option is usually included with the configure script as a means to list the other available options. Because every configure script is customized for a given source code package, the other options may vary. Even --help may not always be available, depending on whether the source code author included it.

Chapter 18: Domain Name Server (Topic 207)

1. A. The file named.conf, located in /etc/ or /etc/bind/, is the default configuration file for the BIND server. The file typically loads or includes other configuration files for specific configurations.

2. B. The allow-query directive sets the hosts from which DNS queries will be allowed for the nameserver. This can be helpful for situations where there may be untrusted clients that can reach the nameserver.

3. B. The -1 or -HUP signal reloads the given process. The -15 signal is the default terminate signal, while -2 is an interrupt signal. The -9 signal is for kill, and it is considered bad practice except in emergencies when the process doesn't respond to normal signals.

4. A. The -a option enables specification of the algorithm to use, while -n specifies the name type to use such as zone, host, or others. There is no -d or -e option.

5. B. The named-checkzone command examines a zone file for obvious syntax errors that would prevent BIND from using the file. The named-compilezone file does the same thing as named-checkzone but sends the output directly to a file instead.

6. A. The lowest priority number wins for MX records, thereby making 0 the highest priority MX record for the domain.

7. D. DNS typically uses UDP port 53, except for zone transfers, in which case TCP port 53 is used because of the size of the request for most zones.

8. A. The directory /var/named stores zones. On Debian, this directory is /var/cache/bind. The /etc/named directory is used by some distributions as a location for configuration files.

9. C. The rndc command is used to control a BIND server, including controlling it over a remote connection. The other commands shown are not valid.

10. D. The axfr type can be used with dig to request a zone transfer. The client from which you request the zone transfer will need to be authorized to initiate a transfer.

11. B. The listen-on directive sets the IP address or addresses on which the daemon will operate. The other directives are not valid.

12. C. The home directory should be set in /etc/passwd, and it should be set to the chroot directory. The other files listed are not valid.

13. A. The dnssec-signzone command is used to sign DNS zones when using DNSSEC. The other commands do not exist.

14. A. Setting -a as an option to the host command sets the query type to ANY. The -c option sets the class, and the -d option turns on debugging. There is no -b option.

15. C. The correct format for a CNAME requires a trailing dot, which represents the only difference between answers C and D.

16. A. The only option, as in forward only, is used to indicate that the server should only forward queries and not attempt to answer them directly. The first option forwards the query, and if no response is received, then it attempts to perform the query itself. The other options are not valid.

17. B. The blackhole option provides a list of addresses that will not be allowed to receive answers for queries. This can be helpful for security reasons. The other options are not valid.

18. B. The daemontools package is required in order to install djbdns. BIND9 is not typically used when djbdns is used, and qmail is not required.

19. D. The named-checkconf command is used to verify the configuration of BIND. When no configuration file is given, it is assumed that /etc/named.conf represents the configuration file.

20. C. TTL, or time to live, values are provided in seconds by default, thereby making 28,800 equal to eight hours.

21. B. The value 1800 represents the retry value for the zone. The refresh is 3600, while the default TTL is 86400. Finally, the serial is 2016070400.

22. C. TXT records are used to create resource records in support of SPF. MX is used for SMTP servers.

23. B. The mail exchanger is defined as Priority MX Hostname in the format shown.

24. C. The .digrc file, found in a user's home directory, can be used to set defaults for use of the dig command. There is no dig configuration file found in /etc.

25. A. The --bind option for the mount command, which has nothing to do with the BIND daemon itself, enables mounting or remounting a portion of the filesystem in another location. This is helpful for facilitating working with BIND configuration files in a chroot environment.

26. D. The zone type of hint is used with the root zone file. When setting up a zone for which the server is authoritative, the type is master or slave. There is no recurse type.

27. A. The `rndc` command can be used for this purpose and, when given the `reload` subcommand, will reload the zones for the server.

28. D. The `allow-transfer` directive specifies the hosts that are allowed to request a transfer of the zone. The other options shown are not valid.

29. D. POP3 servers do not have a specific type in DNS. The MX type indicates mail exchanger, or SMTP server.

30. C. The `allow-recursion` option is useful for situations where certain clients can query the nameserver for its authoritative names but not request recursion.

31. A. The correct format is `named-checkzone <zone> <zonefile>`. No other options are required.

32. D. The only available algorithm for `rndc` is hmac-md5, and the key can be generated with `dnssec-keygen`. The other options shown are encryption or hashing algorithms but are not used for the scenario described.

33. B. The `version none;` directive within a BIND configuration file tells BIND not to return version information. The other directives are not valid.

34. C. The `-z` option tells `named-checkconf` to verify the master zones as part of the verification process. The other options are not valid.

35. B. An individual TTL on a record means that it will take up to that many seconds for the change to propagate. New requests will begin seeing the change immediately after restart, but external resolvers may cache for up to the TTL value before requesting another resolution.

36. A. The `pdns-server` package is available on Debian and `pdns` on Red Hat. Red Hat will require installation from EPEL.

37. B. The `rndc` command can be used for this purpose with the `reconfig` subcommand. Because the scenario includes changes to the `named.conf` configuration file, a simple `rndc reload` is not appropriate.

Chapter 19: HTTP Services (Topic 208)

1. B. The `<VirtualHost>` directive begins a stanza that facilitates serving websites using virtual servers. The other directives are not valid for Apache.

2. D. The `htpasswd` command creates or updates credentials for native Apache authentication using htaccess. The `passwd` command is valid, but it does not work with htaccess. The other commands are not valid.

3. C. The `configtest` option verifies the configuration file syntax, and it is quite helpful in order to prevent a situation where the server cannot restart due to a fatal error in the configuration. The other options are not valid for the `apachectl` command.

4. A. The openssl command is used for this purpose with the genrsa option. An output file is specified with -out. The other commands containing openssl all contain an invalid option, and the final command is openssh and it is not used for this scenario.

5. B. The AuthUserFile directive works with mod_auth_basic and mod_authn_file to tell Apache the location of the file that will be used for authentication.

6. C. The ServerName directive provides the hostname for the virtual server. The other directives are not used.

7. A. The SSLEngine option needs to be set to On for SSL to be enabled for a given site or server. The other options are not valid.

8. D. The index option enables the administrator to set a space-separated list of valid index files for the server, such as index.html, index.htm, and index.php. The other options listed for this question are not valid.

9. B. The acl configuration directive creates an access control list. Access control lists are powerful features of a Squid proxy setup and can include networks, MAC addresses, ports, browsers, and much more.

10. C. It can be desirable at times not to display the version of Apache in use. Some say that doing so might help security. However, this type of "security through obscurity" may not be entirely effective.

11. C. Server Name Indication, or SNI, facilitates serving multiple virtual hosts from the same IP address even when SSL is used. Without SNI, each SSL-based virtual host would require its own IP address. The other technologies are not valid for this scenario.

12. A. The SSLCACertificateFile directive enables specification of a single PEM file containing CA certificates for client authentication.

13. B. The AuthName directive sets a friendly display value that is shown within the authentication pop-up window. The other values shown do not have any effect within Apache2.

14. D. The LoadModule directive is used for this purpose and accepts the name of the module followed by its filename.

15. A. The req option begins the CSR generation process, typically also requiring -new as an additional option. The other subcommands are not valid.

16. B. The DocumentRoot directive sets the default directory from which documents are served, both inside and outside a virtual host stanza. The ServerRoot directive sets the overall root directory for the server and is not related to virtual hosts or document serving. The other two options are not valid Apache directives.

17. D. The file php.ini, typically located within the /etc/ hierarchy, depending on distribution, is used as the primary configuration file for PHP. The other files are not used by PHP.

18. C. The Options directive is used for this purpose and the option to exclude is Indexes. Options are included or excluded by a plus or minus sign, respectively. There is no option named Default.

19. A. The syntax shown will redirect the user to a 404 page in the event that they attempt to navigate to the `.git` directory. The other options will not work because of syntax errors.

20. B. The `SSLCertificateKeyFile` directive points to the location of the private key for an SSL configuration. The other options shown are not valid directives.

21. B. Squid listens on port 3128 by default. The other ports listed are valid but are not the default port for Squid.

22. C. The `mod_authz_host` module is used for authorization based on IP address or host-name. The other modules are not valid for a default Apache configuration for the purpose described.

23. A. The default name for the primary log file for Apache is `access_log`. This file may some-times be called `access.log`, depending on the distribution. The name of the file along with what is recorded in the log can be customized.

24. B. The `http_access` directive is combined with ACL directives to define access to use the Squid proxy. The other directives are not valid for use in Squid.

25. C. The `AccessFileName` directive can be used to set the access filename to something other than `.htaccess`.

26. B. Apache explains within the documentation that higher performance is achieved by stor-ing the directives related to user authentication within the main server configuration when possible. The only reason not to do this is so that the authentication directives are accessible by the user. There is no scenario to store user authentication configuration information in a `mod_rewrite` block or in a module, as was the case for two of the four options for this question.

27. D. The `AuthGroupFile` directive facilitates the scenario described. Users must be authenti-cated, and then a directory or other resource can be associated with the group file to enable users in the file to access the resource. The other directives shown are not valid.

28. B. The `apachectl` command can be used for this purpose, and when given the `status` argument will print status information for the server. The other arguments for `apachectl` are not valid.

29. A. A 405, Method not allowed, response will be sent when TraceEnable is off. A 100 code is continue, while 302 is redirect and 200 is OK.

30. C. The `-c` option creates a new file. The `-b` option is batch mode. The `-e` and `-f` options do not exist for `htpasswd`.

31. A. Log format sequences begin with a percent sign, and `%D` logs the time taken to service the request in microseconds. The `%T` sequence logs the time taken to service the request, but it requires a preceding unit of time to log. The `%t` sequence is the time of day when the request was received.

32. B. The `Alias` directive is used for this purpose. The format calls for the destination fol-lowed by the location to be aliased, thereby making option B correct. There is no `Connect` directive in Apache.

33. B. The SetHandler directive is used for this purpose. SetHandler should be set to perl-script for mod_perl to work. There is a LoadModule required for mod_perl, but its arguments include mod_perl and the location of the mod_perl module.

34. C. The proxy_pass directive, found within a location stanza in nginx, enables proxying of requests for that location to the specified URL. The other directives are not valid for nginx.

35. C. The StartServers directive determines the number of child processes that will start initially. This number will change as requests are received, especially simultaneous requests. On busy servers, the StartServers directive may need to be increased, as will other related directives to ensure adequate performance.

36. D. The LogFormat directive sets the parameters that are stored in a log file. The LogFormat directive sets up a logging profile that can then be used elsewhere within the configuration. The other options are not valid.

37. C. The Require directive is used for this, and when requiring a specific user, the directive is followed by the keyword user and then the user to allow. The other directives shown are not valid for Apache.

Chapter 20: File Sharing (Topic 209)

1. B. The configuration files for Samba are located in /etc/samba. The directory is not named for a specific version of Samba. The other directories listed do not exist by default.

2. B. The nmbd daemon is responsible for NetBIOS name service request handling. The smbd daemon is responsible for file and print sharing and winbindd provides user and group information. There is no daemon called samba.

3. D. The smbcontrol command can be used to send messages to smbd, nmbd, or winbindd. When using the destination of all, the message will be sent to all three daemons. There are several message types that can be sent with smbcontrol, one of which is reload-config. There is a shutdown message, but that would be disruptive to users and would not reload the configs until restart.

4. D. The file /etc/exports contains definitions of filesystems to be shared using NFS. The other files are not valid for use with NFS.

5. A. Spacing is important within an NFS export configuration. This is the primary difference between option A and option C, regarding a space between the hostname and the (rw) configuration directive. With option A, where there is no space, www.example.com is allowed read-write access to the share. With option C, where there is a space, www.example.com is allowed only read access while everyone else is allowed read-write.

6. B. The -k option enables Kerberos authentication for the net command. The -a option indicates that non-interactive mode should be used, and -l sets the log directory. There is no -b option.

7. D. The `username map` option, which is set to a file containing the username mappings, is used to provide translation between a Windows username and the username on Linux for each user. The other options shown are not valid in a Samba configuration.

8. C. A percent sign (%) is used to separate the username from the password, as in this example with a username of `Administrator` and a password of adminpass: `-U Administrator%adminpass`.

9. C. Wildcards are specified with a * or ? for NFS; therefore `*.example.org` indicates that all hosts directly under `example.org` can connect. Note that the wildcard match is not hierarchical, meaning that subdomains underneath `*.example.org` are not included (`www.chicago.example.org`, for example).

10. D. The cifs filesystem type is used for mounting Samba shares. The vfat filesystem is used to mount native Windows filesystems, and ext4 is a native Linux filesystem. There is no win type.

11. C. The `mount` command can be used for this purpose, and when given the `-t cifs` argument it will show all mounted CIFS filesystems. There is no smb filesystem type, and the `ls` command with `-cifs` options will display various file listings but none specific to the CIFS filesystem.

12. D. Setting the security parameter to `share` indicates that share-level security will be used. The parameter is set as in `security = share`. The other options shown for this question are not valid.

13. B. The `-m` option to `rpcinfo` displays statistics for `rpcbind`. The `-s` and `-l` options are used to display lists of programs and entries for the specific program. There is no `-e` option for `rpcinfo`.

14. B. The `showmount` command is used for this purpose, and when given the `-e` option it displays the exports for the server. Among the other options, the `mount` command is valid but not with the given options.

15. C. The `/etc/fstab` file utilizes a specific format calling for the filesystem device, in this case `src.example.com:/source`, followed by the mount destination, in this case `/srv/source`, and then followed by the filesystem type. For this scenario, the filesystem type is nfs. Options for the filesystem along with default mount order are typically also included in `/etc/fstab`.

16. A. The `-3` option shows only NFSv3 statistics. There are also corresponding `-2` and `-4` options for NFSv2 and NFSv4, respectively. The other options shown do not exist.

17. B. The `/proc/mounts` file shows currently mounted filesystems. The `/etc/fstab` file shows filesystems that could be mounted but may not currently be mounted. The other files shown are not valid.

18. A. When used with TCP Wrappers, as in `hosts.allow` and `hosts.deny`, the `portmap` service must use IP addresses. Therefore, option A is correct.

19. B. The -L option displays a list of locks. The -l option sets the base directory for logging. There is no -o or -m option for smbstatus.

20. B. The smbpasswd command is used for management of Samba credentials. When given the -a option, a new user is created. Of the other commands, the passwd command is valid but does not have a -samba option. The other commands are not valid.

21. A. The browsable option, set to yes or no, configures whether a given share can be seen by browsing. When set to no, users must know the share name in order to interact with it.

22. D. The dbcheck command for samba-tool verifies the location of the Active Directory database. The other commands are not used with samba-tool.

23. C. The [global] section of the Samba configuration file enables setting of the log file. The other sections shown are not valid.

24. C. The testparm command can be used to verify the syntax within Samba configuration files. The other commands shown are not valid.

25. B. The exportfs command is used for several administrative tasks related to NFS. When given the -ra option, the /etc/exports file is reread, a new export list is created, and the shares are created.

26. A. The -R option specifies the resolve order for names used with smbclient. For example, setting the value of the -R option to wins specifies that the WINS server should be used for name resolution. The -d option specifies the debug level.

27. C. The -l option logs all successful mountd requests. Of the other options, the -n option allows non-root requests, and -r allows regular files to be served through RPC requests.

28. B. The read only option, set to yes or no, defines whether users connecting to a given share can perform read/write operations on the share. The other options shown are not valid for Samba.

29. C. The smbd daemon listens on TCP ports 139 and 445. Port 443 is used for HTTPS, and ports 161 and 162 are used for SNMP.

30. C. The root_squash option changes the privileges of root when using an NFS share from a remote client. The root user will have the lowest privileges possible. The other options are not valid for NFS.

31. B. The net command is used for this solution, and when given the groupmap list sub-command and option, a mapping of Windows to Linux groups will be shown. The other commands are not valid.

32. A. The -p option shows current portmappings for the various RPC-related services on the host. The -m option shows statistics. There is no -c or -f option for rpcinfo.

33. B. The -x option deletes a user from the Samba user database. The -d option disables the account. The -e option enables the account. There is no -o option.

34. C. The `smbclient` command can be used for this purpose, and when given the `-L` option and a hostname, the command will show the services available on that host. The other commands shown are not valid.

35. C. The configuration shown, with `%S.log`, will create a separate log file for each share. All of the other options contain syntax errors that make them invalid for the Samba configuration file.

36. D. The `nmblookup` command can be used to test NetBIOS-related services on a network.

37. D. The `exportfs` command with the `-u` and `-a` options unexports all directories. Another way to accomplish this task would be to stop the NFS daemons, but that option was not given among the choices.

Chapter 21: Network Client Management (Topic 210)

1. A. The `ddns-update-style` option configures whether a server performs a DNS update when leases are created or confirmed. The other options are not valid for use with DHCP.

2. A. The subnet keyword is used for this purpose as well as a `netmask` parameter. The netmask shown will provide 126 usable addresses.

3. B. The `hardware ethernet` directive is used to specify the MAC address for a given host to which the reservation will be tied. The other options are not used within DHCP.

4. C. The directory `/etc/pam.d` stores configuration files for individual PAM-aware services. Each service typically has its own file that is managed for that service according to its usage of PAM. Of the other options, none of the directories are the default directories used for PAM.

5. A. The standard port for LDAP is 389, and that is the port on which `slapd` listens for connections. Port 3389 is RDP, while 3306 is MySQL. Finally, 110 is POP3.

6. D. The `ldapadd` command is used to add entries into the OpenLDAP database.

7. C. DHCP traffic, which uses UDP, communicates on ports 67 and 68. Of the other ports, only 143 is widely used but as the port for IMAP and not related to UDP.

8. D. The `slapd_db_recover` command can be used to help recover an OpenLDAP database that has become corrupt or otherwise invalid. The remaining options for this question are not valid commands.

9. C. The domain suffix search order can be set through a DHCP option. The option name is `domain-search` and the values are separated by a comma.

10. A. The directory /var/lib/ldap stores database files related to the OpenLDAP deployment on a given server. The other directories shown are not valid for this purpose.

11. C. The pam_nologin.so module facilitates a scenario whereby non-root logins are prevented when /etc/nologin exists. This module must be specified within the configuration file for a given service. For example, within the sshd PAM configuration file, the following line creates this configuration for ssh:

account required pam_nologin.so

12. D. The LDAP Data Interchange Format (LDIF) is an open format, defined in RFC 2849, which enables import and export of LDAP entries. The file formats TXT and CSV are valid but not for the purpose described. There is no specific file format known as LDAP.

13. C. The pam_unix.so module is used for standard login. The man page for pam_unix.so indicates that it is for "traditional password authentication." The other modules listed are not standard PAM modules, though there is a similar pam_auth or squid_pam_auth module for Squid.

14. B. The clients section within an interface in radvd.conf enables configuration of specific clients to which route advertisements will be sent. The other options listed for this question are not valid directives in radvd.conf.

15. B. Debug level 64 provides configuration processing debug information. Debug level 1 traces function calls, while level 8 shows connection management. Debug level 0 is no debug.

16. B. The max-lease-time directive, followed by the number of seconds, specifies the amount of time that a given host can have a lease before it is purged. The other options shown are not valid in a dhcpd.conf configuration file.

17. B. The DHCPDISCOVER message being logged is coming from a client. The client is beginning the process of obtaining an IP address from the DHCP server.

18. A. Within nsswitch.conf, the passwd line contains information about authentication. The format is as shown in the correct answer. Local authentication is accomplished using the files keyword for the normal passwd file. There is typically a similar line called shadow, assuming that the server is using shadow passwords. The shadow line follows a similar format.

19. B. The pam_cracklib.so module enforces password strength options. The other files listed are not valid PAM modules.

20. B. The -c option specifies an alternate configuration file for sssd. The -f option sends debug output to a file. There is no -a or -m option for sssd.

21. C. DHCP failover communicates on port 647. DHCP failover is helpful to provide redundancy for this important service. Ports 67 and 68 are used for normal DHCP traffic, while 389 is for LDAP.

22. C. The routers option defines the default gateway for a given DHCP lease. Like other options, routers can be specified at the subnet level or for an individual host. The other options are not valid for the purpose described.

23. C. The `slapcat` command dumps the slapd database in LDIF format. The other commands are not valid.

24. D. The `pam_limits.so` module is responsible for enforcement of limits such as those mentioned in the problem as well as several others like the maximum size of files, memory usage, and so on. The other modules listed are not valid.

25. C. The `slapindex` command generates indexes based on slapd databases. The other commands are not valid.

26. D. There are multiple ways to specify log levels and debugging for `slapd`, including by keyword, by integer, or as shown in the question, by hex. All of the values shown are valid for loglevel. No debugging is 0, trace is 1, stats logging is 256 or 512 depending on type, and packets sent and received is integer 16 or hex 0x10.

27. D. The `-j` option enables specification of a line from which the import will be started. It is useful in the scenario described where the import needs to be restarted due to error. The `-f` option specifies an alternate location for the `slapd` configuration file. The `-q` option is quick mode, with less checking, and `-l` specifies the input file.

28. D. Beginning with OpenLDAP version 2.3, `slapd-config` is used for configuration of OpenLDAP, as documented at `http://www.openldap.org/doc/admin24/slapdconf2.html`. The other commands are not valid.

29. B. The `changetype add` creates a new entry in the LDAP database. The other changetypes are not valid.

30. B. Specifying one `-L` indicates LDIFv1 format. The next `-L` turns off comments in the output, and a third `-L` suppresses the version. The other options are not valid for the described scenario.

31. C. The port for LDAPS or LDAP over SSL is 636. Port 389 is standard, non-SSL LDAP. Port 443 is used for HTTPS, and 3128 is used for Squid proxies.

32. B. The `pam_listfiles.so` module is used to create scenarios whereby you can create files that control authentication and authorization through the PAM system. The other files are not valid for the scenario described.

33. A. The `-n` option shows the results without actually making changes to the LDAP database. The other options are not valid for the scenario described.

34. B. The filter `(objectClass=*)` is used when there is no filter provided for `ldapsearch`. The other filters shown are not valid with `ldapsearch`.

35. A. The `pam_sss.so` module is used for integration of SSSD into the PAM authentication system. The other modules are not valid.

36. B. The `ldap_uri` option sets the URI of the LDAP server for use with SSSD. The other options are not valid for use in `sssd.conf`.

37. B. The `deny unknown-clients` configuration directive will cause the DHCP server to deny addresses when a client requests an address through DHCP. The other options shown are not valid.

Chapter 22: E-Mail Services (Topic 211)

1. A. The postsuper command is used for management of various items with Postfix, including deletion of individual messages from the mail queue. The other commands will not work for the purpose described.

2. C. The /var/spool/postfix directory contains directories and files related to the mail queue for Postfix. The other directories listed are not valid for this scenario.

3. B. PEM format is used for public and private keys with a Postfix TLS configuration. The other methods listed are valid cryptographic algorithms or systems but not for the scenario described.

4. D. The fileinto keyword is used to define the destination for mail that matches one or more conditions within Sieve. The other configuration keywords are not valid.

5. D. The directory /etc/postfix contains files related to the configuration of Postfix on a given server. While the other directories shown are valid names, they are not the default location for Postfix-related configs.

6. B. The file .procmailrc, found in a user's home directory, is used by Procmail for processing messages on a per-user basis. The other files are not used by Procmail in a default configuration.

7. D. The format is local-address: destination-address. Each destination address is separated by a comma. The difference between answers C and D is that the question specifically asked for addresses @example.com, and since the question didn't specify whether this server was the server for @example.com, the destination addresses needed to be fully qualified.

8. C. The mailq command displays the current mail queue for a Postfix server. The other commands are not valid, though there is popular mail server software named qmail.

9. A. The postqueue command will be used for this purpose, and when given the -f option, it will flush the queue immediately. The other commands and options do not meet the intended purpose for the scenario.

10. B. The postsuper command is used for this purpose, specifically with the -d option. When given the ALL keyword, all messages will be deleted from the queue.

11. A. The newaliases command will rebuild the /etc/aliases database so that changes will be noted by the mail daemon. The other commands shown are not valid.

12. B. The keep action causes the message to be preserved in the mailbox. The other verbs shown are not valid Sieve actions.

13. D. The postcat command shows the contents of a message from the Postfix queue. The other commands shown are not valid.

14. D. The doveadm command is used for this solution. The option called who produces a list of the users who are currently logged in, their PIDs, and their IP addresses. There is no list option for doveadm or dovecot, and likewise there is no users option for the dovecot command.

15. B. The discard keyword is used to specify that a message should be deleted. It is usually followed by the stop keyword in order to indicate that no further processing needs to be done for that message.

16. A. The postqueue -p command and option view the pending queue. The postqueue -f command and option cause the queue to be flushed. The other commands shown are valid but their options are not.

17. C. The redirect action will be used but must be accompanied by the :copy keyword in order to retain a copy of the message. There are no forward or :duplicate keywords in Sieve.

18. B. The :days keyword sets how frequently the vacation auto-responder will reply to a given sender. For example, setting :days 1 means that the same sender will receive a vacation auto-response once a day at most. The other keywords are not valid.

19. C. The qshape command displays information regarding the number and age of the messages in the Postfix incoming and active queues. Other queues can be viewed using the command as well. The other commands shown as options for this question are not valid.

20. A. The doveconf command displays configuration parameters related to Dovecot, including the setting name and its value. The dovecot command is valid, as is the doveadm command. However, the options shown for both of those commands are not valid. There is no doveconfig command.

21. A. There is an implicit keep action if no other action takes precedence or otherwise handles the e-mail within a set of actions. There is a discard action, but it is not the default. There is no action called shred or forward.

22. B. The mynetworks parameter sets the networks or hosts that are allowed to relay through the Postfix server. The other options are not valid. Note that there are parameters related to relaying, such as relayhost, but those are typically used to set the destination for relaying rather than allow relaying through the server.

23. D. The doveadm command, when used with the auth option, tests authentication for a given user. There is a dovecot command, but the command does not have auth or testauth options. Likewise, there is no testauth option to doveadm.

24. D. The m4 command compiles a native Sendmail configuration into the final Sendmail configuration file. A standard redirect is used to send the output to its final destination.

25. A. The postconf command is used for this purpose, and when given the -d option it displays all parameters in the current Postfix configuration. Note that the only other command shown that is valid is postfix, but that command uses -c to specify the configuration directory and not for the purpose described in the scenario for this question.

26. C. The file /var/log/mail.err contains errors related to mail delivery. However, on some systems, mail-related errors may go to a different log such as /var/log/mail.log or /var/log/mail.info or similar.

27. B. The inet_listener directive creates a stanza for a listening port within Dovecot. Additional parameters can be specified relating to the given listener within the inet_listener stanza.

28. A. SMTP uses TCP port 25 by default. Port 110 is POP3, and 143 is IMAP. Port 2525 is not a well-known port.

29. C. The mailq_path parameter contains the path to the mail queue for Postfix. You can use this to diagnose problems with the queue directories. The other parameters shown are not valid in Postfix.

30. D. The EHLO command indicates Extended Hello syntax, and it is followed by the host from which communication has been initiated. Of the other options, the HELO option is valid, but it is not the Extended Hello syntax specified in the question.

31. B. Sieve uses elsif for definition of an alternate condition. The other forms of this keyword are valid for many languages but not for Sieve. There is no alt keyword.

32. B. The :contains keyword looks through an object such as an address to see if there is a matching string within it. The other keywords shown are not valid.

33. A. The process_limit option specifies the maximum login processes for a Dovecot server. The parameter is set on a per-service basis.

34. D. The :domain keyword matches on just the domain portion of an address in Sieve. The other keywords shown are not valid.

35. B. The default port for IMAPS is 993. POP3 uses 110 for unencrypted communication and 995 for encrypted communication. The default port for unencrypted IMAP is 143.

36. A. The Exim configuration file is /etc/exim/exim4.conf by default on Debian, but it may be named as shown for the other options when using other Linux distributions.

37. B. The postscreen_tls_security_level option sets the security level for the postscreen server. This option should be used instead of the postscreen_use_tls and smtpd_use_tls options.

Chapter 23: System Security (Topic 212)

1. A. The PermitRootLogin directive, set to yes or no, determines whether the root user can log in directly. The other options shown are not valid.

2. B. The file vsftpd.conf contains the configuration for vsftpd. The file can be found in /etc or within a subdirectory such as /etc/vsftpd.

3. B. The PREROUTING chain, part of the nat table, contains rules that are applied as packets arrive. A common use for this chain is to apply redirect rules. Among the other answers, REDIRECT may appear valid, but it is in fact a target and not a chain. The other options shown are not valid.

4. A. The primary configuration file for OpenSSH is /etc/ssh/sshd_config. The other options shown are not valid.

5. C. The iptables-save command creates a file with the currently running iptables rules. The file can then be applied the next time the server is restarted. The other commands shown are not valid.

6. B. The -H option causes Pure FTPd not to resolve host names. The -n option is used for quota enforcement, and the -r option is used to indicate that existing files should not be overwritten. The -z option allows anonymous users to read directories and files that are preceded with a dot.

7. D. The ssh-keygen command generates a public and private key pair that can be used for user authentication between a client and server. The other commands shown are not valid.

8. B. The telnet command can be used for this purpose and, for SMTP, requires the use of a port as shown in the correct answer for this question. There is no smtptest command, and specifying the port by name or not specifying the port will not work.

9. D. The iptables -n option causes iptables not to resolve host names or port names. The -L option lists current rules. There is no -a option.

10. C. The -i option disables uploads by anonymous users. The -a option keeps users in their home directory unless they are a member of a specified group. The -m option prevents anonymous download if the CPU load on the server is above a threshold. The -n option is used for quota enforcement.

11. A. The Port option specifies the port on which the OpenSSH server daemon will listen. Clients will need to specify the port using -p or with colon notation in order to connect to the server. The other options shown are not valid.

12. B. The push directive is used to send a route to clients on connection. In this case, the network and netmask are sent, with 255.255.255.0 being appropriate for a /24. The other options are not valid.

13. B. The nmap command is used for this purpose, and the -sT option performs a TCP Connect to the specified host or network. The other commands are not valid.

14. D. The /etc/fail2ban directory contains configuration files related to fail2ban. The other directories shown are not valid.

15. A. The -i option specifies the identity file or key that will be used for authentication. The server must have a copy of the public key and be configured for key-based authentication in order for the authentication to be successful. The -p option specifies the port. The -k option disables forwarding of GSSAPI credentials and is not related to the described scenario. The -l option specifies the username to use for authentication.

16. B. The `ip6tables-save` command saves the currently running IPv6 iptables configuration. The other commands shown are not valid. Most of the IPv6 commands related to iptables are of the form `ip6tables`.

17. B. The `PermitEmptyPasswords` directive, when set to `yes` or `no`, specifies whether empty passwords can be used for authentication. Enabling empty passwords would be a specialized use case and generally not recommended. The other options shown are not valid.

18. C. The `-P` option sets the policy for a given chain in `iptables`. In this case, the chain is `INPUT` and the policy necessary is `DROP`.

19. B. OpenVPN listens on UDP port 1194 by default. The other combinations are not the valid OpenVPN configuration.

20. B. The `Protocol` directive specifies the version of the SSH protocol that should be used. Currently, version 2 is recommended. The other options shown are not valid.

21. B. The `DROP` target silently discards packets that match the rule. An ICMP unreachable message is sent back for `REJECT`. In general, `DROP` is preferred in order to reduce the chances of Denial of Service (DoS) or other information-gathering issues.

22. D. The file `authorized_keys` contains keys that can then be used for authentication when the corresponding private key is sent by the client. The other files are not valid.

23. B. The `-m` match limit, along with the configuration options shown, creates the scenario described. There will be three log entries per minute. This can be useful to prevent Denial of Service by filling up log files or overwhelming the server I/O while another attack is under way.

24. C. The `-X` option enables X11 application forwarding through an SSH connection. The `-A` option is used for authentication agent forwarding, and `-F` indicates a per-user configuration file. There is no `-X11` option.

25. C. The `lsof -i` command and option can be used for this purpose. A list of processes and ports will be shown and can then be used to determine which actual process is listening on the port. Of the other commands, `tcpdump` is valid but will not show the information necessary to solve the problem described. The other commands are not valid.

26. A. The `INPUT` chain is used, and when used with the `-A` option, it will append a rule to the chain. The `-p` option specifies the protocol, ICMP in this case, and the `-j` option specifies the target, ACCEPT, in this case. The `-P` option specifies a policy and is not used for this scenario.

27. D. The `AllowTcpForwarding` configuration directive determines whether port forwarding will be allowed through the SSH server. When enabled, clients can forward ports through their SSH connections. The other directives are not valid.

28. B. The `INPUT` chain will be used, and a rule needs to be appended with `-A`. The ALL option when specifying protocol means that all protocols will be included in the rule. The `-s` option specifies the source, which in this case is a single IP address. Finally, the `DROP` target silently discards packets. There is no BLOCK or DISCARD target, and the ACCEPT target will not block but will accept all traffic.

29. A. A rule will be appended to the INPUT chain with -A. In this case, the protocol should be specified with -p TCP and a destination port of 2222. The source address indicated, 0/0, applies the rule to all hosts. The ACCEPT target will be used.

30. B. Echoing a 1 to the /proc/sys/net/ipv4/ip_forward file enables forwarding of IP packets. This is necessary in order to utilize NAT and for other uses. There is no /proc/sys/net/ipv4/nat file.

31. D. The listen_ipv6 directive is used to indicate that IPv6 will be enabled for vsftpd. The other directives shown are not valid.

32. C. The PubkeyAuthentication directive determines whether key-based authentication can be used with the server. The other directives shown are not valid.

33. A. The logpath directive determines the log file that will be monitored for failures by fail2ban. This file is used as part of a larger configuration for a given jail. The other directives are not valid for fail2ban.

34. D. The ssh-copy-id command sends an identity to a remote server that can then be used for key-based authentication. The other commands shown are not valid.

35. B. The ip6tables command is used for creation and maintenance of a firewall for IPv6. The ip6tables command is similar to the iptables command in form.

36. C. The push directive is used, and it requires the use of dhcp-option, in this case, DNS 192.168.2.1. The other formats and options are not valid.

37. A. The local_enable directive specifies whether users will be able to log in to the server. This option would not be used in cases where the FTP server is anonymous only.

Chapter 24: Practice Test 1

1. B. The /proc filesystem stores information about running processes on the system. The /etc filesystem is used for configuration information, and /dev is used for device information. The /environment filesystem does not exist on a default Linux system.

2. C. The /etc/modprobe.d directory contains information related to the modprobe configuration. This can be overridden with the -C option on the command line.

3. A. The -g option to wall sends the input to the specified group. Answer B will send the output to all users, while answers C and D will not work.

4. B. The SIGTERM signal is the default signal sent with the systemctl kill command.

5. B. The -e option to dmesg displays the time in local time and the delta in a format that is typically easier to work with. The -rel option does not exist. The -f option specifies the logging facility, and -t does not display time at all.

6. B. The init process is typically associated with the initial process ID of 1 to indicate that it is the process from which others are spawned. Killing PID 1 will typically and immediately halt the system.

7. C. The lspci command shows the PCI devices in the system, and the -k option shows the kernel driver being used by the given device. The lsusb command will not accomplish the task requested, and the ls command with -pci will not display the correct information. There is no showpci command.

8. C. The --no-wall option will cause telinit not to send a wall command to logged-in users about the state change. The other options listed in this problem do not exist.

9. A. The class/net hierarchy within /sys contains information on the network configuration for the computer. It is a symlink to the devices hierarchy, where the device will be listed by its address rather than the logical eth0 name.

10. D. A logical location to begin troubleshooting is within the system BIOS to ensure that the drive is being detected by the computer.

11. C. The dbus-monitor program, which requires an X display, can be used to monitor dbus. The other programs and options listed for this question do not exist.

12. A. The udevd service is called systemd-udevd.service within a systemd environment.

13. A. The system can be scheduled to shut down at a certain time, and that time should be entered in 24-hour format, as shown in the answer.

14. C. The -s option changes the signal to be sent from its default of SIGTERM. The new signal must be one of the main signal types such as SIGINT or SIGSTOP.

15. D. The list-unit-files command shows the files available, while --type=service limits those files to the services, in the same way that chkconfig --list returns a list of services.

16. A. The -C option sets the location of the cache to be updated instead of the default /etc/ld.so.cache. The lowercase option, -c, changes the format of the cache, while -v sets verbose mode. The --f option does not exist.

17. C. The -P option to dpkg will purge a package from the system, including the configuration files associated with the package. The apt-cache clean command will clean the package cache but not an individual package, and the apt-get remove command will remove a package but not associated configuration files.

18. C. The deb-src prefix is used to indicate that a given repository contains source packages. The deb prefix in option A would indicate normal packages. The other options are not valid.

19. B. The -U option is used to upgrade a package. Adding -v for verbose and -h for hash marks will print additional information and progress, as requested by the problem.

20. A. The -y or --assumeyes option will do what it says, that is, assume that you will answer yes and therefore not prompt. The other options do not exist.

21. A. The exclude option within /etc/yum.conf is a space-separated list of packages that accepts wildcards and cannot be installed or upgraded. The other options listed in this question do not exist.

22. C. The ldconfig command is used to work with the library cache and the -p option prints the directories and libraries in the cache. The -C option informs ldconfig to use a different cache. The ldd command prints the library dependencies for a given command, but the options given don't exist for ldd.

23. D. The baseurl option is used to set the URL and must be fully qualified, meaning that it must include the protocol such as http:// or file://.

24. B. The apt-cache dump command will display a listing of the available packages and their respective dependencies. The other commands and options listed in this problem do not exist.

25. A. The /boot directory almost certainly exists but has not been partitioned into its own space. The /boot partition would not be hidden from lsblk if it was indeed a separate partition.

26. B. The /var/cache hierarchy contains cached data for both package management tools. In the case of yum, cached data is stored in /var/cache/yum, and in the case of a Debian-based system, cached data is stored in /var/cache/apt.

27. A. The Master Boot Record (MBR) is the typical location for the bootloader to be stored on a BIOS-based system.

28. D. The / filesystem is the root filesystem. If separate partitions have not been created, the / filesystem will be the beginning of the hierarchy and will contain all other directories in the same partition.

29. A. The --output option configures the location for output of the command instead of STDOUT.

30. C. The tilde key (~) is used as a substitute for a given user's home directory. The other options shown here will not work for the purpose described.

31. A. The dd command is used for this purpose, and in this case it takes an input file with the if option and an output destination with the of option. The bs option signals that the block size for writing should be 1 megabyte.

32. D. The history command displays history from the current session and can be used for the purpose described. The .bash_history file is written on session close, by default.

33. C. The --boot-directory option will install the boot images into the directory specified. This might be helpful for non-standard installs or at times when you need to mount the boot partition separately. The other options listed in this question do not exist.

34. A. The update-grub command should be executed in order to make changes take effect in the menu and when changes have been made to the GRUB configuration. The other commands listed in this question do not exist.

35. B. The export command is used for this purpose and accepts a name=value pair, as shown in the answer. The other commands are not valid with the exception of the echo command, which will simply echo the argument to the console.

36. C. The HISTFILESIZE option configures the number of commands to keep in the history file. The other variables are not valid within Bash.

37. D. The -b option configures the body numbering format for nl, which by default will not number blank lines. The -a format option will number all lines including blanks. The -a option is not for the nl command, and the -n option configures the numbering format and would require an additional argument in order to be valid.

38. D. The od command is used to create octal output. The cat command will show the file as it exists on disk. The other two commands are not valid.

39. A. The pr command formats text for printing, including the date and page numbers at the top of each page. Adding the -d option causes the output to be double-spaced. The cat command will display output but will not be paginated in such a way. The other two commands are not valid.

40. A. The -n option is used to change the number of lines. Adding the +N after the -n option begins the tail process at the Nth line within the file.

41. C. The -i option causes the unique test to be done while ignoring the case of the element to be matched.

42. C. The awk command shown can be used for this purpose. The -F option sets the field separator, and the OFS option sets the output field separator.

43. C. The -a option is equivalent to the -d and -R options, which preserve links and copy recursively, respectively. The -b option creates a backup, and -f forces the copy.

44. A. When in command mode, typing a number followed by an uppercase G will immediately move the cursor to that line number. The /23 option will search for the number 23 in the file. The i23 option will insert the number 23, and finally ZZ will exit Vi.

45. A. The -d option changes the update interval and can be helpful on a busy system where top may be affecting performance. The -n option sets the number of iterations to run. There is no -t or -f option for top.

46. B. The ps -e command is used to display all processes, while the -o option configures the columns to display.

47. A. The grep command can be used for this purpose. Note the difference between grep -r and grep -ri. The question did not ask for case insensitivity, and therefore the use of -i in option B makes it incorrect.

48. B. The find command will be used for this purpose. Setting the directory from which to begin the find is required, along with the expression, which in this case is files beginning with DB.

49. B. Load average information is gathered from /proc/loadavg, while uptime information is stored on /proc/uptime.

50. C. The -f option will force the umount to occur. The --fake option is essentially a dry run in that it won't actually unmount a filesystem. The other two options do not exist.

51. C. The -r option will perform an interactive repair. The -f option forces the operation, while -y and -a are both variations of non-interactive repair.

52. D. The /etc/mtab file is updated dynamically as filesystems are mounted and unmounted. The /etc/fstab file is not dynamically updated.

53. B. The -s option displays output in human-readable format. The -p option is used to print the raw grace period. The -h option displays help, and the -f (lowercase) does not exist, though -F (uppercase) would change the report format.

54. B. The -B option changes the format and -T sets the scale to terabytes. The other options do not exist.

55. A. The e2image program can be used to create an image of metadata that can help with drive recovery. The resulting image file can be used with programs like dumpe2fs and debugfs.

56. C. The -c option checks for bad blocks. The -b option sets the block size. There is no -a or -d option.

57. B. The chown command is used for this purpose, and it can be used to set both the user and group for ownership.

58. B. The HISTSIZE value is the current session history. HISTFILESIZE configures the number of lines to keep in the .bash_history.

59. C. The GRUB_RECORDFAIL_TIMEOUT option is used to configure the behavior of the system in the event of a failed boot. Setting the value to -1 will display the GRUB menu and not continue booting. Setting to 0 will cause the menu to not display. Setting to a value greater than or equal to 1 will cause the menu to display for that many seconds.

60. A. The -s option displays a summary, while -h displays it in a human-readable format.

61. D. The -L option tells find to follow symlinks. The -H and -P options are both variations to tell find not to follow symlinks, while the -S option does not exist.

Chapter 25: Practice Test 2

1. A. The /etc/hosts.deny file is part of TCP Wrappers along with /etc/hosts.allow. Both provide a basic mechanism for configuration of access from remote hosts to network services.

2. B. The WHERE clause can be used to limit the rows returned or affected by a SELECT, UPDATE, or DELETE statement. Within a GROUP BY, the HAVING keyword is used.

3. C. The `alias` command uses the alias name followed by an equals sign followed by the command to be aliased. In this case, because the command to be aliased contains spaces, it needs to be contained in quotation marks.

4. C. Shell scripting syntax uses the format shown, with square brackets around the condition to be tested and double-equals for a string test. Variables are preceded by a dollar sign as shown.

5. A. The `export` command is necessary so that any variables that are manually defined in your current session become available to child processes. The `source` command executes the file and can be used for the purpose described, but it requires an additional argument. The `let` and `def` commands are not valid.

6. C. The `source` command is the functional equivalent of a single dot (`.`). The `set` command exists, but it is not used for this purpose. The other commands are not valid.

7. A. The syntax for setting the PATH separates the new path with a colon, as shown in the correct option. A primary difference between the correct and incorrect options for this question is in how the actual specified path is shown.

8. A. The correct syntax is as shown. Note that a semicolon is required when the commands are included on one line, as shown in the answer.

9. C. The `mail` command with `-s` for the subject is necessary, followed by the e-mail address for the mail. Then input is redirected to the `mail` command using `/etc/hostname`.

10. C. The `/etc/skel` directory contains files that are a skeleton of a user's home directory when their account is created. The other directories listed do not exist by default.

11. B. The syntax at a minimum sees the UPDATE keyword, followed by the table name, and then followed by the SET keyword.

12. A. The command shown launches speech output for Orca. The other commands contain options that are invalid and thus will not work.

13. D. The Universal Access section, which can be found by typing Universal Access from within an Ubuntu GUI interface, enables configuration of accessibility options.

14. B. The `kbdrate` command is used for the purpose described and can help with accessibility. The other commands shown are not valid.

15. A. The configuration files can be found in the `/etc/lightdm` hierarchy or `/usr/share/lightdm`. The other directory locations do not exist by default.

16. A. The DISPLAY variable controls the destination and screen for displaying GUI applications. Setting this variable facilitates forwarding of X applications over ssh.

17. D. The `xwininfo` command is used to gather information about windows. The other commands shown are not valid.

18. B. The `xhost` command is used to control who can make connections for both users and hosts to a given X server. The other commands are not valid.

19. B. The -f option sets the days between expiration and disabled for an account. The -g option is used to set the group ID, while -e is used to set the overall expiration date.

20. A. The getent command can be used for the purpose described, and it will display the aliases on the server by examining the aliases database. The other commands are not valid, and in the case of the mail command shown it will simply attempt to send mail to an address known as aliases.

21. C. The ALL: ALL syntax will cause all hosts to be denied. This means that you must explicitly authorize hosts and networks using /etc/hosts.allow.

22. B. The current at jobs for all users are shown when atq is executed as superuser.

23. A. The tzconfig command can be used on a Debian system to set the time zone. The other commands listed do not exist.

24. C. The -r option to the crontab command removes all cron entries for a given user. The -l option lists cron jobs, while the -e edits the crontab. There is no -d option.

25. A. The -u option specifies the user. The -l option lists the cron jobs and -e edits them. There is no -d or -m option.

26. C. The locale command is used for this purpose, and the -m option displays the available character maps. There is no charmap or mapinfo command.

27. B. Timezone information is found within the /usr/share/zoneinfo hierarchy. The other directories listed do not typically exist by default.

28. A. The userdel command, given no other options, does not delete their home directory. When given the -r option, the command will delete the home directory and mail spool file. There is no -h or -p option for the userdel command.

29. D. The -gid option is used to specify group ownership for the find command. The -group option does exist, but since the question specified that the group had already been deleted, the -gid must be used instead. There is a -user option, but that searches by name and not group ID.

30. B. The groupmod command is used for this purpose, and the -n option followed by the new group name is used to change the name. There is no groupchg command.

31. D. The journalctl command is used to view and parse log file entries on systemd-based systems that maintain logs in a special format. The logger command can be used to create log entries, and the other commands shown do not exist.

32. A. The default location on a Red Hat system is /var/lib/ntp/drift. The other locations shown do not exist by default. Within /etc/ntpd.conf, the location of the drift file can be changed with the driftfile option.

33. A. The -o option, followed by either 1 or 2, enables ntpdate compatibility with older NTP servers. The default, when no -o option is specified, is version 3. The -v option tells ntpdate to be verbose, while the -e option sets the authentication timeout.

34. D. The directory /var/log/journal is used to store journal log files for systemd-based systems. The other directories do not exist by default.

35. C. The -m option sets the mail program to use when mailing logs. It is set to /usr/bin/mail -s by default. There is no -o option and -v is verbose. The -s option to the logrotate command sets the state file to use.

36. A. The -u option configures the output to UTC regardless of the time zone. The -s option sets the time, and there is no -v or -t option.

37. D. The lprm command is used to remove print jobs on a system that uses the lp system for printing. There is no lpdel or rmprint command. There is an rm command, but it's not used for working with print queues.

38. C. The <<< character combination reads input from STDIN or Standard Input and uses it as the body of the message for the mail command.

39. C. The groupdel command is used to remove a group from a system. There can be no members of the group remaining or the command will fail.

40. C. The lpr syslog facility sends messages from the lp subsystem to syslog. The auth facility is used for security-related messages. The other listed options are not syslog facilities.

41. D. The 255.255.254.0 subnet mask is equivalent to a /23. The 255.255.255.0 subnet mask is a /24. The subnet mask 255.255.255.255 is /32 and 255.255.0.0 is a /16.

42. A. The /etc/hosts file will be examined first, and then a DNS query will be sent based on the configuration shown.

43. D. Standard LDAP traffic is TCP port 389 on the server. TCP port 25 is SMTP, 443 is HTTPS, and 143 is IMAP.

44. C. The -l option to ssh changes the username sent for authentication. This can be useful for scripting scenarios where the @ notation cannot be used. The -v option is verbose mode, and -i is the identity file to use. There is no -u option.

45. D. The -n option disables name resolution for addresses involved in the ping request/reply. The -D option returns a timestamp, while -d sets the SO_DEBUG option. Finally, -f is a flood ping.

46. A. The ifconfig command shows various statistics about the interfaces on a Linux system, including whether the interface is up or down, its packets and bytes, queue length, and other information. The other commands listed do not exist.

47. B. The -6 option causes dig to use IPv6 for communication.

48. B. The current limit is six domains and 256 total characters for the search option in /etc/resolv.conf.

49. C. The -C option shows SOA for each of the DNS name servers listed as authoritative for the domain. The -a option sends an ANY query, while -N sets the number of dots for the domain to be considered absolute. There is no -n option.

50. A. The entire 127.0.0.0/8 range is available for local host addresses. Therefore, an answer would need to be in this range. The proper format for /etc/hosts is IP address followed by name followed by alias, which makes answer A correct.

51. C. The --ignore-errors option tells ifup to continue even if there are otherwise fatal errors. The -h option outputs help. There is no --C or --continue option.

52. C. The -u option unlocks an account that was locked using the -l option. The -w option sets the warn days, and -S prints the status.

53. C. When connecting to an alternate port, you can use the -p option to set the port or use a colon to separate the host from the port.

54. A. If /etc/cron.allow exists, then /etc/cron.deny is ignored and only those users listed in /etc/cron.allow can create cron jobs.

55. B. The mailto configuration option sets the destination for e-mails related to sudo. The other options listed are not valid for sudo.

56. B. The who command displays who is currently logged in and the date and time they logged in. The whois command displays information about domains. The other commands are not valid.

57. C. Port 123 is used for NTP communication by default. Port 161 is SNMP, while Port 139 is NetBIOS and Port 194 is IRC.

58. D. A UDP scan can be initiated with -sU. A scan of -sT is a normal TCP scan, and -sS is a SYN scan. There is no -sP option.

59. C. The ssh-keyscan command can be used to retrieve a host key from a remote ssh host, and it is helpful in scripting scenarios to prevent prompting for a host key on initial connect. There is an ssh-keygen command, but it is used to work with keys that are local.

60. B. The +D option is used to search an entire directory tree for files that are open by processes. The -d option does essentially the same thing, but it does not go into subdirectories. The -f option is typically used in combination with other options to control path name interpretation. The -i option lists files or processes with open ports.

Chapter 26: Practice Test 3

1. A. The --delay option sets the interval between checks of array health. The argument value is in seconds. The other options shown are not valid.

2. A. The --assemble option starts an array that has been previously stopped. The other options are not valid.

3. B. The sfdisk command can be used for this purpose, and when given the --id argument, you can specify the disk and partition on which to operate. The partition type fd is Linux RAID.

4. D. The WWID, or World Wide Identifier, is a unique and system-independent way to identify an individual SCSI device such as that which might be seen when using a SAN or iSCSI device. Of the other options, a /dev/sd device is not persistent across systems or reboots. The other options do not exist.

5. A. The discovery mode is used to discover iSCSI targets. The other options are not valid modes for iscsiadm.

6. C. The vgscan command is used to build the LVM cache file. The cache file keeps a list of current LVM devices. The other commands shown are not valid.

7. B. The sysctl command can be used to view various kernel parameters including the current hostname. That is the primary difference between looking at sysctl and examining /etc/hostname or /etc/hosts. The sysctl command will give the current value, which was specified as a criterion in the question.

8. A. The Banner option within the sshd_config file provides a means by which an administrator can display a message to people logging in with ssh.

9. D. The --prefix option sets the destination prefix or directory into which the resulting compiled code will be installed, typically meaning the binaries from a compile process. The other options shown are not valid in most configure scripts.

10. D. The archive option, invoked with -a, is equivalent to several other options with rsync, such as recursive, preservation of groups and ownership, and others.

11. A. The -D option disables printing of messages to the console. The -E option turns such printing back on. There is no -O or -off option for dmesg.

12. B. The -g option displays multicast information. The -r option displays route information, and -a displays sockets. There is no -m option for netstat.

13. C. The -r option causes the ip command to attempt to resolve IP addresses. The -f option specifies the protocol family. There is no -n or -a option to the ip command.

14. A. The ss command is used, and when given the -o option, timer information is displayed. The netstat -rn command shows route information but not sockets or timing, and ping -f is a flood ping and not related. The ls -l command displays files in a long listing format.

15. D. The dd command typically takes arguments for input file (if) and output file (of) in the format shown.

16. C. All of the addresses shown are in private ranges. The only one with the correct netmask is 255.255.255.0, which is equivalent to 24 masked bits.

17. B. The -b option creates a backup of destination files. The -a option is archive, -c uses a checksum for determining which files to transfer, and -d includes directories but not necessarily recursive copying within the directories.

18. D. The -p option preserves permissions. The -x option extracts, while -z unzips with gzip. The -v option is verbose.

19. C. The !H sequence indicates host unreachable. Network unreachable is !N.

20. A. The -m option specifies how the packet should be marked or tagged. The -a option is audible ping, while -p enables specification of custom padding. There is no -k option.

21. D. The environment variable TAPE can be used to specify the device on which mt will operate. The other environment variables are not used by the mt command.

22. C. The /etc directory and its subdirectories typically contain configuration files that would be necessary in order to re-create the system in a restoration scenario. The /var directory usually contains variable information, while /opt may be used for several other purposes. The /bin directory contains binaries that can usually be reinstalled.

23. B. The -i option tells patch to ignore whitespace. This might be necessary when the patch file doesn't match exactly what's needed. The -p option sets the level of directory for the patch, while -e informs patch to interpret as an ed script. There is no -w option for patch.

24. C. The -i option sets the interval between ping requests for iscsiadm. The -a option sets the IP address in ping mode, -o sets a database operation, and there is no -e option.

25. B. The -C option checks the power mode on drives that support the operation. The -a option gets or sets the sector count, -d gets or sets the using_dma option, and the -f option syncs and flushes the buffer cache for the drive on exit.

26. D. The file /proc/swaps contains information on the swap spaces available on a given computer. The other files do not exist by default.

27. B. The rescue target boots the system into rescue mode, from which system recovery can be performed. The other targets listed are not valid.

28. B. The -r option displays a report including CPU time and exit status about the just-completed fsck operation. The -f option forces whatever operation is being requested, -s serializes fsck operations, and -l creates an exclusive flock.

29. C. The allnoconfig target answers no to every question when creating a new config for kernel compilation. Of the other options, only the config target is valid and is used to create a normal config, prompting for answers to portions of the kernel to include.

30. D. The file /proc/meminfo provides a wealth of information about memory usage and utilization. Much of this information is displayed by various commands, but the canonical source for those commands is usually found in this file. Of the other options, only /proc/cpuinfo is valid and that file provides information on the CPU(s) for the computer.

31. B. The -p option shows the parameters for a given module. The other options are not valid for the modinfo command.

32. C. The -k option displays the kernel driver for a given PCI device. The -d option selects devices from the specified vendor. The other options are not valid.

33. D. The udevadm command should be used for this purpose, and the hwdb mode works with the hardware database. The -u option updates the database.

34. A. The systemd-delta command helps to sort out the scenario described by showing overridden, masked, and other file conflicts and ordering. The other commands and options shown are not valid.

35. B. The grub-install command is used for this scenario. SCSI disks are located in /dev/sd* by default, with the first disk being /dev/sda and the second /dev/sdb. Option D is incorrect because it lists both /dev/sdb and the partition number (2).

36. D. The blkid command displays the UUID and other relevant information for appropriate devices. The other commands shown are not valid.

37. C. LUKS encryption is the default mode for the dm-crypt command. Other modes include plain, loopaes, and tcrypt.

38. B. The -b option accepts a parameter of the file containing the El Torito boot image. The boot image must be 1200, 1440, or 2880 KB in size. The other options are not valid with mkisofs.

39. C. An exit code of 64 means that some disks failed the trim process. An exit code of 0 is success, 1 is general failure, and 32 is all failed.

40. D. The correct option is -s for the arp command, and the format is address followed by hardware address. The -d option deletes an entry, and -a displays all entries.

41. B. The txpower option displays available transmit power for the interface. The power option is available, and it lists the power management modes for the interface. The other two are not valid.

42. D. An Xmas scan is available using the -sX mode of nmap. The -sT mode is a TCP connect and -sS is TCP SYN. There is no -sP option.

43. A. The -s option sets the snapshot length, or snaplen, of the capture instead of its default of 65535 bytes. The -l option provides line buffering, -c stops after the indicated count of packets is received, and -d dumps compiled packet-matching code into a format that is readable.

44. B. The -r option reverses the journal, displaying the newest entries first. The -n option shows the most recent N events, -f is follow, and -b tells journalctl to show a message from a specific boot ID.

45. B. The file /etc/lvm/.cache, which is built using the vgscan command, is the default location for LVM devices that have been discovered on the system. The other file locations described are not valid for the purpose described.

46. D. There is no port for ICMP. The protocol itself does not use ports.

47. D. The emergency target can be used in situations where rescue mode cannot recover the system. The other targets are not valid.

48. A. As specified in the question, you need to remove both group and user ownership; therefore, both -g and -o are needed. The other options are not valid, though you can remove individual options from an archive process with --no-g and --no-o, which would be equivalent to removing the -g and -o options from the command.

49. B. The -r option bypasses the routing tables and enables sending packets directly using an interface. The -A option is adaptive ping, while -b enables sending pings to a broadcast address. The -q option is quiet output.

50. A. The traceroute command uses UDP by default and chooses 33434 as its first port. This setting can be configured to another port or to use ICMP but not IGMP.

51. C. The devices at /dev/nst* are non-rewinding tapes; therefore, index 0 would be the first such device. The devices at /dev/st* are normal SCSI tape devices.

52. A. The /var directory typically contains temporary or changeable information. However, mail spool files are usually stored in /var/mail or /var/spool/mail. The /etc directory contains configuration information, and /usr contains binaries and other files that can be reinstalled if necessary. The /mail directory does not exist by default.

53. B. The -b option makes a copy of the original file before patching. This can be particularly useful in a scripted scenario where several files are patched in succession. The -d option causes a change directory prior to patching, while -c tells patch to interpret the patch file as a normal diff file. The -s option causes patch to work in silent mode.

54. D. The -g option shows drive geometry that includes the specified information. The -h option displays help, and the -w option performs a reset of the device. There is no -e option to hdparm.

55. B. The --no-wall option suppresses the warning from being sent to logged-in users. The other options are not valid.

56. C. The -C option can be used to display a progress indicator on the fsck operation. The -f option forces the operation, while -p and -d do not exist.

57. C. The tinyconfig target provides the smallest possible kernel config. The other targets are not valid for the kernel.

58. D. The file /etc/udev/hwdb.bin contains the hardware database for udev, gathered from information in /usr/lib/udev/hwdb.d/ and /etc/udev/hwdb.d/.

59. B. The --diff option displays differences among overridden files with systemd-delta. The other options shown are not valid for use with systemd-delta.

60. B. The -U option enables specification of the UUID for a given mount. The -t option specifies the filesystem type, while -i keeps the mount internal-only and does not call the filesystem helper command. There is no -u option to mount.

Chapter 27: Practice Test 4

1. C. The notify directive, set to yes or no, specifies whether slave servers will be notified of changes to the zone. The other options are not valid.

2. A. The -b option enables specification of the key size. The -a option specifies the algorithm. The -f option sets the flag in the key/dnskey record. There is typically no -e option, but it may tie into a large exponent on certain versions of Linux.

3. B. The -q option suppresses output entirely, thereby making the command print nothing on success. The exit code of 0 for success is returned, however, so the command could still be used in a scripted scenario. The -f option specifies the format of the zone. The -s option has no effect for named-checkzone, and there is no -p option.

4. B. The class of record for most BIND zones is IN, meaning an Internet class. The other options are not valid classes.

5. C. The rndc command listens on port 953 by default. Port 53 is used for DNS but not rndc. Port 530 is RPC and port 1053 is not one of the defined well-known ports.

6. C. Start of authority records are known as SOA records. NS records are name server, and A is a normal address record. IN is the class for the record and not directly related to the question being asked.

7. A. The @ symbol can be used as a means to set the server for the dig command query. The other options shown are not valid.

8. D. The forwarders directive is a list of addresses to which requests will be forwarded from the server. The other options are not valid.

9. A. The query-source directive sets the IP address from which queries will appear to originate. This is useful in multi-homed scenarios where the server may not correctly choose which interface to use. The other options are not valid.

10. A. The -D option dumps the zone file in canonical format. The other options are not valid for this purpose.

11. B. The -t option, followed by the directory, tells named-checkconf to read included files relative to the specified directory.

12. A. The -B option specifies that the program should use bcrypt for passwords. The -C option sets the computing time used for bcrypt. The -b option sets batch mode, and the -m option specifies md5 for the passwords.

13. C. The ServerTokens directive affects how the version number, or even whether the version number, is returned on server-generated documents. The other directives shown are not valid.

14. D. The file httpd.conf is the primary configuration file for Apache2 servers. It is typical for httpd.conf to include one or several other files and directories that contain further

configuration information. The httpd.conf file is typically located within the /etc/ hierarchy, though its exact subdirectory varies greatly depending on the distribution of Linux.

15. B. The http_port directive sets the port on which Squid listens for connections. By default, Squid listens on port 3128. The other options shown are not valid.

16. B. The SSLCertificateFile directive sets the location of the public key file for an SSL hosting scenario. The SSLCertificateKeyFile sets the location of the private key. The other directives are not valid.

17. C. The SSLCipherSuite directive enables the selection of cryptographic ciphers available on a server. This can be quite helpful for limiting the ciphers to ones that are believed to be secure at any given moment.

18. C. The format is GroupName: name1 name2 name3, thereby making option C the correct answer.

19. A. The %b sequence is used to log the number of bytes including the HTTP header. The %B sequence logs the number of bytes excluding the HTTP header. Log sequences are preceded with a percent sign, thus making the other options incorrect.

20. C. The -newca option begins the process of creating a new certificate authority through the ca.pl script, which is a helper for the openssl commands related to certificate generation and management.

21. C. Files related to SSL are typically stored in either /etc/ssl (or a subdirectory therein) or within the /etc/pki hierarchy. There is no /etc/private or /usr/share/ssl directory.

22. D. The nmbd daemon listens on UDP port 137. Ports 139 and 445 are used by the smbd daemon, and port 143 is IMAP and not related to Samba.

23. A. The force-election message type, sent to nmbd, forces a browse master election. The other message types are not valid with smbcontrol.

24. B. The ads mode enables integration within an Active Directory environment. The rpc mode is available for remote procedure call environments. The other two modes are not valid.

25. C. The @ character is used to specify an NIS netgroup to use an exported NFS filesystem. The other syntax examples shown are not valid.

26. A. Credentials are included as an option. Options are specified with -o. The username and password can be specified as shown. There is no credentials command-line argument.

27. C. The security level of domain is used for Active Directory–based domain security mode. A trust is established between the domain controller and the Samba server in this scenario.

28. A. The -a option displays the hostname or IP address along with the mounted directory for NFS exports. The -d option displays only the directory. There is no -b or -c option.

29. B. The smbstatus command is used for this purpose. When given the -S option, a list of shares is displayed. The other commands shown are not valid.

30. B. If a user already exists when smbpasswd receives the -a option, the user's password is simply changed to the new password.

31. B. The port can be set with -p. It's worth noting that attempting to run Samba on a non-standard port will likely cause problems for devices that cannot specify a custom port for the share. The -d option sets the debug level, while the other options are not valid.

32. D. The fixed-address directive reserves the specified IP address for the given host in DHCP. When that host asks for an IP address, it will receive the specified address. The other options are not valid in a dhcpd.conf configuration file.

33. A. The ldapadd command requires that the OpenLDAP server be online when adding entries. Slapadd does not have this requirement. Both work on local databases.

34. C. The IgnoreIfMissing option within an interface section of radvd.conf changes the behavior of radvd when the given interface does not exist at startup. The other options shown are not valid for radvd.

35. B. The default-lease-time option, followed by the number of seconds for the lease, is used to specify the time that a client can have a lease before asking for a new lease. The other options are not valid.

36. C. The file /etc/nsswitch.conf contains information for Name Service Switch (NSS). The format is as shown in the correct answer. Local files are known as files, and LDAP is known as ldap within the /etc/nsswitch.conf file.

37. C. The [sssd] section defines general parameters for use with the SSSD system. Sections are noted with brackets, as in the answer shown.

38. A. The file limits.conf, located in /etc or /etc/security, provides basic configuration related to the pam_limits.so module. Other related files may also be found in /etc/security/limits.d on certain distributions.

39. B. The -l option enables specification of a file to which output will be written rather than to STDOUT. The -f option enables the command to point to a different slapd configuration file. The -d option specifies debug and -o enables specification of extended options.

40. B. The modify changetype specifies that an entry will be changed. The other changetypes are not valid.

41. A. The mail attribute resides in inetOrgPerson. Other attributes in inetOrgPerson include homePhone, gn (givenName), and others. Of the other options, only organization is a valid objectClass.

42. D. The gt operator is used to test for greater-than conditions with Sieve. The ge operator tests whether a value is greater than or equal to. The other operators are not used with Sieve.

43. B. The /etc/dovecot directory is used for configuration files related to the Dovecot e-mail daemon. The other directories are not used by default for Dovecot.

44. B. The `sendmail` command to view the queue uses the `-bp` option. For mail servers like Postfix, there are emulation commands like `sendmail -bp` that are available for compatibility purposes.

45. C. The `postsuper` command is used for this purpose. When given the `-d ALL` argument, all messages will be deleted. However, because the question specified only the deferred queue, then the keyword `deferred` is added in order to limit the scope of the deletion.

46. D. The `-b` option causes `postcat` to display only the body of the message rather than the envelope (`-e`) and header (`-h`), which are the default (`-beh`) for the command. There is no `-m` option.

47. B. An `if` statement will perform a conditional test with Sieve. In this case, the `size` test is needed and will use the `:over` structure for comparison. The `messagesize` and `message` will not work, but it's worth noting that the greater-than sign can be used with Sieve.

48. B. The `doveadm` command is used, specifically with the `pw` argument. The command will then prompt for a password (twice) and display the resulting encrypted password as output.

49. A. The `message_size_limit` parameter is used to set the default maximum message size for any single message delivered by or to a Postfix server. The default is 10,240,000 bytes.

50. C. The `:all` address-part is the entire Internet address, and it is the default when no other `address-part` has been specified. The other options are not valid `address-part`s.

51. A. The `RCPT TO` portion of the SMTP conversation is where the destination address is specified. The other options shown are not part of the SMTP conversation for mail delivery.

52. D. The `REDIRECT` target is used for creation of a redirection within iptables. It is typically used within the PREROUTING chain. The other targets are not valid.

53. A. The `-T` option limits bandwidth for authenticated users. The `-t` option does the same but for anonymous users. The `-B` option starts Pure-FTPd in the background, and `-b` indicates that Pure-FTPd will ignore the RFC standard in order to work with FTP clients that don't adhere to the standard.

54. B. The `nc` command can be used for this purpose and requires that a port be specified, which is 80 in this case. The other formats for the `nc` command will not work.

55. C. The `-F` option flushes or clears rules out of a given `iptables` chain. The option is useful at the beginning of an `iptables` script in order to clear existing rules in preparation for a new ruleset. The `-P` option sets the policy for the chain.

56. A. The `AllowUsers` directive is used to specify users who will be allowed to log in to the server. The other options shown are not valid.

57. B. Echoing 1 to `/proc/sys/net/ipv4/conf/all/rp_filter` prevents packets from exiting on a different interface than the one on which they arrived. The `rp` in `rp_filter` is an abbreviation for reverse path.

58. D. The -L option sets up local port forwarding, and it is therefore required for this scenario. It is followed by the local port and then the host/port to which connections will be forwarded. The other options are invalid for the purpose described in this scenario. The -p option connects on a specific port but does not create a port forward.

59. B. The file /etc/services contains port-number-to-name translation for a given server. The file contains well-known ports and can be customized on a per-server basis.

60. A. The --log-prefix option specifies the string that will be prepended when a log entry is created by iptables. The other options shown are not valid for use with iptables.

Index

A

E

J

jail configuration, 230
jobs
  cron. *See* cron jobs
  deleting, 79
  executing, 76
  information, 81
  scheduled, 78
jobs command, 36
joins, inner, 58
journalctl command
  disk space used, 90
  log files, 88, 248
journalctl -f command, 92
journalctl -r command, 262
journald.conf file, 93
journals
  disk space used, 90
  displaying, 173
  filesystems, 44, 156
  systemd, 249

K

kbdrate command, 246
keep action for mailboxes, 218
Kerberos authentication, 201
kern facility, 88
kernel
  Braille display, 67
  dkms, 133
  documentation, 135
  drivers, 135, 260
  final configuration location, 133
  information on, 137
  loaded modules, 8
  messages, 88
  minimal configuration, 265
  options, 9
  parameters, 164
  printing information on, 30
  SAN modules, 44
  source code compression, 174

source directory, 132
symbols, 137
unzipping, 132
updates, 22
upgrades, 132
version, 22, 135, 180
kernel ring buffer
  messages, 137
  viewing, 6
key pairs
  GnuPG, 116
  ssh, 225
keyboard models, configuring, 67
keyboards
  delay and repeat rate, 246
  on-screen, 68, 70
keys
  algorithms, 185
  authentication, 117, 228
  OpenSSH, 230
  PBKDF2, 154
  RSA, 117
  size, 268
  SSH, 227
  SSL, 193
  TLS configuration, 217
kill command, 185
kill -9 command, 34
kill -HUP command, 35
killall command, 37
killing processes, 37, 232, 234
klogd -f command, 91
kmag program, 68

L

l key for htop, 126
LANG=C option, 80
large files, directories for, 46
last command, 117
last -f command, 112
layout options for servers, 72
LC_ALL variable, 80
LC_MONETARY variable, 83
LC_TIME variable, 78

LDAP
  databases, 213
  firewalls, 250
  mail attribute, 274
  server URIs, 214
LDAP Data Interchange Format (LDIF)
  changetype, 274
  creating, 212
  databases, 210
  ldapsearch with, 213
LDAP over SSL, 106, 214
ldap_uri option, 214
ldapadd command, 273
ldapadd -f command, 210
ldapmodify -n command, 214
ldapsearch command, 214
ldapsearch -L command, 213
ldconfig command, 16
ldconfig -C command, 234
ldconfig -p command, 235
ldd command, 20
LDIF. *See* LDAP Data Interchange Format (LDIF)
leading slash removal for paths, 177
leases in DHCP, 211–212, 273
less than signs (<) for STDIN messages, 250
/lib/systemd/system folder, 7
libraries
  caches, 235
  dependencies, 20
LightDM
  automatic logins, 70–71
  configuration files, 71, 246
  guest logins, 66
  reverting to terminals, 70
lightdm.conf file, 68
limits.conf file, 274
line numbers, prepending, 36
linear acceleration, 67
lines, numbering, 237
links
  /etc/rc.d/*, 118
  files, 43
  shared libraries, 16
  wireless devices, 168

Comprehensive Online Learning Environment

Register on Sybex.com to gain access to the comprehensive online interactive learning environment and test bank to help you study for your CompTIA Linux+ and LPIC certifications.

The online test bank includes:

- **Practice Test Questions** to reinforce what you learned
- **Bonus Practice Exams** to test your knowledge of the material

Go to `http://www.wiley.com/go/sybextestprep` to register and gain access to this comprehensive study tool package.

30% off On-Demand IT Video Training from ITProTV

ITProTV and Sybex have partnered to provide 30% off a Premium annual or monthly membership. ITProTV provides a unique, custom learning environment for IT professionals and students alike, looking to validate their skills through vendor certifications. On-demand courses provide over 1,000 hours of video training with new courses being added every month, while labs and practice exams provide additional hands-on experience. For more information on this offer and to start your membership today, visit `http://itpro.tv/sybex30/`.

A Wiley Brand